T0340230

CAMBRIDGE SOUTH ASIAN STUDIES

VILLAGE REPUBLICS

A list of the books in the series will be found at the end of the volume

VILLAGE REPUBLICS

*Economic conditions for
collective action in South India*

ROBERT WADE

*The Institute of Development Studies at the University of Sussex
The World Bank, Washington DC*

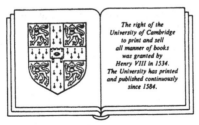

The right of the
University of Cambridge
to print and sell
all manner of books
was granted by
Henry VIII in 1534.
The University has printed
and published continuously
since 1584.

CAMBRIDGE UNIVERSITY PRESS

CAMBRIDGE

NEW YORK   NEW ROCHELLE

MELBOURNE   SYDNEY

CAMBRIDGE UNIVERSITY PRESS
Cambridge, New York, Melbourne, Madrid, Cape Town, Singapore, São Paulo

Cambridge University Press
The Edinburgh Building, Cambridge CB2 8RU, UK

Published in the United States of America by Cambridge University Press, New York

www.cambridge.org
Information on this title: www.cambridge.org/9780521301466

First published 1988
This digitally printed version 2008

A catalogue record for this publication is available from the British Library

Library of Congress Cataloguing in Publication data
Wade, Robert.
Village republics.
(Cambridge South Asian studies; 40)
Bibliography.
Includes index.
1. Agriculture, Cooperative – Kurnool (District)
– Case studies.   2. Kurnool (India: District) – Rural
conditions – Case studies.   3. Panchayat – India – Kurnool
(District) – Case studies.   I. Title.   II. Series.
HD1491.I392K878   1987   334'.683'095484   86-33389

ISBN 978-0-521-30146-6 hardback
ISBN 978-0-521-05178-1 paperback

To Freddy Bailey, who taught that anthropology is the better part of politics and economics. And to Syed Hashim Ali, IAS, professor of integrity.

CONTENTS

ILLUSTRATIONS

Figures

Maps

TABLES

PREFACE

When will villagers come together to supply themselves with goods and services that they all need but could not provide for themselves individually? In what circumstances will those who face a potential 'tragedy of the commons' be able to organize a system of rules by which the tragedy is averted?

Many writers on collective action and common property are inclined to think that the circumstances are very limited. A long line of collective action theorists has been concerned to elaborate the proposition that people placed in a situation in which they could all benefit from cooperation will be unlikely to cooperate in the absence of an external enforcer of agreements. An equally long line of theorists on property rights has argued that common property resources are bound to be over-exploited as demand rises. The only solution is private enclosure, according to some theorists, or state regulation, according to others.

This book is about villages in one small part of South India. Some villages in this area have organized the public aspects of resource use to a more sophisticated degree than has been reported previously in the literature on Indian villages, while others have not organized at all. Only a few miles may separate a village with a lot of organization from one with none.

From the literature on collective action theory we would not expect to find villages maintaining a steady pattern of collective control. From the literature on 'peasants-in-general' we would not expect such a range of variation between villages in the same area, for that literature prefers to characterize peasants as broadly individualistic or communitarian, according to the author's predilection. From the literature on Indian villages we would not expect to find that caste, factions, marriage rules, inheritance rules, and other such sociological variables, are unimportant in explaining the observed pattern of variation between villages.

This book offers an explanation of the variation and an account of how the collective action problems are overcome in those villages with a large amount of organization. It is a study, in other words, of the emergence of a 'public realm', of the origins of small polities and formal politics. The public realm is here concerned with 'efficiency' rather than 'dignity', with providing public goods and services in the vital agricultural sphere rather than symbolically representing the village to itself and the supernatural. It bears similarities to the open-field form of village organization found over much of medieval western Europe, and is in part a response to the same problems of mixed arable and animal husbandry as gave rise to that medieval form. But it is also a response to the hazards of irrigation, which introduce complexities not found in western Europe. If, with some political theorists, we look upon the state as based on a conjunction of contract and coercion, and if the first states are thought of as representing a relatively advanced stage of evolution of a public realm in local communities, we might draw on an understanding of how the combination of contract and coercion is sustained in these Indian villages today for insights about how it emerged in the agricultural communities of pristine states.

We shall at the end of the story examine why most collective action theories – including Prisoner's Dilemma, Hardin's 'tragedy of the commons', and Olson's 'logic of collective action' – fail to give accurate predictions in the present case, and thereby see why their sweeping pessimism about voluntary organization is unwarranted. We shall also specify some general criteria for identifying the conditions in which one would expect more, or less, collective action on the part of those faced with the need to regulate their use of common property resources. Clearly there can be no general presumption that collective action rather than privatization or state regulation will work – the dismal frequency of degraded grazing commons, despoiled forests, over-exploited groundwater and depleted fisheries is testimony to the contrary. On the other hand, there are many cases, in addition to these, where villagers *have* been able to sustain common property management arrangements over long periods of time. Privatization or state regulation is therefore not always necessary for successful management of resources of this type. The third option of locally-based collective action needs to be taken seriously. For one thing, it is likely to be much cheaper in terms of state resources than either of the other two. Already over-stretched states should encourage local systems of rules where they can be expected to work – hence the usefulness of establishing the conditions which are more, or less, favourable.

The research project began in 1977, as a by-product of another study on the operation of large-scale canal schemes. In the course of talking to farmers about their experience of the water bureaucracy I stumbled quite accidentally across a number of villages whose water organization seemed remarkable in relation to what was then known about Indian village organization. I made a quick study of 24 irrigated and 8 dry villages, the results of which called for a more intensive inquiry. I returned in 1980, together with Jeremy Jackson and Rosemary Jackson. They lived in Kottapalle village for 7 months in 1980. I lived in the village and nearby market town for 8 months over several periods between 1980 and 1982. Altogether we studied 31 irrigated and 10 dry villages. The present tense in what follows refers to 1980–1 except where otherwise noted. Further details on the field-work are given in chapter 8, n. 1, p. 135.

I thank the following people and groups of people, without whom *Village Republics* would not have been completed. The Institute of Development Studies at the University of Sussex is my own community, whose ability to surmount collective action problems in supplying a supportive research environment no doubt coloured my sense of the possibilities for Indian villagers. The Social Science Research Council of the United Kingdom (since renamed the Economic and Social Research Council) funded the study. Syed Hashim Ali gave it his blessing. Jeremy Jackson provided core ideas in my interpretation of the institution of field guards, and much help besides. Lakshmi Reddy was our indefatigable research assistant and translator. Tirupal Reddy, Norman and Pamela Reynolds, Hunter and Avelda Wade, and Ray Pahl helped in various crucial ways. Freddy Bailey, Ronald Dore, Michael Lipton, and especially Bruce Graham commented on parts of the argument. Elizabeth Crayford and Fernando Leobons helped prepare the manuscript for publication. Susan Joekes did her best, as always, to put the project to bed.

The manuscript was completed in the interstices of other work at the World Bank, and I thank that organization for its support. In particular, Hans Binswanger's commitment to scholarship was essential, for without it the devotion of machine bureaucracies to 'on time' or 'overdue' as the chief planning criterion would have brought the project to a premature end. Finally, a special thanks to Elinor Ostrom, who gave generously of her insights on common property resource management, and emanated an enthusiasm wonderfully infectious for a writer approaching the end of a long manuscript.

Kurnool district is the real name, but most names below this level are invented, for reasons which will become clear in chapter 5. In particular, 'MN' and 'TS' canals are pseudonyms.

1

The village as a corporate group

This book is about how and why some peasant villagers in one part of India act collectively to provide goods and services which they all need and cannot provide for themselves individually. And why some do not.

Ever since Henry Maine, scholars have proffered generalizations about *the* Indian village. 'An Indian Village Community,' said Maine, 'is an organized society, and besides providing for the management of the common fund, it seldom fails to provide, by a complete staff of functionaries, for internal government, for police, for the administration of justice, and for the appointment of taxes and public duties' (1905:262). Nowdays such a picture is generally scorned as idyllic, owing more to wishful thinking than to empirical evidence. The new hard-nosed school offers a rival picture of *the* Indian village in terms roughly the reverse of Maine's. 'Indian rural society today,' says V.R. Gaikwad, 'is an atomized mass, composed of individuals who are not in any organized fold except the family and the extended kin-groups which form the sub-caste' (1981:331). The obvious truth is that villages vary, some being more like Maine's communitarian ideal than others. Why? What accounts for variation between villages even within culturally homogeneous areas?

My answer is that several factors bear on the situation, related to ecology, internal social structure, demographic composition, relations with external markets and the apparatus of the state. Of these, I argue that the ecological factors – particularly scarcity and risk – are very important, yet do not seem to have interested students of Indian village organization very much. I argue that variations in scarcity and risk in the vital agricultural sphere explain much of the variation to be found in village organization within one small part of upland South India. Nevertheless, when all that is explainable by these kinds of factors is stated, much variation remains unexplained. Perhaps new variables will be discovered to reduce the randomness; perhaps some of it is unexplainable. In the meantime a certain modesty is in order.

The debate

Much current literature boldly generalizes not just about *the* Indian village but about *the* village in peasant society, no less. For instance, political scientist James Scott portrays the village in pre-capitalist peasant society as a key institution, characterized by a variety of social arrangements designed to insure village members against a subsistence crisis. These arrangements include labour exchanges, the use of communal property for the livelihood of orphans and widows, rent reductions at times of crop failure, and gifts by patrons at the birth of a child or the death of a farmer. The underlying principle is 'all should have a place, a living, not that all should be equal' (1976:40). To the extent that the village elite respects this principle by protecting poor members of the community against ruin in bad years, their position is considered legitimate; they are leaders of a moral community. In similar vein, economist Yujiro Hayami identifies the village as the basic unit of rural life in Asia, not simply the place where people live but also 'a community which mobilizes collective actions to supply public goods essential for the security and the survival of community members. The village mobilizes labour and other resources collectively to construct and maintain social-overhead capital such as roads and irrigation systems. Also it stipulates and enforces rules and regulations to coordinate and reduce conflicts on the use of resources among villagers' (1980:27).

On the other hand, many other scholars have presented the peasant village in quite different terms. According to what might be called the 'scarcity consciousness' or 'peasant pie' approach, peasants typically behave as if all possible 'good fortune' accessible to them is strictly limited. The result is strong social pressure towards normative and static behavior patterns, and extreme individualism in social relations. The anthropologist George Foster, whose theory of 'the Image of Limited Good' is perhaps the best known example of this approach, argues that 'People who see themselves in "threatened circumstances", which the Image of Limited Good implies, usually react in one of two ways: maximum cooperation and sometimes communism – burying differences and placing sanctions against individualism; or extreme individualism. Peasant societies seem always to choose the second alternative' (1965:301). 'Traditional peasant societies are cooperative [he continues] only in the sense of honoring reciprocal obligations, rather than in the sense of understanding community welfare, and ... mutual suspicions seriously limit cooperative approaches to village problems' (308).

Samuel Popkin (1979) takes a broadly similar position. Arraying himself against Scott, Popkin stresses the tenuousness and the difficulties of collective action at village level, the limited abilities of peasants to generate villagewide insurance or welfare arrangements. His view, like Foster's, is a world apart from Hayami's image of the Asian village. Organizing to supply themselves with public goods is precisely what peasant villagers find very difficult to do, according to Foster and Popkin.

This selection of views about the nature of the peasant village demonstrates the hazards of mounting exalted generalizations about 'peasantry' as a social type. Hayami takes Japan as his primary reference point, and villages in Japan do show a great deal of village-based collective action.[1] Foster takes his primary material from Mexico, where the amount of village-based collective action is often rather limited.[2] Scott and Popkin both take their material primarily from Indochina, Scott from Annan, a densely populated area of ancient settlement, Popkin from Cochinchina, a more recently settled economic frontier region. It is perhaps not surprising that Scott emphasizes the conservative sense of community, the natural collectivism of pre-capitalist 'peasants in general,' while Popkin stresses the entrepreneurial individualism of peasant life (Baker 1981).

The fact is that rural societies of the non-western world are marked by greatly varying features and tendencies, both in their internal ecology and culture, and in their connections with markets, state structures and other external influences before and during western penetration. We must seek generalizations, of course. But our generalizations should be less about the essential nature of peasant society than about the factors – ecology, markets, etc. – which make for more, or less, community organization, thereby expanding the proportion of social structure which can be explained in terms of a universal human nature acting in different kinds of situations and reducing the explanatory recourse to culture as a residual variable.

The Indian village

The picture of village India which emerges from existing village studies is a long way from Hayami's picture of the Asian village or Scott's account of the pre-capitalist peasant village. It is true that the existence of a formally constituted body for arbitration and adjudication on

---

[1] For examples from a huge literature, Beardsley 1964; Eyre 1955; Dore 1978; McKean 1984.

[2] For non-religious purposes. See for example, Foster 1948; Lewis 1951; Wolf 1971.

matters unresolvable by the participants themselves is often noted, though more for the nineteenth century than for the twentieth. Hugh Tinker, writing of 'traditional Indian village government', took a village *panchayat* (council) to be nearly universal. 'Although Indian village government has never been "democratic" in western terms, there was a sense in which the whole body of villagers took their part in affairs. The old *panchayat*, whether as a caste tribunal or as a judicial or administrative body, normally conducted its deliberations in the presence of all those who cared to attend. The onlookers although having no direct share in the proceedings formed a sort of "chorus"...' (1954:20). Bernard Cohen, drawing on studies of twelve dominant caste villages in the twentieth century, found village *panchayats* to be common though hardly universal: three or possibly four of the twelve had inter-caste *panchayats* (1965).

However even in the nineteenth century village-based arrangements to mobilize 'labor and other resources collectively' and to enforce 'rules and regulations to coordinate and reduce conflicts on the use of resources' – Hayami's central features – were weak or absent altogether. So were Scott's villagewide insurance and welfare arrangements. Today, according to the existing studies, a concrete political or public realm is even more attenuated. A number of men may be widely regarded as 'big men', as being in some sense first in the village; and they may overlap with village officers empowered by the state. But there is no clearly defined social domain or institution separate from state authority where choices and activities of a 'public' nature are organized; no center of community management other than the bottom levels of the state apparatus; no administrative staff; and no machinery for raising resources for public purposes other than through state-sanctioned taxation.[3] Indeed, in Louis Dumont's celebrated sociology of Indian society, *Homo Hierarchicus*, the village vanishes altogether as a significant social unit, appearing only as a locus for the great principles of caste and kinship to work themselves out on the ground.

However, the importance of the sub-caste in Indian villages also distinguishes them from the peasant villages of Foster and Popkin. While they stress the individualistic character of peasant life, Indian villagers are emotionally dependant on and derive their identity from, groups – and in that sense are not individualistic (Hofstede 1980; Kakar

---

[3] A study of popular involvement in India and three other countries makes a similar point. 'Even though civic organizations exist in India, the small number of people who participate in them and the limited role they have in local communities make organizational participation a weak basis for evaluation of popular involvement' (ISVIP 1971:245–6).

1981). It is just that *territorially-defined* groups like villages are not a focus for their identity and needs. Indeed, the strength of attachment to non-territorial groups like the sub-caste is said to obstruct emotional attachment to the village.

Studies of village power relations emphasize a complex web of patron–client ties within the village and stretching upwards to higher levels of politics and administration. They also show the actual management of disputes to be often a matter of self-help in feuds, revenge, and exacting reparations. Commentators frequently remark on how laden with menace relations between villagers are perceived to be. 'In their interpersonal relations the people are hypercritical and very sensitive', said Dube about a village a few hundred kilometres north of our area. 'They do not easily let go an opportunity of commenting on and criticizing their neighbors, their relations are never very smooth and certain... It is common to suspect others' motives, and not unusual to be always on the alert to read hidden meanings into the seemingly innocent utterances of others' (1955:181–4). One of Carstairs' informants warned him, 'These people are not to be trusted, they will be sure to rob you ... You should not trust me either. How can you know what is really in my heart?' (1958:40, 42). Comparative studies have shown that in India the idea of 'trust' is closely associated with the idea of 'treachery' (Triandis *et al.* 1972:256). At the level of elite political culture, Hindu political philosophy emphasized to a degree unusual in other major cultures the need for the ruler to use punishment as a technique of rule (Pye 1985). Comparisons of Indian and western civilization have often stressed the despotic character of central power in India – nowhere more succinctly than in Marx's dictum, the *locus classicus* on Oriental Despotism, that the 'prime necessity of an economical and common use of water, which, in the Occident, drove private enterprises to voluntary association, as in Flanders and Italy, necessitated in the Orient where civilization was too low and the territorial extent too vast to call into life voluntary association, the interference of the centralizing power of Government' (1853). Given all this, the absence of a concrete political realm in Indian villages, autonomous from the state, comes as no surprise.

The 'corporate' exceptions

However this book will show that within one small area of the South Indian uplands some villages sustain a public realm of a sophistication which to my knowledge has not previously been reported for Indian caste villages. Their level of organization approaches Hayami's picture of 'the Asian village in general,' and indeed is not so very far from Henry Maine's generally discredited account.[4] In contrast, other villages in the same area show almost no village-based collective action at all, in line with Foster's and Popkin's characterizations of peasant villages in general and with Gaikwad's characterization of Indian villages today. Only a few miles may separate a village with a great deal of public organization from one with very little.

Take Kottapalle, with its population of just over 3,000. It has a *council* of about nine members, with general authority to take decisions affecting all the village. The members are expressly chosen year by year, and are quite distinct from the statutory village council of local government legislation, the *Panchayat*, which in virtually all villages in the area is moribund. (I shall adopt the convention of *Panchayat* to refer to this statutory council and *panchayat* to indicate non-governmental councils.) The council administers the village's *standing fund*, which spends some Rs. 10,000 a year (in an economy where a male agricultural labourer gets Rs. 4 a day). The village fund pays the salaries of a work group of village *field guards*, employed by the council to protect the crops against depredations of livestock and thieves. Four field guards are employed for the whole year, and six to eight near harvest time. The village council also employs a work group of *common irrigators* to distribute water among the village's irrigated rice fields and to bring more water through the government-run irrigation canal. About 12 common irrigators are employed for up to two and a half months, for about 1,200 acres of irrigated rice. At the time of the rice harvest, the common irrigators supplement the field guards, giving Kottapalle some 20 village-appointed men for crop protection. In addition, the council lays down regulations to govern harvesting and animal grazing, which the field guards are to enforce. Fines are levied for infractions of the rules.

While crop protection and water distribution are the two central services, the council also organizes the supply of other public goods important in village life. These include the construction of an animal clinic, ridding the village of monkeys, repair of wells and field-access

---

[4] Dutt brings together examples of the Maine genre. 'Every village with its twelve Agagandeas, as they are denominated, is a petty commonwealth, with its... chief inhabitant at the head of it, and India is a great assemblage of such commonwealths', wrote the Madras Board of Revenue in 1808. Again, 'In pursuit of this supposed improvement [assessment of land tax on each field in the Presidency, instead of collective village tax assessment] we find them unintentionally dissolving the ancient ties, the ancient usages which united the republic of each Hindu village, and by a kind of agrarian law, newly assessing and parcelling out the lands which from time immemorial had belonged to the Village Community collectively...' (1963:96, 101).

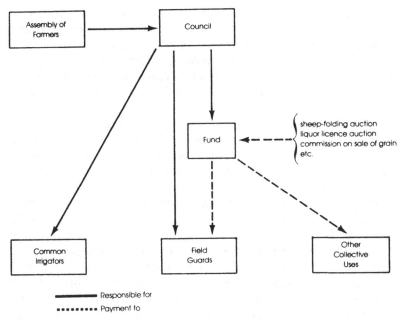

1.1 Village-based corporate institutions

roads, donations towards the cost of a new primary school building, contributions towards prizes at the local high school, provision of a male stud buffalo to service the village's female buffalos, and so on (table 6.1, p. 97). The village council is loosely accountable to a *general meeting* of the village's cultivators. Between 40 and 100 men attend the annual general meeting.

The council and the general meeting, then, constitute a mechanism by which Kottapalle's cultivators supply themselves with a range of public goods, including the public good of 'law and order'. The mechanism is wholly local and autonomous, in the sense that authority is not derived from the state. Indeed state officials outside the village barely know of its existence. Figure 1.1 shows the relationship between the main components.

Kottapalle is not an isolated case. In a sample of 31 canal-irrigated villages, all in Kurnool district of Andhra Pradesh (map 2.1, p. 20), 8 villages have all four of the main corporate institutions – council, fund,[5]

---

[5] I refer to the fund as an 'institution' for expository convenience. It is not an institution in the sense of a group of people whose activities are coordinated towards some goal. However the fund does need to be distinguished from the council, because either can be present without the other.

field guards, and common irrigators; 11 have some but not all; and 12 show no trace of any of them (table 8.1, p. 136). The sample was not drawn randomly (but rather with an eye to ease of access and a representative range of water supply conditions),[6] so one cannot read off from these proportions how frequent the corporate forms are in canal-irrigated villages of Kurnool district as a whole. But it is clear that they are not rare.

Moreover, many dry villages have some of the same institutions. In a sample of 10 dry villages in the same area, 8 have field guards, 6 have a village council, and 6 have a village fund (table 8.2, p. 138). So some of the dry villages have more corporate organization than some of the irrigated villages.

How does this type of organization differ from the traditional village *panchayat*? First of all, the Kottapalle type of council is *not* involved in what is normally identified as the central task of the village *panchayat* – the settlement of disputed claims and the administration of justice (other than in cases which directly involve its own authority); and there are good reasons why not. Most such tasks are performed by ad hoc musters of big men, or by government courts. Second, the Kottapalle type of council *is* involved in resource management within the village boundaries, in regulating what can and cannot be done and in sanctioning those regulations. Resource management is not identified as a usual function of village *panchayats*. Third, it has the authority to extract resources from village society for pursuing these purposes. Fourth, it has a specialized staff responsible to it for execution of its decisions. Finally, it is formally constituted, with a membership selected and re-selected year by year at a meeting of the general assembly and formally accountable to that assembly – so that it must keep written records of village fund expenditure and present these accounts (orally) to the general meeting.

In these ways the Kottapalle type of council is significantly different from what is normally understood to be or to have been the village *panchayat* of village India. In another respect it is similar. It is no more representative of the main groupings in the village than the traditional *panchayat* was. Tinker says in his account of Indian village government in general that '(the *panchayat*) was rarely representative of the village as a whole; it might be drawn from the members of the founding families or from the Brahmins and superior cultivators' (1954: 19). Most villages in our area are dominated by the Reddy caste, which is the main land-controlling and political office-controlling caste in the wider region. The

---

[6] For details on the selection of the sample see chapter 8, n. 1, p. 135.

Reddys are not a numerical majority in each village but collectively own more of its area than any other caste grouping and hold the main positions at village level of the state administration. They also tend to monopolize councils of the Kottapalle type.

Dumont is scornful of those who fail to see the significance of the unrepresentative nature of ostensibly village-wide bodies like the traditional *panchayat* (or the Kottapalle council). It means, he says, that one cannot speak of a 'village' *panchayat* but only of a 'dominant caste' *panchayat*, and this is an important part of his argument that caste, not the village, is the primary unit of thought and action in Indian society. Dumont bases his argument only on the social composition of the *panchayat*, not on what the *panchayat* does (a question in which he is, indeed, not much interested). Yet if the *panchayat* or council makes decisions in the agricultural sphere which are binding on all cultivating households – regardless of caste – it can sensibly be referred to as a *village* organization.

The roots of corporateness: scarcity and risk

My approach to the question of why some villages sustain a high level of corporate organization while others in the same area do not, places central importance on the net material benefits to be obtained from such organization by all or most participants. Features of social structure – the sorts of things described by the classic sociological variables – are also relevant, to be sure. But the impetus comes from the attempt to secure certain benefits, or avoid certain costs, which could not be secured without deliberately concerted action by cultivators. The benefits relate to reduced risk of crop loss and of social conflict in the agricultural sphere. In 'corporate' villages these risks tend to be higher – as I shall show – than in 'noncorporate' villages,[7] because of differences between corporate and noncorporate villages in two kinds of scarcities. One is of grazing land, which tends to be scarcer in relation to the number of livestock in corporate villages. The other is of canal irrigation water, which also tends to be scarcer and more unreliable in corporate villages. Both kinds of scarcities are likely to be found in widely differing peasant societies, which makes an account of how some Indian peasants respond to them of more than parochial interest. I now discuss these scarcities and social responses to them in more detail.

Exclusive possession (freehold) is one extreme on a continuum of

---

[7] Corporate and non-corporate are used as shorthand to refer to the presence or absence of the four institutions.

property rights. No property, as in ocean fisheries or the atmosphere, is the other extreme. In between lies common property, where the rights to exploit a resource are held by persons in common with certain others. These rights may take a variety of forms: they may allow unlimited exploitation for those within a specified group (as in commercial fisheries under national jurisdiction, until recently), or they may stipulate limits on exploitation for each user (as is commonly the case for commercial fisheries today, or as in 'stinting' on a grazing commons).

Whether a resource is used under private or some form of common property rights depends in large part (revolutions aside) on the cost of excluding others from the resource. Whereas it is easy for a farmer to demarcate an area of crop land and exclude other people from its use, it is more difficult for him to demarcate an area of grazing land and exclude unwanted animals from it (Coase 1960). To do so reliably requires fencing, and fencing may be expensive in terms of materials, labour, and land taken out of production.

So crop land in peasant societies is often owned privately while grazing land is owned in common by a local group. As low-cost fencing is introduced, grazing land may – sometimes only with protracted struggle against those who benefit from the commons – also be made private.

In many parts of the peasant world population pressure has reached the point at which most waste land has been put under the plough and little land is left fallow from one year to the next. At prevailing yield levels most of the produce has to go to feed humans rather than animals. Yet animals are needed not only as almost the sole non-human means of traction but also to provide manure on which the yield of the crops depends. As the English bishop Latimer declared in the sixteenth century, 'A plough land must have sheep; yea, they must have sheep to dung their ground for bearing of corn; for if they have no sheep to help fat the ground, they shall have but bare corn and thin' (Kerridge 1953–4: 282).

A standard solution has been to put the fallow land and the stubble left behind after the harvest in common; that is, to restrict the rights of landowners to rights over the crops, leaving the fallow grasses and crop residues for the village's animals in common. An animal owner can choose to cut grasses or crop residues and carry them to his animals in their stalls; or tether them; or let them graze under the watch of a shepherd. But stall feeding is expensive in labour time; tethers can be slipped and in any case are not feasible for large numbers of sheep and goats, which are the main source of manure; and young shepherds may run away and play games. Where there are no natural obstacles separating crops from animals and where fencing is ruled out for cost reasons, it is difficult to protect the crops from the depredations of straying animals.

The danger is worse the smaller and more scattered are the plots of each landowner, and the more uneven the harvesting dates. Scattering of holdings – the division of each holding into several or more plots in different locations – is common in peasant societies, from Japanese paddies to Swiss meadows. McCloskey (1975, 1976) argues that scattering is to be understood primarily as a means of reducing the risk of crop loss, by holding land in a diversified portfolio of locations (also Lipton 1968; Farmer 1960). Small scattered plots of course greatly increase the cost of fencing – the cost of excluding animals. When the harvest is not regulated, there will be times of the year when animal owners have the right to graze their animals on small scattered plots of fallow or stubble land adjacent to small plots of standing crops. The risk to those crops is then very high. All the more so because the incentives on tethering and watching are, unlike fencing, asymmetrical: whereas A's fence protects A's crop from B's animals as it protects B's crop from A's animals, A's tethering or watching is only to protect B's crop from A's animals – and A may not be unhappy seeing his animals getting fat on B's grain. So B's protection is contingent upon A's good will, A's fear of B's anger, or on the force of law (McCloskey 1976). Alternatively, crop watchers may be placed on each plot, night and day, whenever animals are in the fields. But this is expensive, if not in cash then in terms of other work which these crop watchers might otherwise be doing.

The social and economic implications of these conditions have received strangely little attention from students of present-day peasant societies. On the other hand, they have been among the central concerns of economic and social historians of medieval northern Europe. Across the Great European Plain, from England to east-central Europe, a single type of agricultural system prevailed throughout the later Middle Ages. This 'open-field' system[8] had four main features: the land of each village was unfenced; the holdings of each farmer were scattered in several or many parcels about the land of the village; the fallow and the stubble was grazed in common; and an assembly of villagers regulated cropping, grazing and other facets of farm management (Hoffman 1975, Blum

---

[8] I skirt a controversy among English medieval historians as to the meaning and utility of 'open-fields', 'common-fields', and 'sub-divided' fields (Thirsk 1967; Baker 1979). I use open-fields in a morphological sense to describe land ownership where the land is divided into separately owned parcels without fencing around the parcels or around the larger blocks in which the parcels are located.

1978, McCloskey 1975, Campbell 1981). Medieval historians have given much attention to the by-laws enacted by these village assemblies for the regulation of cropping and grazing (Ault 1972).

In our 'corporate' villages of South India all four features of the classic European open-field system are found, and much of our attention will be on how that system operates in the specific ecological conditions of upland South India today. We shall see that whereas the medieval by-laws commonly gave emphasis to regulation of the cropping, the corporate organization of our villages emphasizes regulation of the livestock. The institution of village field guards has the function of making the balance of incentives on tethering and animal shepherding less asymmetrical, by increasing the animal owner's liability for what his animals do.

Water scarcity is the second main impetus to corporate control. Canal (or tank) irrigation water, even more than grazing land, is difficult to privatize because of the high cost of excluding others. Water does not come in neat packages, and tends to escape wherever the ground slopes downwards. One tends to find, then, a system of common property rights in canal water (once it has passed out of the government-owned and operated canal). The general feature of common rights is that the use of the resource is determined on a first come, first served basis: anyone within the unit of common ownership can use the resource and cannot exclude others who are already using it. With water, those owning land closest to the canal outlet have first access and under simple common rights cannot be prevented from taking as much as they wish by those lower down who see themselves disadvantaged by excessive use higher up – no more than drivers on a road can be excluded by later arrivals who find the road congested. Because of this, top-enders are inclined to waste water and to skimp on maintenance of field channels, and may dispose of their drainage water in ways inconvenient to tail-enders.

How serious are the consequences for tail-enders depends very much on how scarce water is, as well as on crop type, topography and the density of field channels. It makes sense to suppose that as water scarcity increases, the risks to downstream farmers of crop loss due to inadequate water supply will increase. It might be possible for them to agree to compensate top-enders for not taking more than their share of water (Coase 1960), but the transaction costs of such agreements would clearly be very high, the difficulties of policing it considerable. A more likely outcome is that tail-enders facing water shortages will push for strong community organization and formal rules of water allocation, while top-end farmers will have little such inclination.

If the whole village is in a downstream location – far down a distributary from the main canal – all or almost all irrigators may have a strong common interest in bringing more water to the village as a whole. And if, as in Kottapalle, the fields of many irrigators are scattered rather than concentrated in one place, some in top-end, some in tail-end locations, they may each prefer formal rules and community control over unregulated, conflict-laden access to water. In Kottapalle, the institution of 'common irrigators' embodies this preference.[9] Indeed, it has been noted worldwide that communities which depend on surface-flow irrigation tend to have a more clearly defined authority structure, a 'denser' community organization, than those which do not (Hunt and Hunt 1976, Beardsley 1964, Coward (ed.) 1980).

Water scarcity and the population-pressure-induced mixing of live-stock with crops are both aspects of a fundamental problem which affects farmers almost everywhere. Farmers are in varying degrees interdependent in production, in the sense that what one farmer does will have repercussions for others in the neighbourhood. In classic peasant villages, with the land held in small, scattered plots, this interdependence in production can be very high. Yet peasant farmers make decisions about production in a private, fragmented, uncoordinated way. They do not themselves have to take account of the costs or benefits which their actions impose on others. The greater the interdependence in production, the greater these 'neighbourhood effects' or 'externalities' of benefit and cost are. So decisions which make sense from the individual producer's point of view may turn out in the aggregate to be socially irrational; they may cause harm not only to the village as a whole but also to the apparently rational individuals themselves. The consequences of 'external' costs may be to reduce the incentive to apply optimal inputs to the land, for if the fruits of X's labor and investment are dissipated by Y's actions, X's incentives to cultivate his land are attenuated. Or, in the crop/livestock context, X may have to spend unproductive labour in crop-guarding against Y's animals, labour which could be better used for other things.

But to suppose that these externalities of grazing and water *are* an important source of crop loss and social conflict is to suppose that villagers take no steps to reduce the risks. This is where village-based corporate organization, with its functions of regulating, rationing, and policing, intervenes. It represents an adaptation to the disjunction between the interdependence in production and the private decisionma-

---

[9] The *warabandi* rules of water allocation in Northwest India represent an alternative way of circumscribing common rights to water; see chapter 5.

king system which directs agriculture, by which the scope of private decisionmaking is reduced and the scope of collective decisionmaking increased. In this way some at least of the more costly externalities are 'internalized' (Barkley and Seckler 1972). Being under the regulation of a common authority, each private farmer in the village is no longer free to ignore the effects of his actions on others.

However, many villages in our area are *not* corporate in this sense: they have no village council or fund or field guards or common irrigators. It is not because the grazing and irrigation water has been privately enclosed. Rather, the interdependencies in production are handled informally, with external costs being reduced by mutual restraint between neighbours, especially that which proceeds from the danger that A will damage B's crops if B allows his livestock to damage A's. So a village-based response to these interdependencies, with the group acting as a single unit rather than as a collection of individuals, is by no means inevitable. That is just what the Foster–Popkin image of peasant villages highlights.

The collective action pessimists

I shall argue that corporate organization of the Kottapalle type is likely only when external costs are high – when, in other words, the interdependencies in production are such that any one cultivator is exposed to a high risk of crop loss and social conflict as a result of the activities of other people. The organization once in existence can then be elaborated to pursue common interests not closely related to the original defensive aims. This hypothesis not only explains much of the variation in corporateness within the sample of irrigated villages, but also explains why – surprisingly in view of those anthropological generalizations about irrigation causing a centralization of (local) authority – some dry villages have more corporate organization than some irrigated villages.

At first glance the hypothesis makes obvious good sense. It is only a special case of orthodox group theory, which explains group formation in terms of the benefits of membership to rational, self-interested individuals (Truman 1951). It could even be seen as a special case of the familiar Marxist interpretation of the role of the state in capitalist society: that the self-interested actions of individual capitalists (cultivators) are in sharp contradiction to the need of the system of production as a whole, because competition compels them to take certain actions which, if unchecked, would be disastrous for the continuation of the system within which they are major beneficiaries; so the role of the state (council) is to intervene to provide the general conditions for non-destructive production and reproduction (Althusser 1971).

The problem common to both these sorts of explanations is that they make an unproblematic jump from the functions to be served by group action to the fact of group action; they take identification of the benefits to rational self-interested individuals, or of the needs of capitalists, as sufficient to explain the institutional response. But the dismal frequency of degraded grazing commons, depleted fisheries, and overexploited ground water is sufficient reminder that groups often do not form and collective action frequently is not forthcoming, even when the benefits to rational, self-interested individuals are clear. If the disjunction between interdependence in production and private decisionmaking always gave rise to a socializing adaptation, the long-term future of the human race would indeed be assured (Cowgill 1975).

The problems in the way of that adaptation have been familiar to political theorists for a long time. David Hume, in the eighteenth century, put the difficulties like this:

two neighbours may agree to drain a meadow, which they possess in common; because 'tis easy for them to know each others mind; and each must perceive, that the immediate consequences of his failing in his part, is the abandoning the whole project. But 'tis very difficult, and indeed impossible, that a thousand persons shou'd agree in any such action; it being difficult for them to concert so complicated a design, and still more difficult for them to execute it; while each seeks a pretext to free himself of the trouble and expense, and wou'd lay the whole burden on others. Political society easily remedies both these inconveniences (*A Treatise of Human Nature*, 1965:538).

In other words, collective action is easier to organize on a voluntary basis in small groups than in larger groups. Hume's use of 'political society' as the *deus ex machina* for resolving the problems of large groups will strike the modern eye as quaint. But the underlying argument remains cogent. The distinction between individual and group interests means that collective action requires more than intensity of need; it requires ways by which the inconveniences of each person's attempt to lay the burden on others, and of having to reach agreement on a single level of supply, can be overcome.

This is a classic problem in what has come to be known variously as the theory of 'collective action' or 'public goods'.[10] Public goods, in contrast to private goods, have the quality that no individual can be

[10] Some writers treat the theory of public goods as a special case of the theory of collective action (e.g. Snidal 1985).

excluded from benefiting from them once they are provided (the quality of 'non-excludability'). Or at any rate, public goods have the quality that exclusion is costly or difficult. If people cannot be excluded from using the good it is intuitively clear that they may be reluctant to contribute towards the provision of the good; they may be tempted to 'free ride', to obtain the good without themselves contributing. Why should a shipowner voluntarily contribute to the cost of lighthouses if he can benefit from the lighthouse service without paying? He may value the service highly, but unless he and other shipowners are prepared to pay, their collective demand will not be translated into effective demand. Without sources of finance other than voluntary contributions there may be no lighthouses to warn ships off the rocks.

It is also intuitively clear that if a group contains diverse preferences about how much of the public good should be supplied (how thoroughly the meadow should be drained, in Hume's example) it may be difficult to reach a consensus. Yet there can be only one level of supply in the case of a public good, so a consensus must somehow be reached. Where there are more than a handful of individuals whose preferences must converge, the transaction costs of obtaining the agreement may be high. Even if there was perfect consensus the free rider problem would remain; but the need to reach consensus adds to the difficulties facing any group or potential group that would provide itself with public goods.

This line of thought has led many analysts to be pessimistic about the chances that those who confront the problem of providing themselves with public goods can find satisfactory solutions by agreement within the group.[11] Mancur Olson has captured this pessimism in a now celebrated theorem: 'unless there is coercion or some other special device to make individuals act in their common interest, *rational, self-interested individuals will not act to achieve their common or group interests*' (1971:2). Olson talks of common 'interests', which are also public goods; by definition the achievement of any common goal or the satisfaction of any common interest (that is, a goal or interest that cannot be obtained by an individual acting on his own) means that a public or collective good has been provided. So Olson's theorem

[11] Russell, commenting on a set of papers applying public choice theory to rural development analysis, states that, 'identifying what will not work nearly exhausts the capability of the theory, for its strongest results are impossibility theorems... When it comes to positive results, to solutions to the problems of collective choice in general or of public goods provision in particular, the theorists have been much less successful' (1981:8). While this is a central tendency of the public choice literature it is no more than that. Some theorists within the same intellectual tradition do have a much more constructive orientation; such as Elinor Ostrom (1985a and b), R. Hardin (1982), Michael Laver (1981), Richard Kimber (1981), Ford Runge (1984).

maintains that interest group membership, in the sense of contributions to a group objective, must be accounted for not by the rational, self-interested choice of individuals, but by their being compelled or offered inducements to belong. (The punishments and inducements must be 'selective' so that those who do not contribute can be treated differently from those who do.) Without either selective punishments or inducements, individuals will free ride, and the public good will not be supplied or will be supplied in sub-optimal amounts.

Garrett Hardin captures the same pessimism in his account of the 'tragedy of the commons'. He asks the reader to imagine a finite pasture 'open to all'. Each herdsman is assumed to be a rational utility maximizer who receives positive utility from selling his own animals and negative utility from overgrazing. When the aggregate of all herdsmen's activities begins to exceed the sustainable yield of the pasture, each herdsman is still motivated to add more and more animals since he receives all of the proceeds from his extra animals and only a partial share of the additional cost resulting from his own overgrazing. The denouement is appalling: 'Each man is locked into a system that compels him to increase his herd without limit – in a world that is limited. Ruin is the destination towards which all men rush, each pursuing his own best interest in a society that believes in the freedom of the commons' (1968:1244).

In more measured terms, Hardin's argument is that if a group of people are placed analytically in a situation where they could mutually benefit if all adopted a rule of restrained use of a common resource, they will not do so in the absence of an external enforcer of agreements. Each individual has an incentive to ignore the social costs of his resource use for fear that others will capture the benefits of the resource before he can. The lack of exclusion from the resource thus creates an incentive for a rate of aggregate use which exceeds the physical or biological renewal of the resource (Ostrom 1985a).

Far-reaching proposals for institutional change in the management of common property resources have been justified by this kind of argument (Ostrom 1985b, Runge 1986). According to one school, the establishment of full private property rights over the commons is a necessary condition for avoiding the tragedy. 'The only way to avoid the tragedy of the commons in natural resources and wildlife', says Robert Smith, 'is to end the common-property system by creating a system of private property rights' (1981:467; see also Demsetz 1967, North and Thomas 1977, Johnson 1972, Picardi and Siefert 1976). Another school, however, is equally emphatic that only the allocation to the state of full authority to regulate the commons can hope to succeed (Ehrenfeld 1972,

Carruthers and Stoner 1981, Hardin 1968). William Ophuls, for example, argues that 'because of the tragedy of the commons, environmental problems cannot be solved through cooperation...and the rationale for government with major coercive powers is overwhelming...' (1973:229). For proponents on both sides, the policy issue is simply how to get the desired change accomplished with the least opposition from those involved.

Yet here we have a case in rural India which fits neither of the prevailing approaches. In villages where the potential externalities of water and grazing are high, there has been no move to privatize these resources – this option is largely ruled out on cost grounds; nor does the state lay down rules of resource use – it would in any case be too weak to enforce them. Rather, the villagers themselves have constituted an authority to impose rules of restrained access. So in this case the people who face the problems *have* been able to devise and sustain rules which serve to keep costs and conflict within tolerable limits. To do so they have created a differentiated and active public core, extending authoritative regulation into village society in the form of water rules, grazing rules, harvesting rules, road maintenance, well repairs, and other things. Compared to other villages, more of their social interactions are 'political' in the sense of being in relation to a distinct political institution. If we follow Eckstein (1982) and take political development to be the growth of the political domain of society, we can talk of these corporate villages as politically more developed than those without such organization. How and why has this come about, and what does this experience say about prevailing theories of collective action and common property resource management?

2

The circumstances of village organization

Peninsula India has three distinct ecological zones. A coastal plain rims
the perimeter; mountain ranges bound the coastal plain; and in between
is a vast upland, 500 to 3,000 feet in elevation, generally flat but dissected
by river gorges and punctuated by stark rocky outcrops (maps 2.1, 2.2,
2.3). The climate of the upland is semi-arid; rainfall is generally less than
750 millimetres a year concentrated in a single season. Agriculture is
based on sorghum and millet, the typical food crops of the semi-arid
tropics.[1] Agricultural operations are almost entirely unmechanized.
Oxen provide the draught power, men and women with simple tools
provide the rest. Most of the population lives in large villages, tightly
clustered and regularly spaced settlements usually of between 1,000 and
4,000 people, surrounded by a patchwork of open fields. Being
constructed of stone and mud with few houses higher than a single
storey, the villages seem to grow out of the land. There are no
fences or hedgerows to define the landscape, and what trees are seen
are clustered around villages and along the margins of roads, rivers,
and canals.

Agriculture is a hazardous undertaking in this dry and unadorned
setting. How village cultivators respond to the hazards is a matter
not only of village characteristics, but also of the wider structures of markets, states, and inequalities into which villages
are – more or less – integrated. This chapter examines these larger
circumstances.

Governments, markets and inequality

We must begin in the nineteenth century (with a glance still further
back), for while little is known of the history of the pattern of corporate
organization it is clear enough that it is not a recent, post-independence
phenomenon, a local off-shoot from governmental development efforts.
There are hints that something like it was not uncommon in the late
nineteenth century.

[1] On millets and their distribution see Mann 1968: Ch. 31.

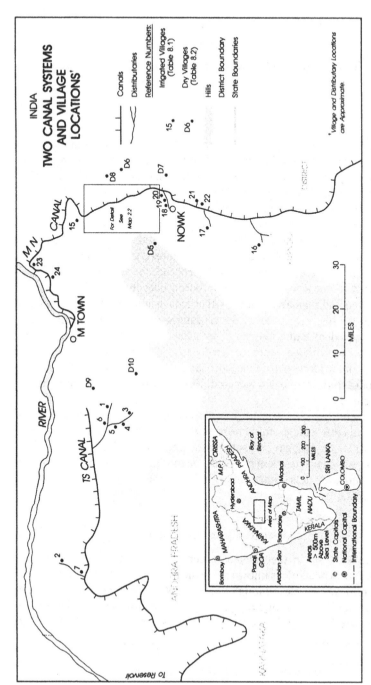

2.1 Two canal systems and village locations

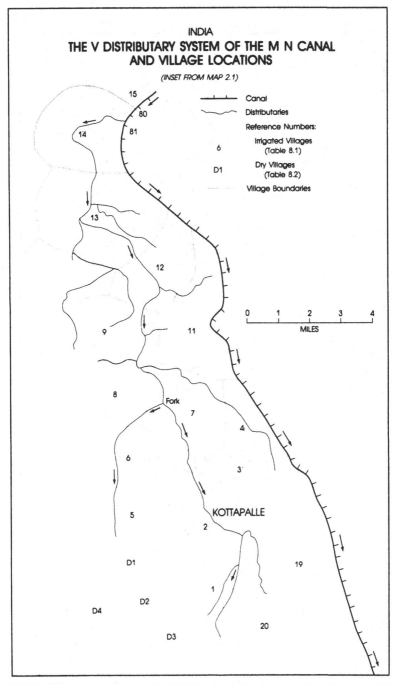

2.2 The V Distributary System of the MN Canal and village locations (inset from map 2.1)

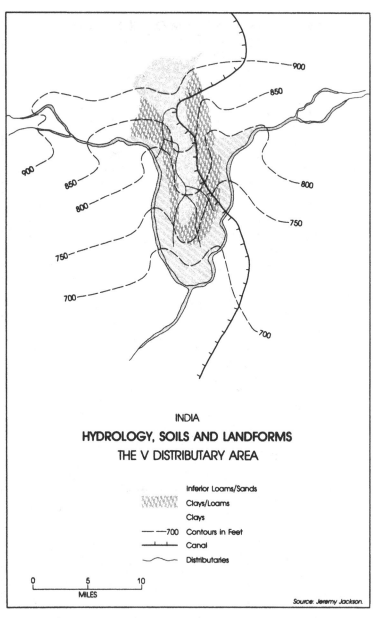

INDIA

HYDROLOGY, SOILS AND LANDFORMS

THE V DISTRIBUTARY AREA

	Inferior Loams/Sands
	Clays/Loams
	Clays
——700	Contours in Feet
⊢⊢⊢	Canal
∿∿	Distributaries

0   5   10
MILES

Source: Jeremy Jackson.

2.3 Hydrology, soils and landforms: the V Distributary area

The circumstances of village organization

The South Indian uplands in historical perspective

The British colonial government took over the administration of most of the uplands of South India in the late eighteenth and early nineteenth centuries.[2] For many centuries prior to the arrival of the British, the political history of the uplands was a constant succession of wars and skirmishes between small feuding states and chiefdoms, each centred upon a town or small city (Beals 1974:13–15). There were periodic unifications, but these often meant little more than the exacting of tribute from subordinate chiefs and princelings, who themselves were exacting tribute from their often poorly controlled villages and towns.[3] In particular, the sophisticated kingdoms which evolved on the fertile eastern coastal plain periodically spread westwards into the uplands in an attempt to control the watersheds on which their livelihoods were based. But the cost of control over large distances and the infertility of the soil caused them repeatedly to withdraw, leaving behind petty states and chiefdoms as the basic units of political organization above the locality – run on the basis of brawn, ceremonial pomp, and warlike display. State 'administration', such as it was, was concentrated in the principal towns. Local power rested with those who dominated the land and its labour; and their political orientation was almost exclusively confined to very restricted localities, to face-to-face relationships. They had, in Washbrook's terms, a 'local-level' rather than a 'state-level' political culture (1977). In the countryside, groups of 'urban' or 'state-level' culture which might have formed the agents of direction in localities, were few in number. On the well-watered tracts of the eastern coastal plain, on the other hand, such groups were much more important even in countryside localities. For there, abundant rainfall and irrigation made cultivation operations sufficiently routine to be left in the hands of low status labourers, while the landowners could detach themselves from the direct management of agriculture and devote themselves to more 'urbane' pursuits. Outside these lowland riverine tracts, more hazardous rainfall and more restricted irrigation made such

---

[2] 'South India' is today sometimes used to refer to the states of Andhra Pradesh, Karnataka, Tamil Nadu and Kerala. It is also sometimes used to designate the entire peninsula. Stein's usage is more precise: 'that portion of peninsula India south of the Karnataka watershed (excluding modern Kerala) on the west, and the Krishna-Godavari delta on the east. Within this portion of the peninsula, there has existed a region characterized by a high degree of sharing of significant social, cultural, and political elements and an order of interaction such as to constitute a viable unit for the study of certain problems' (1980:32–3).

[3] Stein 1980:44–5.

detachment by landowners from management of their lands less feasible (Stein 1980:27–9).[4]

When the British arrived the village was already established as the basic economic unit, in the sense that all its fields were worked under the direction of and almost exclusively with the labour of its residents, and most income rights from the land were restricted to persons of the settlement (Stein 1980:417). It had also been established as the basic political unit in a wider structure of rule. The rulers of the last great empire before the British, the Vijayanagar Empire (from the fourteenth to the sixteenth centuries), introduced a set of village officers and servants which the British were later to revive: namely, the headman (often called the *Reddy*), the accountant (*karnam*), and the watchmen (*talaiyari* – known today in our area as *tallari*). Just what these 'watchmen' did is not clear (today, they assist the village accountant as crop inspectors, revenue collectors, runners and general dogsbodies). The village functionaries were paid in the form of rights to particular plots of village lands, which were exempt from regular tax payments (Stein 1980:424).

Inequality and market relations

With the arrival of the British colonial government war-lords every-where lost their military power, and in many places much of their economic power as well. At village level, however, the existing structure continued. Villages tended to consist of a small number of landlords and a great mass of people who depended on both wage labouring and petty cultivation, the latter being comprehensively dependent on the former. Even worse off were the estimated 10 to 20 per cent of the population which depended entirely on labouring on the fields of others; such people were seldom more than 'predial serfs' (Washbrook 1977:68). In

---

[4] Stein emphasizes that local assemblies (of supra-village size) were important during the medieval period in South India. 'A distinctive feature of medieval South Indian states was the primacy of assemblies of all kinds in the governance of the numerous localized societies of contemporary South India. It was an assembly of some sort which most consistently articulated and took responsibility for the decisions to allocate agrarian resources to various purposes, at least from the ninth to the fourteenth centuries. With regard to agrarian resources, the polity was less one of regal ... raj [rule], than one of assembly, or sabbha raj' (1980:47). Later, however, he qualifies this generalization, saying that assembly rule was largely limited to the fertile, well-watered tracts of the plains; while in the dry uplands hereditary, highly localized chieftainships prevailed, the chiefs belonging to the dominant local peasantry (110, 142). Moreover, even in the areas of 'assembly rule' it is difficult to see from his account just what the assemblies did, and in particular whether they exercised control over cropping and livestock other than on lands apportioned to temple maintenance (161, 168).

the late nineteenth century, probably only about 5 to 10 per cent of cultivators would have enjoyed a comfortable degree of economic independence or better.[5] In the part of the uplands where Kurnool district is located, this class of independents was composed very largely of members of the Reddy caste.

It was mainly the big landowners who responded as the uplands became more closely integrated into international markets. By the 1870s some parts of upland peninsula India had as much as 30 to 50 per cent of cultivated area under commercial crops, mainly cotton and groundnut; elsewhere 15 to 25 per cent was quite common.[6] But it is to be noted that even big landlords had most of their land under food crops and obtained their own food from their own land; the degree of specialization in commercial crops was not large.

To promote this expansion of market relations the British constructed roads, railways, and canals.[7] A railway linking Madras and Bombay was built in the second half of the nineteenth century, crossing the southern part of Kurnool district in 1870. Nowk, the market town near to which most of our villages lie, was connected to the railway network in 1887. By 1886 Kurnool district had 900 kilometres of made-up road (in an area of 18,200 square kilometres), having had none in 1839 (Rajagopal 1974:128–32). Canals were intended to provide navigation as well as irrigation. In mid nineteenth century a plan was mounted (astonishingly ambitious it seems even today) to build a chain of navigable canals right across the country between Madras and Bombay.

---

[5] Washbrook 1977:71, see also Brakenbury 1915:87. Eleven per cent of Kurnool landowners paid more than Rs. 30 in the 1880s, 63 per cent paid less than Rs. 10 (Benson 1889:102).

[6] Banaji 1978:361–2. Commercial crops in Banaji's calculation include wheat, cotton, oilseeds and 'miscellaneous crops'.

[7] Roads, railways and canals were intended not just to promote commercial agriculture, but also to protect against famine. Early colonial administrators frequently exclaimed about the severity of the environment. 'No high mountain ranges, no thick forest, the paucity of perennial rivers, a low rainfall, an enervating climate – these are part of what nature has given to this land and no wonder its material progress is hampered', wrote one. 'At first glance', remarked another, 'the great black plains, the aching wilderness of stone, the bare dusty roads and summer air, half dust and wholly heat, realize vividly the abomination of desolation' (Government of Andhra Pradesh, Finance and Planning Department, 1973:113 and 31 respectively, no source given for first, second from J.C. Molony in his Census Report for the Deccan Division, 1911). In the Great Famine of 1876–8, some 250,000 people died or fled Kurnool district out of a population of just under a million at the start of the 1870s; twenty years later the population had still not regained its pre-1876 level. This was the last big killer famine. The westerly part of the district suffered a population fall of 37 per cent between the 1871 and 1881 censuses, the Nowk valley tract, 25 per cent, and a more easterly, good rainfall *taluk*, since detached, less than 25 per cent, giving a district average of 26 per cent (Benson 1889).

Only one upland link in this proposed chain was built. It is the MN Canal, from which most of the villages of this study are irrigated. It was constructed between 1860 and 1890, 300 kilometres (190 miles) long.

The expansion of market relations did not do much to reduce one of the generic characteristics of South Indian peasant society – its localness and autonomy. Compared to the Indo-Gengetic Plain, heartland of successive North Indian civilizations, Brahmins and other Sanskritized, 'urban-oriented' groups were thin on the ground; there was little connection between the religious organization of the towns and that of localities; the poverty of dry cultivation did not encourage extensive, urban-based trade network of the sort that developed in the North; and the method of tax collection used by the British in the South – direct collection of tax from each landowner, rather than tax-farming by intermediaries – meant that South Indian localities were not connected to towns via links with supra-local tax or rent receivers. Hence the social structure of South Indian peasant society continued to be characterized by territorially segmented clientage relationships between land control- ling groups and their dependents, while socially-horizontal, territorially-extensive relationships were much more important in the North (Washbrook 1975). The contrast can still be seen today in marriage patterns: the typical radius from which village brides are obtained in North India is of the order of 200 to 300 villages, in the South, 20 to 30 villages (Srinivas and Shah with reference to 1960, cited in Stein, 1980:9).

On the other hand, villages in South India have not been 'closed' in the sense used by Wolf (1957), at least since the early colonial period. Most villages had no communally owned arable land, no clear notion of village membership, and no restriction on outsiders owning land (though on the uplands difficulties of travel and the absence of legally defined tenancy made ownership at a distance more problematic than in the North). The British soon gave up an attempt to implement collective tax assessment village by village.

The colonial government

Under colonial government the Madras Presidency had the 'thinnest' administration of any area of British India. It had vast districts (sometimes twice the size of districts in North India), and a tiny cadre of provincial – centrally appointed and mobile – officials, whether British or Indian. It had vast responsibilities, for over three-quarters of the Presidency the British used a different method of land revenue collection to that used in much of North India and to that which had prevailed in the South prior to their arrival. Instead of relying on tax-farming intermediaries (*zamindars*) and/or collective village assessment, the government stripped away intermediary layers of authority between itself and the cultivator and undertook to measure and assess land revenue to be paid on each field – in a Presidency of some 140,000 square miles and 30 to 40 million people, most of them in villages.

The government concluded that the only way its small core of officers could effectively govern was simultaneously to utilize and circumscribe the powers of the pre-existing village establishments which had been created under the Vijayanagar Empire. The dilemma was to sustain a village and sub-district administration strong enough to raise revenue, keep order and undertake some limited civic responsibilities – but not strong enough to shut the government out.

One line of approach was to build up intermediate levels of government between village and state. Hence it attempted to create a three-tiered arrangement of government within each district, of 'Union *Panchayats*' (councils for clusters of villages), '*Taluk* Boards', and 'District Boards'. The intention was to make these institutions responsible for many conservation and development tasks and to give power in them to local Indian notables, so ensuring that the local powers had an interest in seeing that the work got done. 'Between the 1890s and the 1920s, local committees to enforce forest conservation, to control the siting and size of liquor shops, to hear appeals against the income-tax, to select policemen, to settle communal disputes and to control the distribution of water from irrigation schemes were set up in many areas [of the Presidency]' (Washbrook 1977:62).

It is not clear how much, if any, presence this local government structure had in villages. In particular, it is very doubtful that the 'Union *Panchayat*' at the bottom had even as much significance as its successor, the village *Panchayat* of today.[8] On the other hand, this government structure of committees and special funds, operating at a level not very far above the village, may have provided institutional models for village-based institutions. Just as the government got a considerable portion of its revenue from liquor licensing (by 1882 liquor licensing formed as much as 15 per cent of gross government revenue in the Presidency), so the Kottapalle council has learned ways of instituting its *own* liquor licensing, to raise money for the village fund.

The second line of approach was to strengthen the establishment of village revenue and law functionaries, in particular, the offices of

---

[8] The vast majority of villages were not touched by a Union *Panchayat*, at least up until 1922 (Rajagopal 1974:10).

accountant (*karnam*) and headman – the headman was normally from the dominant landowning caste (the Reddy caste), while the accountant was commonly a Brahmin. These were the two roles through which passed most communication between government and village populace; they were the pivot of the revenue and law and order systems. As executors of government, and under only remote and flexible supervision, they enjoyed considerable power and perquisites. Until early in the twentieth century it remained a fairly simple matter for them to make (illegally) their own distribution of the tax demand within the village, collecting their cut on the way. In short, 'At the base of the sprawling superstructure of imperial government, the British had built a little monolith' (Baker 1979:30).

For our purpose three points about the political institutions of the colonial government are important. First, the village was taken as a single unit in the overall structure of government. Second, the government's ability to intervene was very limited. The administration tended, in the absence of effective supervision or social controls, to become 'a series of despotisms within despotisms from the village to the district capital and beyond' (Washbrook 1977:27). As long as the revenue flowed out of the localities and order was maintained, the British government left its officials alone – for it had no choice. 'Indigenous, non-official powers, by one means or another, absorbed and controlled the functions of the state in the locality' (1977:47).

Third, the new pattern of political institutions which the British created did not create *new* channels along which the resources could be passed – from tenant to tenant, from Muslim to Muslim, or other such socially-horizontal networks which did emerge in North India. Rather, the new arrangements supported the existing socially-vertical relationships of local clientage, passing resources down these lines. So, as Washbrook sums up, 'Political development elongated the factions of local Madras, it did not cut across or undermine them' (1975:17).

The village in colonial government

The village officer establishment was paid out of a 'village service fund' until early in the twentieth century. This fund was filled from the produce of certain lands which belonged nominally to the state and were made available to the functionaries at much reduced rates of tax; and secondly, from a small portion of each farmer's crop.[9] One calculation for coastal Andhra in the 1840s suggested that about 8 to 12 per cent of

---

[9] The small proportion was called *mera*, the Telegu version of *jajmani*.

gross village tax revenue was apportioned for the village service fund. In addition to provisioning the village officers and servants, the fund was also used to make payments to sub-district (*taluk*) office personnel, temple maintenance, village entertainments, and the like (Rao 1977:25). And at least in the government's administrative models – to what extent in practice is difficult to tell – the village officers also controlled a number of other special funds, such as a fund for maintenance of tanks (local earthern-dam reservoirs) financed from tax exemptions on certain lands, a forest conservancy fund financed from a tax on sales of forest produce, and other funds from sources as diverse as road tolls, grass rents and fishing rents (Gopalakrishnamah Chetty 1886:ch. 16). There is also some indication that ad hoc collections were made from village households for specific purposes, either to supplement a fund or to make up for a fund that did not exist. Rao reports for coastal Andhra in the 1840s that, 'a portion of the gross [village] produce was in general appropriated apparently for repair of tanks and the like, but its outlay was always so inefficient that the *ryots* [farmers] were frequently obliged to make a collection among themselves for this purpose' (1977:21).

Today the local fund principle is continued in the *Panchayat*'s income arrangements. The *Panchayat*'s fund is to be paid a percentage of the value of all registered land transactions which take place within the village; a percentage of the land tax, a population grant, a house tax. The *Panchayat* may demand licence fees for temporary occupation of sites for market or other purposes, and may levy fines for stipulated offences, to be paid into the fund. In practice, however, such provisions are little used.

Here then are a series of more or less close parallels with the institutions of Kottapalle's 'autonomous' organization. The ideas of management of village affairs by village officers, of standing funds for 'public' village purposes, of franchises with which to raise revenue for the funds, of village work groups paid from the village fund (and probably selected by the village officers), of fines for certain kinds of offences to be paid into a village fund – these ideas were familiar in governmental ordinances for village governance (and presumably reflected patterns already in use). And the long-existing principle of dispute settlement – the ad hoc grouping of a number of people, normally an uneven number between five and nine, to hear a dispute and pass judgement, emphasizing not so much the question of what is the law but what is a workable compromise – this principle was written into the formal ordinances for village governance; the village magistrate (*munsif*) was to be given powers to call such a *panchayat* to settle disputes, provided both sides agreed in writing to abide by the verdict.[10] This is not the same thing as a standing committee for village resource management, but it does embody the idea of a committee of villagers nonetheless.

Post-independence government

Despite Independence in 1949, the structure of local administration has continued virtually intact from the days of British rule. The district remains the major administrative unit under the state. Responsibility for law and order and collection of tax revenue is concentrated in the hands of the collector, a civil service official appointed from above by the state government. Below the collector, the district is divided into a number of units of general administration, the relevant one for our purpose being the sub-district (*taluk*), with roughly 100,000–200,000 people.

Ten years after Independence India launched a program to create a new hierarchy for carrying out development tasks and for increasing popular participation in development. This was the system of *Panchayat Raj*. A new hierarchy was created parallel with the old administrative hierarchy, to specialize in carrying out development programs. In Andhra Pradesh (but not in all states) the Collector is also responsible for this hierarchy. The level of this hierarchy which corresponds to the sub-district, is the 'block,' comprising 50 to 150 villages. It has a staff of extension officers and village-level workers. There is no lower-level unit in this hierarchy. Alongside the development hierarchy was created a set of tiered electoral bodies, to which considerable powers were to be devolved. These are called, collectively, *Panchayats*. At the lowest level, villagers directly elect members of a *Gram Panchayat* or statutory village council. These bodies are then represented on the *Panchayat Samiti*, covering a development block. At the third level, the *Zilla Parishad* functions for an area coterminus with the district. The *Panchayati Raj* system is separate from the general legislative process. The legislative assemblies of each state and the national parliament are directly elected from constituencies that usually have some correspondence with *taluks*. There is no formal connection between the *Panchayats* and the legislatures, except that the members of the Legislative Assembly may be ex-officio members of the *Samiti* and *Zilla Parishad*.

This is the structure. Much has been written on why, on the whole, it has not worked; and why, in particular, it has failed to root develop-

---

[10] In practice the use of a 'public' *panchayat* of this form was very restricted (Gopalakrishnamah Chetty 1886:237).

mental decisionmaking in the hands of villagers through their elected representatives (ISVIP 1971:173ff, Gaikwad 1981). Part of the answer is that the scope for local autonomy is in fact severely restricted. As one study puts it, 'with Panchayati Raj, the *power* of decision remains concentrated and centralized in the political and administrative hierarchies, though in form it seems dispersed through the various organs of local self-government' (ISVIP 1971:183). In Andhra Pradesh the village *Panchayats* are moribund virtually everywhere (for example, no elections were held between 1970 and 1981). They do receive a small grant of income to be spent on village development purposes; but in practice this is spent largely at the discretion of the *Panchayat* president (*sarpanch*). State governments over the 1970s have seen to it that the powers and resources of the middle-tier *Panchayat Samiti* are very restricted.

Government, whether electoral or administrative, is for most villages another world. The 'block' office has officials who might be helpful to cultivators, such as agricultural extension officers and veterinary officers. But such officers rarely set foot in villages, and then generally as a result of special pleading. The lowest level employees of the Irrigation Department – the channel men who patrol the banks of the canal network and their foremen – move freely in and about the irrigated villages. But the next higher official, the Supervisor, the lowest rank to wield significant authority, spends his time between office and major water control structures, rarely moving along the canal roads unless specifically requested to by concerned farmers. Police, too, are rarely seen in the villages. They tend to be much feared, and brought into a case only if it is very serious, as for a murder. Villagers say with wry cynicism, 'police keep the company of criminals only'.

At the local level, then, the state remains for most of the population a grace-and-favour state. Officials are seen and see themselves as dispensers of favours. It is widely assumed that if an official wishes to do something for you he can, and the problem is how to make him want to. If you fail, it is because you do not have enough influence or have not paid enough money. Politicians make all kinds of promises before an election, and they might pass through your village to muster support. But that's the last you see of them and their promises, till the next election (Bailey 1971).

Access to governmental power is much easier for some than for others. Wealth helps; so does being a Reddy. The Reddy caste is the dominant caste in the southern uplands of Andhra Pradesh, in the sense that its members own more land than other castes and also dominate the legislative bodies and (to a somewhat lesser extent) the bureaucratic hierarchies of the state.[11] They are, however, a farming caste, people of the soil. Whereas in other parts of South India the dominant castes (often Brahmins) have long since disengaged from the active management of land, living on rents and making the business of rule their original vocation, this is not the case amongst the Reddys (Elliott 1970). So today, as in the past, effective management of land and effective political authority are combined in the hands of one ascriptively-defined group.

The Congress Party has long been the dominant party in Andhra Pradesh; indeed, the state is known as one of its national strongholds.[12] This is not due to a lack of competition from other parties or independents; in every Assembly election there are normally several contestants per seat. But the main challenges to Congress have come from rival groups within the party, not from without. Voting turnout has averaged 60 to 70 per cent of the electorate, and a 1972 study showed that four-fifths of the (sampled) electorate could correctly name the winner in their Assembly constituency, and four-fifths correctly named the Prime Minister. But membership of a political party is limited to less than 1 per cent (Sharma and Madhusudan Reddy 1979:457–90).

Kurnool district

Kurnool is a rural district. Over 80 per cent of its population (just under 2 million in 1971) is classed as rural. Population density is 105 people per square kilometre,[13] which on Boserup's scale is group 8, 'dense' as distinct from 'medium' and 'very dense'. There are over 900 villages, most with between 1,000 and 4,000 inhabitants; and 10 towns.[14] The district headquarters, Kurnool town, has a population of 140,000, and four other towns have over 20,000 people. One of these is Nowk, a bustling marketing centre of 63,000, the nearest town to many of our irrigated villages. The district is crossed by important interstate road and rail routes. Hyderabad, the state capital, population nearly 2 million, is seven to nine hours away from Nowk by several-times-daily

---

[11] Since the formation of the state of Andhra Pradesh in the mid-1950s, Reddys, Velmas and Kammas have held 45 to 58 per cent of Cabinet seats, with the Reddys being the largest group (28 to 38 per cent till 1971) (Sharma and Madhusudan Reddy 1979:470).

[12] The elections of 1983 brought a regional party to power at the state level, ending the era of Congress dominance.

[13] The state average is 153 persons per sq. km. This and other data in this paragraph come from the 1971 census.

[14] Towns are defined as settlements with more than 5,000 people of whom at least three-quarters depend on non-agricultural pursuits.

buses and trains. Madras is ten to twelve hours away. So the district is by no means isolated from access to major urban centres.

That 80 per cent of the district's 2 million people are classed as rural is one index of the level of 'development'. Another is electrification: 34 per cent of villages are supplied with electricity (as of 1971). Another is literacy: male literacy is put at 34 per cent, female literacy, at 13 per cent. Using these and other such indices, Kurnool district comes about halfway down the rank order of districts of its state, Andhra Pradesh, neither among the most 'developed' nor the poorest districts.[15] Andhra Pradesh is itself one of India's more prosperous states, especially because of extensive canal irrigation on the coastal deltas.

Agriculture

By the 1880s Kurnool already had over a fifth (22 per cent) of its cultivated area under 'commercial' crops produced wholly for sale. Cotton was by far the most important commercial crop; followed by castor and indigo. Seventy per cent of the area was under cereals, mostly sorghum and millet; the remainder under pulses (Benson 1889:70-1, 165). Little if any of the grains and pulses were exported from the district, suggesting a very low productivity.

Population density was about 53 people per square kilometre in the early 1870s. This corresponds to Boserup's density group 7, at which she predicts a predominance of 'short fallow' (one or two years of cropping followed by one or two years fallow), and a cropping frequency of 40 to 80 per cent (1981:19). Consistent with Boserup, the district's cropping frequency is put at 75 per cent in the late 1880s, with 25 per cent of the arable land being left fallow (Benson 1889:102).

There was, however, substantial variation within the district. On the easterly side, in the Nowk valley, rainfall averaged 750 millimetres a year (30 inches) and soils were relatively good. Here, according to a contemporary observer, 'the land is practically never at rest as long as the seasons are favorable' (Benson 1889:110). It seems likely that already by the 1880s areas like the Nowk valley were running short of waste and long fallow on which livestock could be grazed at will. On the westerly side of the district, rainfall averaged 600 millimetres, and soils were poorer. Here 'short fallow' was common.

Today agriculture remains oriented towards food production; 70 per cent of cultivated area is still under food crops. Average rainfall is 620 millimetres a year, concentrated in one season, with high variance

[15] Government of Andhra Pradesh, Finance and Planning Department, 1973.

around the average.[16] Most of the area is rainfed; only 12 per cent of gross cropped area is irrigated (1970).[17] Most of the irrigated area is fed from either the MN Canal or the TS Canal, which irrigate about 320,000 acres and 110,000 acres a year, respectively. The MN Canal was completed in the late nineteenth century, the TS Canal in the 1950s; but the MN Canal's physical structures (water gates, barrages, conveyance channels, etc.) were extensively upgraded in the 1950s to equal those of the TS Canal. There is little use of groundwater, and only one river of any significance, the Tungabhadra. (MN and TS are pseudonyms.)

A handful of farmers in the district have recently begun to use sprinkler irrigation systems for high value crops like groundnut and cotton. Tractor ownership is confined to the wealthiest landowning families, roughly one tractor per one or two villages in canal irrigated areas (fewer in dry areas).[18] This indicates the upper limit of agricultural transformation in the district. Most cultivators plough the land with a pair of oxen and a steel-tipped wooden plough, and transport their produce in a wooden-wheeled ox-drawn cart.

It remains an agriculture requiring huge amounts of back-breaking labour, much of which is supplied by landless or near-landless labourers working for daily wages. (Tenancy is unimportant.) Indeed, according to the census definition[19] there are more 'agricultural labourers' than 'cultivators' amongst the district's male labour force: 48 per cent are agricultural labourers, and 34 per cent cultivators. We are not dealing with communities of nearly homogeneous peasant households.

Wages are normally paid in cash, but tend to lag up and down behind foodgrain prices. Most of the variation in real wage rates within the

[16] The area is under the influence of both the Southwest and the Northeast monsoons, but by the time they reach it they are largely exhausted. An analysis of rainfall in the four-district region of Rayalseema (which includes Kurnool) shows that one year in five had, over the 1950–70 period, an average rainfall one standard deviation less than the long-run mean (Government of Andhra Pradesh, Finance and Planning Department, 1973). Another analysis of Kurnool district's rainfall, 1942–62, shows that all 11 of the district's *taluks* had an average annual rainfall deficit of more than 7 inches below 30 inches in 7 years or more, and are thus classified as 'chronically drought affected' (ibid.). See also table 3.1, below.

[17] Figures on irrigated area and land use should be taken as broad orders of magnitude only (Wade 1981, 1985a). They come from *Kurnool District Handbook of Statistics 1974/5.*

[18] Source is my own survey (table 8.1). The *Kurnool District Handbook of Statistics 1973/4* gives a total of 10 tractors in the whole district, certainly too low by a factor of well over 10.

[19] The 1971 Census is unclear about the definition of 'cultivator' and 'agricultural labourer', except to say that it refers to time allocation rather than income. See Government of Andhra Pradesh 1973, *District Census Handbook, Kurnool District*, p. 111, and Government of India Registrar General and Census Commissioner 1978. *Census of India 1971*, part II–B(ii), p. xii.

district (over the agricultural year, between recent years, between men and women) is contained in the range of 3 plus or minus 1.5 kilos of foodgrains a day. It is estimated that an adult male or female eats roughly 0.5 to 0.7 kilos of food grain a day. Allowing for the one-third to one-half of the year that a typical labourer gets no wage work, it is easy to see why labourers have little surplus with which to purchase consumer goods, why in material terms their lives are a nullity. With wages at this level, 50 to 70 per cent of a typical labouring household's income has to be spent on food alone.[20] It is also easy to see why at such wage levels India's industrialization is constrained by demand.

One hundred years ago, in the 1880s, the real wage in terms of food grains was probably a little lower than today. One estimate put the district average male wage in agriculture at 1.9 kilos of grain a day, rising to 2.8 or even 3.7 kilos at harvest time (Benson 1889:116). If so, real wage rates have not worsened in the past 100 years, while population has more than doubled; but the melancholy fact remains that real wages have increased very little.

The level of real wages today is exceptionally low by historical western European standards. Converting the real wage into hours of work required to buy one quintal of foodgrain, real wages rarely fell so low as to cross the 200 hour line in western Europe after 1400. Generalizing from western European experience, Fernand Braudel says, 'It is always serious when the 100-hours-for-one-quintal line is crossed; to cross the 200 is a danger signal; 300 is famine' (1981:134). If the Kurnool working day is taken as seven hours and the real wage as three kilos of foodgrain, then to get one quintal the Kurnool labourer must work 233 hours. This is the long-term normal situation, not one of crisis.

Conclusion

Several features of the overarching context of government, markets, and inequality seem to be important for understanding the shape of the Kottapalle type of corporate village organization. (1) Market relations for products and for labour have been important for over 100 years. Whether the fact that wage labour makes up a sizable part of production costs identified this as a 'capitalist' mode of production is a complex question I shall avoid (Harriss 1982). I continue to use the term 'peasant' as a loose descriptive label, even though some definitions of peasantry

---

[20] Bhalla concludes from a mass of evidence that the figure is even higher: 'Food expenditures account for over 80% of total expenditures, for the bottom half of the Indian population' (1980:33).

would exclude these villages because of the importance of market relations (Macfarlane 1978, cf. Moore 1972). (2) Rural social organization in this area is territorially segmented. The village remains a basic economic and political unit, as in colonial times. Most people who live in a village draw their livelihood from within it. A sizable 'gap' remains between the village and the state, despite the elective local political institutions of the post-colonial state. (3) Caste and wealth constitute basic lines of cleavage in the countryside. The Reddy caste has long been the dominant caste in the area of Kurnool and nearby districts. Not only do the Reddy hold more land than other castes, they are also predominant in the institutions of government. However, in the villages they remain people of the soil, actively involved in the management of their land. (4) The bulk of the population is very poor, with little material surplus.

If, then, the interests of different agriculturalists within a village tend recurrently to collide, several features of this overarching context might be expected to help establish and maintain a locally-based system of rules. First, recourse to the external authority of the state is even today costly and difficult, which makes a possible alternative less attractive. Equally, the state continues to have a limited ability to reach into villages and push aside or absorb systems of rule that stand in its way; that is, a limited ability to control or meddle – with the important exception of canal irrigation water. Second, the local government institutions even in colonial times – as stipulated in the ordinances and, to lesser degree, as put on the ground – provided models for such institutional forms as local committees, local funds, and specialized village-based work groups. The existence of such models presumably made it easier for villagers to initiate similar practices for themselves. Third, the supply of leadership for a locally-based organization might be expected to be ample, because of the existence of the Reddy caste. Finally, the size of the relevant group is generally quite small. Villages are usually of between 1,000 and 4,000 people, or roughly 200 to 800 households, and fewer than half of the households will have enough land to get most of their income from it. Given the overlap between work and residence, one would suppose that attempts by some to free ride would be likely to be detected by others. 'Noticeability', in Olson's term, would be quite high.

Yet it is striking that despite these facilitating conditions, a majority of the villages in our area do not have institutions of the Kottapalle type, or have them in very attenuated form.

3

Kottapalle

From the market town of Nowk a single-lane tarmac road heads north across the broad expanse of the Nowk valley. A line of worn-down hills to the east defines the edge of the uplands. The road passes first through dense banana stands owned by the wealthy of Nowk, then emerges into a flat open tract of paddy fields and irrigation ditches. Periodically, close to villages, the road is congested with bullocks hauling carts piled high with produce, streams of labourers moving from one work site to another, herds of buffalo on the way to grazing, schoolchildren returning home, people passing the time of day with their neighbours or waiting for a passing vehicle to take them to town. Buses, trucks, and the jeeps of government officials speed past, braving the potholes. Shopkeepers by the roadside throw water on the road to keep down the dust, to little avail. Abruptly beyond each village the road resumes its passage through a vast flat landscape intensively cultivated but empty of people. Some 10 miles from Nowk, the road comes to a bus stop and a collection of roadside stalls. This is the 'road colony' of Batampur village. At this point one leaves the tarmac, crosses the river by a crumbling concrete bridge, and negotiates the lanes of Batampur to join the road to Kottapalle. This is a dry weather road; in the rainy season it is barely fit for walking, and even bullock carts have trouble advancing along it. A few miles up the road, across a treeless expanse of dry, open fields, there lies a thick band of trees, glittering in the sunshine. This is Kottapalle village.

About 3,100 people, in 575 households, live in Kottapalle.[1] Almost all of the male labour force are engaged in agriculture as cultivators or agricultural labourers or both. The 15 per cent of non-agriculturalists include men whose primary occupation is potter, washerman, barber, or trader; and ten or so government employees, such as Irrigation Department field staff, postmaster and postman, primary school teachers, and veterinary assistant.[2] A handful of men commute to jobs

---

[1] The population figures used here are from the 1971 census, except where otherwise stated. Preliminary returns from the 1981 census suggest a small decline in Kottapalle's resident population, from 3,127 in 1971 to 3,105.

[2] Seven men depend primarily on a government salary: three schoolteachers (the other

or businesses in Nowk, though the journey can take two or even three hours. How much land is owned by Kottapalle residents outside the village boundaries can only be guessed at, but it clearly does not condition the village economy in any important way. Only about 200 acres of the village's land is owned by non-residents, mostly people who have a strong kinship connection with the village. The residents of the village depend overwhelmingly on the produce of the village land.

The village area is 4,600 acres (19.5 square kilometres). About 200 acres are uncultivable, 1,400 are irrigated, and roughly 3,000 acres are under rainfed crops.[3] Each square kilometre supports an average of 159 people – almost double the figure at the turn of the century. Irrigation was first brought to the village sometime between 1907 and 1935, probably in the first half of that period. One can be reasonably confident that Kottapalle has had a large area under canal irrigation for at least 50 years. But the village is located near the tail-end of a 20-mile irrigation supply channel off the main canal, and throughout those 50 or more years its irrigators have often worried about their water supply. Maps 2.2 and 2.3 (p. 21–22) show the village's location on the irrigation distributary; and maps 3.1 (p. 46) and A.1 (p. 220) show the layout of the village land.

This chapter describes several features of the village economy and social structure which are relevant to the establishment and maintenance of a village-based system of rule. I begin with the sequence of agricultural operations – for this sequence tends recurrently to make individuals' interests collide; and then go on to define how much is at stake, especially on the irrigated lands.

Cropping calendar

On the rainfed lands the rhythm of agriculture is set by the rains. The annual average rainfall of about 750 mm (30 inches) is concentrated from June to November, 62 per cent falling in the three months from

---

five schoolteachers live outside the village and, at least in principle, commute to it daily), the postmaster, the postman, one Irrigation Department channel man (*lascar*), the Veterinary Compounder. The village accountant (*karnam*) and village magistrate (*munsif*) receive a salary which supplements their landed income; and they are assisted by five *tallari*, revenue peons.

[3] The only reliable figure in this list is 4,600 acres for geographic area. The others are derived by making more or less heroic assumptions on the basis of our own local knowledge (we did not attempt a survey of our own). The census of 1971 states that Kottapalle has 840 acres under irrigation, 32 acres of cultivable waste, and 3,943 acres of 'area not for cultivation'. The census figures for the other villages of which I have local knowledge are equally foolish.

Table 3.1 *Long-run average rainfall and potential evapotranspiration (PET), mm*

	May	June	Jul.	Aug.	Sept.	Oct.	Nov.	Dec.	Annual total
Nowk taluk	39	96	149	144	181	89	31	5	765
Stan devn.	n.a.	49	70	75	96	85	31	11	
Kurnool taluk	30	76	106	103	146	79	30	6	607
District average	37	67	101	100	143	92	44	7	624
Rainfall – PET	− 159	− 75	− 8	− 1	+ 51	− 37	− 49	− 51	− 298

Sources: Rajagopal, 1974, Tab. 1; *Taluk* Statistical Officer, for 38 year run of figures; C.W. Thornthwaite Publications in Climatology, 1963, for PET.
Notes:
(1) Potential evapotranspiration (PET) is the water potentially evaporated from the leaves of a crop and from the land or water it is growing in. When total water supply (rainfall, soil moisture, irrigation) is enough to satisfy PET, plant growth is at or near its maximum (Levine 1977). Hence the difference between average rainfall and average PET gives a rough indication of average irrigation requirement. It must be noted that the values of PET given in the above table are for the Hyderabad station, over 200 kilometres away on the uplands to the north, about 1,000 feet higher in elevation; this is the only PET data readily available. So the difference between Nowk rainfall and Hyderabad PET must be treated as an extremely rough indicator of irrigation requirement.
(2) Kurnool *taluk* figures are given to illustrate rainfall on the westerly side of the district in the area of the TS Canal. 'Rainfall minus PET' refers to Nowk *taluk*.

July to September (table 3.1, which also gives figures for the western side of the district where the TS Canal villages are located). Variability of monthly rainfall around the average is high. Winters (December–January) are mild, with no frost. Summers are hot, temperatures of over 35°C being normal.

In areas of light soils, planting begins immediately after the first heavy rains at the end of June or early July; for light soils hold water relatively poorly, and if the planting does not take place immediately the water is lost through percolation. In heavier soils planting may be delayed till as late as September, by which time the soil moisture reserves are full. The rainfed crops are typical of the semi-arid uplands of peninsula India: sorghum (*jowar*), millet (*korra*), grams, groundnut, and cotton. Whenever they are planted, all the rainfed crops except cotton and sesame will be harvested by late February. The land is then left fallow until the next agricultural year begins with the new rains in June. Only one crop a year is taken. But rains permitting, little cultivable land is left fallow from one year to the next. Not more than 10 to 15 per cent of the cultivable area is left fallow each year, and this is concentrated in poor soil areas of the village's land. Rather, attempts are made to maintain soil fertility by adding fertilizer and manure, and by changing the cropping pattern year by year. Land is too scarce to keep it fallow.

On the irrigated lands, preparation of the paddy seedbeds begins in late June and early July, to be ready for transplanting a month later – or longer if sufficient canal water has not arrived or if operations on the rainfed lands are delayed. The paddy comes to harvest during December and January. Only a small part of the first season's irrigated land is under a crop other than paddy. (Paddy means rice which is growing or harvested rice still in the husk.)

In the second (dry) season, conventionally defined as from December–January to April–May,[4] the main irrigated crops are hybrid sorghum, groundnut and paddy, with small areas of turmeric, onions and cotton, Both sorghum and groundnut may be planted from November through to January, sometimes even into February, to be harvested by late April or early May at the latest.

The gross irrigated area of 2,200 acres is made up of roughly 700 acres planted with two irrigated crops a year, and 800 acres with only one irrigated crop. Some of this 800 acres takes a rainfed crop in the first season, followed by irrigated sorghum or groundnut in the second season. The rest takes the irrigated crop in the first season and is left fallow in the second season. Land is intensively used[5] and more would be put under irrigation if more water were available; it is the supply of water that limits the intensity of cultivation.

Figure 3.1 shows the main sequence of the rainfed and irrigated crops through the agricultural year. Note especially the large 'hole' in the calendar between March and June. At this time stubble grazing is available over most of the village land; but for much of that time some irrigated and rainfed crops are still standing, and stock need to be regulated even after the first season harvest.

The advantages of irrigation

In Kottapalle an average to good yield for paddy in the first season is reckoned at 20 to 25 bags per acre (3.7 to 4.7 metric tons per hectare).

---

[4] See Wade (1985a) on the difference between the conventional definition and the official one.
[5] I estimate that the cropping intensity on irrigated land (including rainfed as well as irrigated crops) is about 1.35 – but the margin of error is large.

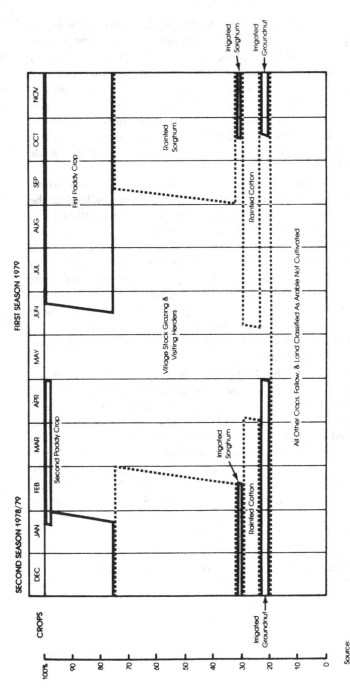

Source:

Village accountant's (Karnam's) records, adjusted by direct observations. Data elaborated by Jeremy Jackson.
The figures are subject to large margins of error. In particular they show less groundnut (wet & dry) than is
normally the case.

3.1 Cropping pattern, crops as a percentage of total cultivable area, Kottapalle

41

Even in good-water-supply villages paddy yields are not much higher than 25 bags (4.7 tons per hectare).[6] (Multiply paddy weight by two-thirds to convert paddy to edible rice equivalent.) This is low by international standards: with controlled irrigation but without 'improved practices', paddy yields in the order of 3 tons per hectare are expected; with improved practices, in field rather than research station conditions, rainy season yields of the order of 4 to 6 tons per hectare are expected (Ruthenberg 1980:243). National paddy averages for Japan and South Korea are around 6 tons per hectare (Wade 1982c, 1982d).

Kottapalle cultivators mostly use an 'improved local variety' (ordinary *mashuri*) rather than a 'higher yielding variety': it is taller than the latter, and of longer duration (135–40 days seed to seed). Its straw is more palatable to animals, being less stiff, and farmers say it gives more straw per acre. It is also more robust in the face of disease and pests, requiring less to be spent on sprays. Application of chemical fertilizer is a normal practice. A rich peasant might apply as much as 150 kilos per acre, which is roughly the same as the average for all crops in Japan and South Korea, though less than the average for irrigated paddy in those countries. It is also much more than the average use of fertilizer for irrigated paddy in Andhra Pradesh as a whole, of about 20 – 27 kilos per acre in the first half of the 1970s.

With paddy prices at Rs. 1.4 per kilo (the prevailing level one to two months after the 1981 first season harvest), a farmer can expect a net profit of around Rs. 1,200–1,400 per acre of paddy, with input costs (including labour) of about Rs. 1,100 per acre.[7] As for irrigated sorghum, a second popular irrigated crop, yields are normally about 3.8 to 5.0 tons per hectare, from which the farmer can expect a net profit per acre of over Rs. 3,000. Irrigated groundnut, a third main irrigated crop, normally gives about 2 tons per hectare, from which the farmer can expect a net profit per acre of over Rs. 1,300. Rainfed lands, on the

---

[6] However, a survey of yields of first season paddy under four other major canal systems in the state showed lower figures than those given for Kottapalle. The average results for plots within the attention of the 'intensive agricultural extension' program (the Training and Visit method) for 1977–8 ranged from 3.0 to 3.7 tons/hectare in the four commands; for control plots not benefiting from the new program, the yields ranged from 1.9 to 2.5 tons/hectare (Government of Andhra Pradesh, Bureau of Economics and Statistics, 1979, table 5.9).

[7] This and following calculations of net profit do not include the cost of seed, or interest payments, or payments to 'common irrigators' or the imputed cost of family labour engaged specifically in irrigation work, or the cost of labour to spread fertilizer, pesticides, etc. The yield is taken to include grain and straw for fodder. The figures come from a small number of detailed farm accounts, and can be taken only as orders of magnitude.

other hand, are unlikely to yield a net profit of more than about Rs. 500 per acre.

These figures highlight the advantages of irrigation: net profits per crop per acre are likely to be about two and a half to three times higher than for unirrigated crops. Further, some of the irrigated land grows two crops a year (in some cases both irrigated, in others, a rainfed crop followed by an irrigated crop in the dry season).

The advantages to the owner of irrigated land are highlighted even more sharply when net profits are compared to the prevailing wage for male agricultural labourers in 1981/2 of Rs. 5 per day, rising to Rs. 6 or even Rs. 7 at times of (short) seasonal peaks. One acre of paddy can be counted upon, if irrigation water is reliable, to produce an income net of most labour costs equal to 200 days of manual labour.[8] Thus, while returns to labour are very low, returns to owners of irrigated land are very high.

But irrigation brings risks. In particular, the irrigator faces the risk that having invested much more in inputs per acre than for dry crops, the irrigation water will not arrive in adequate and reliable quantities. In villages located in the upper two-thirds of a longish distributary (more than two or three miles long) this risk is small for most irrigators; but in villages towards the tail-end, like Kottapalle, it is much higher. Corporate organization is a means of reducing this common risk.

Household distribution of agricultural assets

Government records of land ownership are unreliable, and the more closely they are examined the more unreliable they become. They can provide only broad orders of magnitude. The records of Kottapalle's village accountant suggest that of the village's 575 resident households (1971), 425 own some of the village's 4,550 acres of non-residential land (in addition to a house-site). This means that about a quarter of Kottapalle's households are landless. The landless households include a small number which derive a comfortable income from means other than cultivation; but the overwhelming majority of them are very poor. At the other end, the top 20 per cent of landowning households (85) hold 40 per cent of the non-residential area (1,820 acres); the top 2 per cent of

---

[8] This is calculated by assuming a net income of Rs. 1,250 per acre from paddy, and average wage rate of Rs. 5 per day for men. However one could also calculate the rate of return to paddy land *ownership* as equivalent to the fixed sum rental. The case described later in the text involves a rental of seven bags an acre, which at Rs. 105 per bag of 75 kilos is about Rs. 735. The equivalent in days of manual labour is then about 150.

households own 10 per cent of the area. Twenty-five heads of household are listed as owning 30 acres or more (of irrigated plus unirrigated land); another 157 own between 5 and 30 acres; another 124, between 2.5 and 5 acres. The biggest holding is about 120–130 acres.

Of course, these figures should be qualified according to how much of each holding is irrigated and how much rainfed. On this the official records are widely inaccurate. It is clear though, that most landowning households own some irrigated land and some rainfed; and that a high proportion have some of their irrigated land under paddy. A crude estimate suggests that a household of 6 members with 2 acres of (single cropped) paddy land and 2 or 3 acres of lightly irrigated land is likely to try to supplement farm income with agricultural labouring for others; but that with 2 acres of paddy and 5 acres of lightly irrigated crops it would be a net buyer of labour, buying in more labour than it sells to others. In any case, the key point for our purposes is the sizable number of 'surplus' farmers, who are net buyers of labour and net sellers of food. There are probably at least 100 households in this position.

Of these, perhaps 20–25 are sufficiently wealthy to disengage almost completely from the actual labour of ploughing and hauling, leaving manual work to those they employ. We may call them 'landlords', as distinct from those who, while surplus, are engaged in the manual labour of operating their own holdings, whom we may call 'rich peasants'. It is important to emphasize that this distinction is not a sharp one, and it will be useful to keep the term 'big farmer' to both landlords and rich peasants. Even the 'landlords', with very few exceptions, actively supervise their workers; they themselves, or their sons, will go to the fields and direct them, and even when there is no work to be done will often visit their fields to check on diseases or water levels.[9] They are not big enough to influence the price of labour or food. Nor do they have tenants who depend on them for access to land; for little land is worked in tenancy, and even less fits the classic big landlord–dependent tenant pattern; tenants are as likely to be big farmers as poor peasants.[10] Eight households employ two or more 'permanent farm servants', male labourers on annual contract.

About 20 households own 2 or more pairs of work oxen (all but one of these own 2 pairs, the remaining household owns 3). Roughly another 150 households own 1 pair, giving a total village stock of around 200

[9] Compare Harriss 1982:115–18; Epstein 1962:71; Mencher 1975:253.
[10] Sangeetha Rao's results from a survey of paddy areas in Andhra Pradesh (1980) show 4 per cent of cultivated area is leased-in land. Harriss (1982, ch. 4) reports that tenancy is of slight importance in most of eastern North Arcot district of Tamil Nadu.

pairs.[11] It is reckoned that 1 pair of oxen can work 10 acres of paddy land, or anything from 15 to 50 acres of lightly irrigated and rainfed land (averaging about 20 to 25 acres of lightly irrigated land and 30 to 40 acres of rainfed). But these figures are exceedingly rough, because oxen are not homogeneous and because draught requirements differ greatly according to soil type and crop. A pair of small, light-weight bulls could manage only about 15 acres of (lightly irrigated) groundnut, while a pair of heavy bulls could manage 50 acres of rainfed sorghum on lightish soils. Also, draught requirements are to some extent staggered, and depending on the combinations of rainfed, lightly irrigated, and paddy lands the requirement per holding would be less than indicated by the above coefficients. Hiring of oxen (with ploughman) is common. In Kottapalle, as in most irrigated villages except those where two crops of paddy are grown over most of the village area, water buffalo are generally not used for ploughing, not even for paddy. Buffaloes are kept mostly for milk, not traction.

The main conclusion we need from this discussion is simply that Kottapalle has no tiny oligarchy; on the contrary, there is a sizable number of small landlords and rich peasants – a sizable number of men with enough security and enough at stake to be prepared to determine how the 'public' affairs of village agriculture should be run.

Spatial distribution of land

The second main point about land control is that the fields of any one household tend to be scattered about the village area. In a sample of 8 large landowners (owning more than 14 acres of paddy land), the combined total area of 460 acres was split into 156 different parcels, an average of 20 parcels per holding, and an average parcel size of 1.9 acres (with dry and lightly irrigated fields being larger, paddy fields being smaller). The biggest landowner, with a recorded holding size of 107 acres (and actually 120 to 130 acres within the village boundaries), owns 36 officially-recorded plots, distributed all over the village area (map 3.1, farmer C).

This scattering of holdings can be understood as a means of reducing risks of crop loss, in the same way Marc Bloch explained the persistence of scattered fields in French agriculture: 'If the plots were

---

[11] This is a guesstimate. Harriss' figures for Randam village, North Arcot, show a much higher density of oxen: for a population of 1,300, a cultivated area of 825 acres (of which about 284 are irrigated), there are 153 plough pairs, or 1 team per 5.4 acres (1982:88). This is high by all-India comparison, and by comparison with conventionally defined optimum density.

INDIA

SCATTERING OF BIG MEN'S HOLDINGS

KOTTAPALLE VILLAGE

Farmer A's Holdings

Farmer B's Holdings

Farmer C's Holdings
(Pulla Linga Reddy)

Holdings of Five Other
Big Farmers

Village Boundary

Irrigation Distributary
(Government Operated
Main System)

Roads

To main road and
Batampur Village (#19)

NOTE: This map shows the locations of the holdings of eight big farmers each with more than 14 acres of registered paddy lands. Each block shown also known as a "survey number," contains at least one field belonging to one of the eight farmers. However, an entire block is not necessarily owned by just one farmer.

Village

0   ¼   ½   ¾   1

MILES

3.1 Scattering of big men's holdings, Kottapalle village

dispersed ... everyone had some hope of avoiding the full impact of natural or human disasters – hailstorms, plant diseases, devastation – which might descend upon a place without destroying it completely (1966:233, quoted in McCloskey 1975:113–4). Or in McCloskey's words, 'The object was to hold a diversified portfolio of locations' (1975:114). In peninsula India, and Kottapalle in particular, the land is notoriously variable even within the space of a square mile: in soil type, sub-surface drainage, slope, susceptibility to flash floods, and micro climate. Each type is differently sensitive to weather over the course of the farming season, and suited to different crops. By comparison, the land of the Indo-Gangetic plain is homogeneous; and it is only here that government efforts to consolidate holdings have met with any success (Wade 1976; Agarwal 1971). In the different circumstances of the peninsula uplands, it is sensible for the farmer to have different types of land in a range of locations.

While minimizing risk is likely to be the main reason for scattering, partible inheritance also contributes. Buying and selling of land is common. Land sales per year in the 1970s averaged about 2 per cent of the village land per year, with most being small parcels of less than 1 acre close to the village (such as hay-yards, threshing floors, animal enclosures).[12] 'Debt bondage', which might be a way in which big farmers could consolidate by forcing adjacent small farmers off their land, is unimportant (Bhaduri 1973).

The holdings of big farmers do not tend to be concentrated in one location. Specifically, irrigated land close to the irrigation distributary is not more likely to be owned by big farmers – many blanket assertions about the connection between land control and water control in India to the contrary (Wade 1975b, 1976). We return to this matter in chapter 9.

Since there is a sizable number of big farmers with scattered holdings, it is clear that many households have a direct interest in land in several parts of the village area. They cannot limit their concern to one small corner.

Local orientation

With land control mostly in the hands of those who reside in the village and draw most of their income from land, it is not surprising that the big

---

[12] Based on a study by Jeremy Jackson of 399 cases of change in land ownership registered with the Sub-Registrar of Assurances, Nowk, in the years 1970, 1975, and 1980; of these, 65 per cent were sales, 23 per cent mortgages, 10 per cent gifts. In 1970, 71 per cent of registered sales were of units of less than one acre. Registered changes in land ownership for Kottapalle, in terms of average number per year: 1902–30, 40; 1951–60, 60; 1961–70 (decade of land reform scare), 107; 1971–9, 96. Note that there is no 'community' threshing floor.

farmers are strongly conditioned by the locality. The area has not seen the growing power of merchant capital as a controller of landed production (in contrast to the long-irrigated Krishna and Godavary river delta tracts of coastal Andhra Pradesh).[13] That Kottapalle, like most other irrigated villages away from the most favoured water locations, produces a variety of crops rather than just paddy has helped to restrict trade between the village and the outside more than would have been the case had it concentrated on paddy. Two or three households in the village derive most of their income from merchandising grains and lending money, but village produce is mostly sold to merchants from the local market town. A few men have shares in town-based assets (a share in a transport truck, for example). And a few have been active in Nowk voluntary associations (as elected director of the Land Mortgage Bank, for example). Yet it is striking how limited Kottapalle's rich peasants' and landlords' business or political involvements in the market town are, given that they make the journey fairly frequently.

Status differentials within the village gradually shade from the wealthiest of the public figures through to the Harijans at the bottom; there is no sharp distinction separating landlords from the others (such as is reported from, for example, the area of ancient civilization along the valley of the Cauvery river).[14] The wives of the wealthy tend to come from within a radius almost as small as those of the poor (the wives of the 1980 village council members come from no further than 60 kilometres away). On the other hand, while the majority of village men have never been to the state capital (7-9 hours by bus) virtually all of those here referred to as landlords have, and many of the rich peasants also. Of the nine (small) Hindu temples in the village, five are to gods of the All-India pantheon, one to a local goddess known only in the Nowk area, and three are to the village's main protecting goddess, Sunkularma, worshipped thoughout the southern uplands of Andhra Pradesh. So the gods and goddesses worshipped by the villagers are mostly *not* local figures.

Wealthy households

Let us take some examples of wealthy landowning households. The biggest household has about 120–30 acres of land, of which 40 acres are

---

[13] Washbrook 1977, ch. 3.
[14] Washbrook 1977; Gough 1961; Frankel 1971; also Harriss 1982. The Cauvery river flows across the eastern plains south of Madras.

irrigated. It owns 1 tractor (purchased in 1978, the first and only one in the village); and 3 pairs of oxen (no one else owns more than 2 pairs). It employs 4 farm labourers on annual contract (who double as house-servants), whereas no one else employs more than 2. This is the household of Pulla Linga Reddy (C in map 3.1). He is now an old man of over 80, and no longer takes any active part in village public life. He has 4 sons, all under 40 (the only child from his first marriage died). The sons live in separate households, but the land has not been divided and villagers still think of them as a single household. Nevertheless, when the land is divided, each son will get about 40 acres, enough for comfortable but no grand living. Like their father, all 4 sons depend on agriculture. They actively manage the land, and do all the tractor work themselves. Only the youngest has any post-high school education, but he has been unable, so far, to 'find job'.

As a second case, take a household, also of Reddy Caste, with 41 acres. The father of the present household head had some 160 acres at his death, but division amongst 4 sons gave each 40, to which the present head has added one more by purchase. The household is composed of himself, aged about 55, his wife, of the same age, his married son, aged 25, and his unmarried daughter, aged 16. Another daughter, aged 31, is married and lives in her husband's village. The son has married his sister's daughter, a common practice,[15] but unusually his wife continues to live with her parents and they have no children.

The 41 acres is divided into: 25 acres of rainfed, on which cotton, groundnut, sorghum and green gram are grown; $2\frac{3}{4}$ acres of paddy land; and 13 1/4 acres of land for lightly irrigated crops, mainly hybrid sorghum and groundnut. They rent an extra acre of paddy land, at a fixed rent of 7 bags of paddy an acre (at about 75 kilos a bag). The more common tenancy agreement for paddy land is two-thirds to the owner and one-third to the tenant, with all input costs being shared in the same proportion except land preparation, which is borne by the tenant.

They own 2 pairs of work bulls, one of only about 20 households to own 2 or more pairs; and employ 2 farm labourers on annual contract, one of only about 8 households to employ 2 or more. In addition to crops, they produce milk and meat from 6 buffaloes, and keep 2 or 3 rams for fattening and half a dozen chickens. They use the oxen not only for working their own land, but also for providing all draught power for

---

[15] Throughout South India there is a general male preference for marriage with sister's daughter, mother's brother's daughter, or father's sister's daughter. Thus the tendency of partible inheritance to result in a scattering of land holdings is checked, and property is retained within narrow lineages. Hence also a 'local' orientation is reinforced. See Harris 1982, ch. 4; Stein 1980; Beals 1974.

several acres of other people's paddy in return for straw, valuable as fodder.

Until a few years ago they lived in a three-roomed house, one room above the other and one to the side. One of the downstairs rooms was a stable for the animals, another the storehouse and work space; the family lived in the one upstairs room, where the women cooked and the family ate and – during the monsoon when a roof is necessary – slept. Since then they have built a new house, single storey, with (unusually) the stable attached to the side of the house rather than inside the family's living quarters. The new house has a big veranda where the family sleeps and socializes; an eating room off the veranda and a separate kitchen off the eating room, where the women cook on wood and straw.[16] The kitchen contains the family shrine, a small inset in the wall displaying pictures of the gods. Three smallish storerooms open off the veranda, one of which the son uses as his room. Beneath the floor of the veranda are storage containers for grains. As exceptional as the stable beside the house is the latrine on the other side of the house – only a few wealthy houses have private latrines, and the five public latrines are available only for women; most people use the village border area, pot of water in hand, for this purpose. Even new and wealthy houses like this one, and all the more so the older houses of the village, owe little to urban patterns of design.

Other than the wooden, string-strung bed frames and cotton mattresses, household furnishings are minimal: mortar and pestle, a few pots, two or three brass vessels, some grain baskets, an old transistor radio, a calendar with a Himalayan snow scene, a photo of the son at his high-school graduation, a few metal trunks containing clothes, a steel safe for the family's valuables. No chairs or table. The son has a wristwatch and a couple of pairs of 'western' clothes to wear on visits to the market town. The diet consists of large helpings of rice, garnished with curried dahl, chutney and egg plant, followed by curd and salt – two or three times a day with little variation. Perhaps once or twice a month, on every religious festival and sometimes on Sundays, this household eats meat, followed by sweets.[17] The meat is sheep or chicken. Most festivals, indeed, have no other tangible expression than this luxury food.

[16] The main cooking fuels are the straw of sorghum and of gram, and the stalks of cotton; plus wood in wealthier households. Poor households may use more dung; and even wealthier households sometimes use dung for heating milk. Elsewhere in the district, but not in the area of Kottapalle, some big farmers are beginning to respond to irregular and scarce canal water supplies by putting some of their tail-end plots under fast growing trees (eucalyptus and casurina).

[17] Harriss (1982:90) reports that little meat is eaten in Randam.

While the difference in wealth between this household and the great majority is substantial, the difference in lifestyle, specifically the style and quality of diet and of dress, is much less striking. There is no emphasis on competitive consumption or displays of open-handed generosity, except at weddings. As Elliott (1970) observes in a study of the Reddy caste in the state as a whole, the Reddys are typically hard-working peasant farmers, given to a certain roughness and frugality and displaying neither urban sophistication nor Brahminical piety (which is related to the earlier point that groups of 'urban' culture have historically been weaker in this part of the South Indian countryside than on the fertile eastern coastal plain, the heartland of South Indian civilization). Benson noted in the 1880s that 'the wealthiest and poorest ryots in their homes do not appear to differ much in their clothing, household gear, or habits' (1889:116).[18] In the household under discussion the impression of frugality may change somewhat when the son takes over; for the son attended an English-language school rather than a Telegu-language school in the hope that he would get a job in government service, but he failed the university entrance examination and like virtually all students from the village who have reached this level or higher has had to return to the village to take 'agriculture'. The son also actively works the land, attending to the feeding of the animals, driving the bullock cart, seeing to the irrigation, whenever the farm labourers are otherwise engaged. But he is not a man of the soil by inclination, as is his dour and wiry father. He would prefer to spend his time in the cinema halls of the market town, sporting western clothes.

These two examples of village landlord households illustrate the orientation of the elite towards the locality, in the sense that their household economies are conditioned largely by the produce of their land rather than by assets and enterprise outside the village. When they reach out of the village to make contact with government officers and regional political elite, it is generally to influence the activities of government in their village and its environs.

Workers and the cash nexus

According to the 1971 census, nearly half (48 per cent) of the village male labour force of 981 consisted of 'agricultural workers'; 'cultivators' accounted for another 37 per cent, and 'other' for the remaining 15 per cent. The village is known in the area as one with a lot of 'labour', as a

---

[18] See also Harriss (1982:186). I remain puzzled as to what Kottapalle's wealthy do with their savings.

village from which men and women go to work in surrounding villages, normally within a two-hour walk. Some of these workers also own small amounts of land.[19]

Relations between employers and employees in Kottapalle are more impersonal than might be expected from the fact of joint life-long residence. Well-to-do landowners are not in the business of providing benevolent protection, of foregoing claims on time or paying extra in return for gratuitous loyalty and the hold it gives them on the employee's future service. In dry villages, it is quite usual for the employer to lend a 'farm servant' on annual contract as much as Rs. 2,000 if needed; but if the farm servant wants to change his employer, the second employer must then pay back the loan. This of course greatly reduces the employee's scope for manoeuvre, tending to bond him to one family. In Kottapalle and other irrigated villages, this arrangement is much less common. A small farmer or labourer may request small loans of up to a few hundred rupees from a big farmer for whom he often works; and in most (but not all) cases the granting of the loan does not entail any wider obligation – notably to work for the lender. For bigger amounts he will go either to a bank (where procedures tend to be cumbersome and land is required as security) or to a moneylender. The moneylenders tend also to be merchants, resident in the market town or in Batampur, the big village three miles away. They commonly lend for the working capital costs of groundnut and cotton in return for a promise to sell to them (at a price a little lower than the prevailing market price). And a small farmer who does not have his own pair of oxen may make an arrangement with a big farmer with surplus draught capacity to provide all his draught requirements in return for sending a labourer (such as a teenage son) to the big farmer whenever needed during that season. The labourer will be paid the normal off-peak wage – even in the peak – and must be available to work at night if need be.

But these relations tend to be short-term; and are readily ended if better opportunities appear. Even between employers and their 'farm servants' there is little paternalistic benevolence on the part of the employer. The same impersonality and cash-based calculation in the labour market, for both daily-rated work and for seasonal or annual contracts, has been found in village surveys elsewhere in upland peninsula India (Binswanger *et al.*, 1980). The contrast is with the common image of labour relations in rural India, according to which a few dominant

---

[19] Harriss reports for Randam village, 'More than half of the total number of households in which there are members who take on wage labour is made up of households in which some land is owned' (1982:125). See also Ryan *et al.* (1980:361).

landlords draw off the produce of the soil and redistribute food, clothing and shelter to their dependents, insulating them from the direct pressure of the market. In this type of structure, money is not a significant element in the composition of rural wages or rent agreements, and the price mechanism does not regulate the distribution of food and services within the village. And in extreme cases, long-term debt bondage reduces many cultivators to the status of near-hereditary serfs. Studies of Tanjore and Malabar, in South India, have shown this type of agrarian relationship to exist there; but it is a long way from that of our irrigated villages.[20]

Blacksmiths, carpenters, priests – and others in what are still thought of as 'service' castes – also sell their products or services on the market, at so much per plough or bullock cart axle. The only occupations involved in relations that approximate what are termed in the literature *jajmani* relations (payments in kind for customary services) are that of washerman (*dhobi*) and barber.[21]

Caste

Apart from the distribution of wealth, the other major grouping is by caste. Kottapalle, like most villages in the southern uplands of Andhra Pradesh, is clearly a 'Reddy village', as the people themselves say. Households of Reddy caste are not in a numerical majority – they account for less than a quarter of total households (130 out of 575). But they own almost half the cultivated area.[22] Other high castes (like Brahmins and Vaishyas) account for another 3 per cent of households and 5 per cent of the area. All the rest – the low castes, Harijans, and Muslims (altogether about 16 separate castes are recognized) – account for about three-quarters of the households and 45 per cent of the land. Only about 9 per cent of the Reddy landowners own less than 2.5 acres, compared with 37 per cent of low caste, scheduled caste and Muslim landowners. So while size of landholding does not correlate perfectly with caste (there *are* poor Reddys) it is a moderately strong correlation.

---

[20] See Washbrook (1977), ch. 3; Orans (1968). Alexander *et al.*'s interview data from a survey of 225 Harijans in Krishna district of Andhra Pradesh is consistent with the picture I give for Kurnool (1981:266). See also Ishikawa on pre-Revolutionary China (1975:469).

[21] Compare Harriss (1982:43).

[22] These figures come from the accountant's records. There is however a problem: some people of non-Reddy caste have added Reddy to their name, and will be included in these figures as Reddys although they would not be recognized as such by village Reddys (but have a better chance of claiming Reddy status in the towns). My impression is that there are not more than a few cases of this kind in Kottapalle.

Of the 8 households with 2 or more farm servants on annual contract, 7 are Reddys; of the 20 households with more than 1 pair of oxen, 13 are Reddys, Place of residence within the village is strongly related to caste. Even poor Reddys tend to live in the same part of the village with their richer caste fellows.

Reddys have long occupied the formal institutions of state power in the village. The positions of village president (*sarpanch*) and of magistrate (*munsif*) have always been in Reddy hands, though the position of village accountant (*karnam*) has been held by Brahmins. And Reddys have a virtual monopoly on village 'public' affairs. The other wealthy but non-Reddy households are, with few exceptions, not publicly active. Except for the accountant, the few Brahmin households keep a low profile. A Reddy informant said of the few Vaishyas (Merchants), some of whom are reputed to be wealthy, 'They just keep quiet and make money.' One Boya (Warrior) landowner with 20 acres expressed his feelings in the aphorism, 'Better to be a Reddy with five acres than a Boya with 20 acres.' Better in terms of getting things from government, better in terms of respect within the village and beyond it, better too in terms of education: Reddy children are much more likely to go on to high scoool, and of the 12 university graduates from the village in the latter 1960s and 1970s, all but 2 (a Boya and Brahmin) are Reddys. This figure of 12 university graduates in about 15 years is worth noting; it contrasts with the figure for male literacy, which is probably about the same for Kottapalle as the district average of 34 per cent. Nowhere is the basic inequality of Indian society more graphically shown than in education: primary school provision is so poor that two-thirds of Indians, nationally, remain illiterate; yet the enrolment of the 20–24 year age group in higher education is greater than in all other countries at remotely comparable levels of per capita income, some eight times the proportion in China (Sen 1983).

As for interaction between members of different castes, the rules are today much softened. There is no outcasting (for example in the case of cross-caste sexual relations); it is up to the aggrieved marriage partners to take action, and this may include a lot of criticism or even beating, but nothing as strong as a formal outcasting. With one minor exception, none of the castes is organized into (intra- or inter-village) caste *panchayats* or councils, such as have been reported in some other Indian village studies, as well as in the 1886 *Kurnool manual*, which states that 'almost all castes have their guilds or corporations' (Gopalakrishnamah Chetty 1886:142).

Harijans or 'scheduled castes' (still often referred to by non-Harijans as 'untouchables') live in two separate 'colonies' on the outskirts of the village. Harijans have a 'special' school; they cannot use the clean caste wells, or visit the clean caste temples. Harijan children generally do not play with non-Harijan children, and friendship between adults across the Harijan/non-Harijan divide is rare. A mixed group of Harijan and non-Harijan labourers will commonly sit in separate locations to take their meals out in the fields. Between wealthy Reddys and older Harijans, one can still see something of a forelock touching deference on the one hand, and domineering insouciance, on the other. And there is still an asymmetry in terms of address. A Harijan will not normally call a Reddy, unless a poor Reddy, by his name, but will instead use one of a range of words meaning 'sir' or 'father' in varying degrees of formality and deference (or even, occasionally, to a big Reddy, a term meaning, literally, 'having respect equal to a god'). A big Reddy will commonly use 'fellow' in the disparaging sense rather than the Harijan's name. Still today, Harijan men will normally stand up to address a Reddy of consequence.

Modern India's promulgation of the equal rights of all citizens has only slowly made an impact on Kottapalle. The essence of the Reddy and Brahmin view of low caste people generally, and Harijans especially, continues to be the inequality of their intrinsic worth.[23] This axiom is much stronger in villages than in the towns. For Reddys of the village, the village remains their reference group; they are little involved with affairs beyond the village except insofar as those affairs impinge on their profits from land within the village; and they are correspondingly dependent for their self-esteem on their position of superordination within it.

Community identity

Several factors inhibit the development of a 'natural' collectivism. Caste is one; the strength of attachment to a non-territorial group like caste hinders emotional attachment to the village. Labour relations constitute another; labour for agriculture is hired much more than exchanged. Other occasions, too, which in some parts of the peasant world provide occasions for cooperative help, are organized in the same way: housebuilding, for example, is done by specialists who take the job on contract for all except the crudest houses; cooking for weddings is done (for anyone who aspires to be someone) by a specialist wedding cook from outside the village. In crises one looks to relatives for help, and there

---

[23] Buses of the Andhra Pradesh Road Transport Corporation carry stencilled slogans like 'Untouchability is a Crime' on their sides – incomprehensible to all but the tiny number of country dwellers who read English.

are patterns of mutual help between relatives; but relatives may be scattered territorially, especially the affinal relatives of the elite, who being thin on the ground have to go outside the local area to find partners of suitable status for their sons and daughters.

In more than a dozen annual festivals, only four involve any coming together in processions, games, or entertainments, and none shows much sign of what Durkheim called social 'effervescence', when the individual feels himself 'dominated and carried away by some sort of external power which makes him think and act differently than in normal times' (1964:218). They are almost staid. On the other hand, even if the festivals hardly serve to constitute the village symbolically, the fact that they occur at all is notable. In some other parts of South India such festivals have been called off altogether by the dominant castes, because the festivals turned into occasions when subordinate castes tried to claim equivalence (Harriss 1982:233, Gough 1955, Barnett 1973).

There are virtually no organizations other than the village council with any degree of participation. Officially a 'school committee' exists, which has met just once in its history. There is a 'Milk Cooperative' with a nominally elected president, which organizes the collection of Kottapalle's milk and its transport to a roadside depot; but it is run as a private business, a cooperative in name only. The *Panchayat* has been moribund for as long as anyone can remember, and there is no sign that the new president of 1981 will treat it any differently. People take for granted, with resignation rather than approval, that he will use its income like his predecessors, as more or less his own. He will find the 'light bulb' category of expenditure useful, they say – he likes his liquor ('tasty but no kick', he said of a specially imported bottle of pure malt Scotch whisky) – and there is a certain logic, my informants said with wry amusement, in classifying *Panchayat* money spent on strong liquor as 'light bulbs'. A few years ago a bunch of the young high school and university graduates in the village decided to buy a newspaper jointly; but the scheme fell apart when they could not agree either where to keep the newspaper or whether to have an English one as well as a Telegu one. That is the nearest there has been to a 'youth club'.

The actions of governmental authorities, too, have not generated a sense of the community as a unit. Village government roles, for example, were not elected or shared; they were filled by hereditary recruitment (in practice even today the hereditary principle is strong), and their incumbents were not paid according to how much tax they collected, but (since about 1952) with a governmental salary. There was no collective responsibility for payment of taxes. Historically, the tendency has been for village officers to use their positions to shut out the government, not in order to permit a local democracy to flourish but to enhance their own local control (Washbrook 1977; Baker 1976).

There are no doubt further reasons why, not only in Kottapalle but in Indian villages generally (compared to say, Japanese or western European villages) the ideas of loyalty to the territorially-defined community, of public-spirited concern for the village welfare as the touchstone of public virtue, have hardly developed (Dore 1978; Silverman 1968; Wade 1975a). The new animal clinic (a one-roomed structure) displays above the door a plaque commemorating the man who donated land and Rs. 3,000 for its construction (these exact details are engraved on the stone, together with the man's name, his father's name, and the date, 10.6.1979). This is the one such recognition of 'public spirited munificence' in the village. Two points might be made about it. First, the man who gave the donation was, and remains, a nobody to the Reddys – a small (Vaishaya) shopkeeper near the end of his time, who had no children and wanted a substitute memorial (so Reddy informants say). The Reddys don't see anything 'public spirited' about it. Second, there is nothing to commemorate the village fund's donation to the cost of the building (nor a much bigger donation to the building of the new primary school). Neither the village council, still less the village 'community', has an identity which might be commemorated in that way. Indeed, there is little sense of the village as an entity over time, to which the appetite for honour and immortality might be usefully attached.

The site of Kottapalle has been settled for several generations, at least; but how much longer is difficult to tell for the village gives no obvious clues to its age. Even oral history of the time before grandfather's is virtually non-existent. One thinks of a marvellous remark by Babur, founder of the Mughal dynasty in the fifteenth century: 'In Hindustan, hamlets and villages – even towns – are depopulated and set up in a moment! ... A group collects together, they make a tank or dig a well; they need not build houses or set up walls – khas grass abounds, trees (are) innumerable, and straightway there is a village or town' (in Habib 1963:117).

Conclusion

This chapter has described two sources of conflict and production loss in agriculture which might be held in check by a concerted response, and three features of local social structure which might facilitate such a response. We saw the 'hole' in the cropping calendar between March and

June, in which large areas of crop land become available for stubble grazing; but at the same time, some crops are still standing, and there is thus a danger that animals grazing the stubble will eat the standing crops as well. But the danger to standing crops is present throughout the year, for population density is at a level (159 people per square kilometre)[24] at which virtually no arable land is left in annual fallow, so the village's own livestock must graze for much of the year on the margins of fields and on small patches of fallow or waste. This is one source of trouble. The second source is the unreliability of water supply to Kottapalle, because of its location in the distribution network, and the much greater investment and profits at risk with irrigated crops compared to dry crops.

In terms of social structure, we find that the village has no tiny oligarchy, but rather some 20 to 25 households which are sufficiently wealthy to disengage almost completely from manual labour themselves, though virtually none disengage from active management of the land. Some 100 to 150 households own sufficient land in relation to their household labour force to be net buyers of labour. The second important feature is the scattering of assets: the landholdings of the wealthy households are scattered about the area of the village, which gives each wealthy household a direct interest in several parts of the village's domain. And the third feature is the orientation of the elite towards the locality, in the sense that their household economies are conditioned largely by the produce of their land rather than by assets and enterprises outside the village. On the other hand, we noted several features of the system of social relations which hinder the development of a distinct village identity and feelings of loyalty to it.

[24] Since population pressure is an important parameter of the argument it is worth bringing together the main indicators. Kottapalle's population (1971 and 1981) is about 3,100, its area 4,600 acres, population density 159 persons per sq. km. In 1901 the population was 1,637 in about the same area. The Nowk valley today has 150 persons per sq. km., the district average is 105, the state average is 153. The district average in the first half of the 1870s (before the Great Famine) was 53. The Nowk valley in 1870 had a density of 330 persons per 1,000 cultivated acres; further west, this density was just under 300. Already by the 1880s in the Nowk valley, 'few trees are to be seen' (Benson 1889:129), and Brakenbury reported for the adjoining district in 1915 that 'firewood is very scarce', so the dead cotton plants and roots of sorghum were used as fuel (Brakenbury 1915:77). (But the absence of trees presumably also reflected the effect of the Great Famine.) By the early twentieth century rather little land in the district seems to have been left in annual or several years' fallow. Meat consumption is another indicator: the fact that little meat is now eaten reflects the extension of cereal cultivation for human consumption. Apparently meat consumption was greater some 30 years ago, according to Kottapalle informants. Specifically, pig consumption was greater, whereas it is now very restricted. As areas of natural forage have shrunk, pigs would have had to be fed on cereals as supplements, and so would have been directly competitive with human beings. See also chapter 9, n. 6.

4

The social response to open-field husbandry

The impetus for Kottapalle's corporate organization comes from two kinds of cultivation problems – those inherent in open-field husbandry and those inherent in tail-end location in an irrigation network. This chapter deals with the response to problems of open fields.

Inherent problems of open-fields

Livestock are needed in this type of agriculture for their role in cereal production rather than as a source of food. They are virtually the sole non-human source of traction and an important source of fertilizer (supplemented today by chemicals). Oxen, or in some heavily irrigated villages, water buffalo, provide the traction; but in too few numbers to provide enough manure. The manure has to come mostly from sheep and goats, and what might be called sheep-shit economics turns out to be a vital ingredient in an explanation of corporate organization.

Population density has reached a level where insufficient fodder is available in or near the village land to support enough animals to fertilize the crops with their manure. The district's average population density, it will be recalled, is 105 people per square kilometre. This corresponds to density group 8 on Boserup's scale, at which one would expect to find most land growing one crop a year ('annual cropping'), and little land left fallow for a year or more (1981:9, 19, 20). In the Nowk valley, where Kottapalle is located, average population density is about 150 persons per square kilometre (group 9 on the Boserup scale), and here the pressure on waste land and fallow is greater still. In Europe after the sixteenth century it was the planting of forage crops in the fallow which released farmers from the trap of insufficient fodder to feed sufficient animals to provide sufficient manure to raise crop yields.[1] But in Kurnool district only very small areas are put under forage crops, which compete with cereal crops for human consumption.

Farmers also feed their stock on those parts of their crops not fit for

---

[1] This solution was found in some locations by the late thirteenth century (Slicher van Bath 1963).

human consumption: on rice straw, the stalk of sorghum, and the haulms of groundnut and gram. These parts of the plant are brought in at harvest and stored for later use by the crop owner. What remains in the field after the harvest is for communal use, including the new growth ('ratoons') put out by the sorghum plants, the unharvested cotton bolls, and the grasses growing up on residual soil moisture. Further, throughout the year the grasses which grow spontaneously on road margins, canal banks, and drains are for communal use and these are the main source of fresh fodder while the rainfed crops are growing.

These conditions of fodder supply produce a sharp variation in the amount of animal food available throughout the year. The limited supply of fodder during the main crop growing season places a low ceiling on the number of animals which can be carried throughout the year on the village land. So the village's stock of animals consists mostly of big stock – of oxen for traction and of water buffalo for milk. Only small numbers of sheep and goats are kept, and even smaller numbers of pigs. The big stock are stall-fed part of the time; indeed, during the hottest period of the year they do most of their feeding in the stalls at night. The buffalo in milk are fed daily by the army of women who are everywhere cutting grass from the canal sides, drains, and road margins. But most days the stock must also be taken out to graze and water.

There are no fences, except for the fearsome thorn bushes planted around two small citrus groves[2] and the stone walls around hay yards and threshing floors on the edge of the village. Field fencing would greatly impede access to small scattered plots, would eat up valuable land, and would be expensive to construct.

So oxen and buffalo, sheep and goats, the occasional herd of pigs, all have to be guided past unprotected stretches of tasty crops as they go to and from grazing. The permanent grazing itself tends to be close to unprotected standing crops. Fields kept fallow for a year (and so available for communal grazing even during the growing season) tend to be surrounded by crops. Often the smaller children are sent to watch the animals. If they stop to watch an argument, or run off to play, the animals can do considerable damage in the adjacent fields. Some of the most heated quarrels in Kottapalle and other villages are precipitated by wayward animals.

After the harvest of the rainfed crops and the first season paddy, the area available for common stubble and fallow pasturage increases

---

[2] The natural grazing in these citrus groves is private propery, not communal; but the owners cannot take any sizable number of sheep and goats to graze in them until the date at which the council allows the outside herders to enter the village land.

dramatically. The supply of fodder is now far greater than needed by the village's own stock of animals. This makes it possible for the farmers to obtain sheep manure by allowing sheep and goats to come into the village for the period from the harvest until the time of field preparation for the next season. The outside herders mostly come from the zones of extensive stock-oriented agriculture on either side of the Nowk valley.

So, after most of the rainfed crops are harvested, large numbers of sheep and goats enter the village land – more than 10,000 head at first – and remain for two months or more. But the end of the harvest is not uniform. Even among the rainfed crops, sesame and cotton are still in the ground when the sorghum is harvested, and the sorghum stubble makes especially good fodder. While herder and sorghum grower both wish to get the sheep onto the sorghum soon after the harvest, the neighbouring cotton-grower may well be alarmed at the prospect of a thousand or so sheep and goats grazing next to his cotton, which is much to the liking of sheep and goats. Also, a catch crop is sometimes undersown in the paddy to grow after the paddy harvest on residual soil moisture, and this too needs protection from free-grazing animals. So, even in wholly rainfed areas, uneven harvesting means that the later-harvested crops are at risk from the animals brought in to graze the stubble of the earlier-harvested crops. Where there are second-season irrigated crops being grown, the problem is worse; they come to harvest after even the late-harvested rainfed crops, so are at risk for a longer time.

The danger posed by grazing livestock to standing crops is only one problem inherent in an open-field system. A second is uncontrolled breeding and endemic livestock disease. With male and female animals roaming about the village land breeding is difficult to control and diseases are easily spread. A third problem is the overuse of land because of too many animals clustered on it. In particular this causes soil impaction beyond the ability of land to recover in the next planting season. While the first three problems proceed from livestock the fourth arises from humans: the physical layout of unfenced, scattered plots makes crop theft relatively easy. And since a large number of landless food buyers live close to the fields of ripening grain, the risk of crop theft is by no means negligible.

Social response

These are the sorts of dangers the open-field system creates or amplifies, and it is to avoid or reduce them that village rules intervene. In European open-field villages, much of the emphasis in village regulation was on joint control of cropping. In the classic three-field form, one whole segment of the village land was designated common fallow each year in a three-fold rotation, and the grazing animals could thus more easily be kept away from standing crops than if the fallow were scattered about the arable in small patches. Dates of sowing and harvesting were often controlled jointly, partly to reduce the conflict which resulted when a crop owner slow to harvest held up animal owners anxious to put their animals onto the stubble, and partly to make identification of thieves easier (anyone seen carrying corn before the stipulated harvest date could be presumed to be a thief). Stock numbers were also controlled, so that a landowner (more exactly, a holder of rights in the common) could graze only a certain number of animals, normally based on the size of his land holding. Each village had a shepherd who guarded the grazing animals in the fallow field and saw that other regulations were observed; and the village might also appoint other 'bailiffs' to police and levy fines for infringements (Hoffman 1975; Ault 1972; Baker and Butlin 1973; Campbell 1981).

Cropping

In Kottapalle the emphasis is different. There are, to be sure, two regulations governing cropping which are intended to reduce the risk of animal damage and crop theft. First, the council fixes the date at which sorghum harvesting can begin, so as to minimize patchwork harvesting. Patchwork harvesting would concentrate bird and animal damage on the crops of those who harvest later, and would make it more difficult to protect standing crops from animals grazing the stubble. It would also make crop theft easier; and since the stalk of nearly ripe sorghum is almost as prized as sugar cane for sucking, the standing crops are at constant risk from people en route to harvest more distant fields. The date of planting being nearly uniform for everyone in the village (it is set by the rains), the date at which the crops are ripe is also fairly uniform, so no great loss is incurred by the harvesting restriction.[3] Secondly, the council lays down the rule that when the groundnut is being harvested, the owner or tenant must be present in the field to supervise the gang of harvesters; otherwise the harvesters, left to their own devices, will make off with harvest from the adjoining fields as well. Groundnut, like sorghum, can be consumed on the spot, raw.

---

[3] But if small farmers without their own oxen plant earlier than they would have preferred (so as to avoid the risk that when the optimum planting time arrives they will not be able to find oxen for hire) this restriction of harvesting may cost them more than it costs those – like the councillors – with their own oxen.

The social response to open-field husbandry

In general, though, cropping is unregulated, though the very seasonal nature of the rains and of canal supply sets tight limits on managerial autonomy. Moreover, in a block of land which is under paddy it is simply not possible for some non-conformist to grow some other crop, because drainage from his neighbours' fields will put his field out of action for any crop other than (water-consumptive) paddy. Unless all farmers in the same mini-catchment agree not to grow paddy, none can switch.[4] The environment has a greater role in regulating the cropping in Kottapalle and other South Indian villages than in European villages.

Field guarding: livestock

The emphasis of communal regulation falls more on livestock than on cropping. A squad of four field guards (FGs)[5] is employed for most of the year, excluding part of April, May and June. Towards harvest time in both seasons, two or three extra guards are employed as the need arises. And during the first season paddy harvest the common irrigators, by then not needed for supplying water, switch to field guarding, giving Kottapalle a total of nearly 20 full-time field guards. They are empowered to take straying animals to the village pound,[6] from which the owner has to pay a standard fine set by the council to get them back. For big stock, the fine in 1980 was Rs. 4 per head at night, Rs. 2 during the day. Where many animals are involved (flocks of sheep and goats, for instance) the case is brought before the council, which decides the fine.

The logic, then, is that the dangers faced by unregulated crop growers from animals grazing on scattered plots and road margins near the crops will be reduced by giving the animal owners a strong *disincentive* to allow their animals to wander. It is then less necessary for each crop owner to arrange for the protection of his own crops.

When the outside sheep and goats are brought in after the harvest of (most of) the rainfed crops, extra precautions are taken. Some 9,000 to 13,000 head of sheep and goats enter the village at this time. During the day the flocks graze over the stubble and fallow at will; at night they are folded, flock by flock, to concentrate their dung in one place. The flocks are allocated to fields by means of a regular auction (described later), and at the beginning of the first auction each year a series of written rules are read out and discussed. These rules are worth noting.

---

[4] This is a simplification: the constraints on paddy plot owners vary with drainage conditions and distance from water source.
[5] Field guards are called *kavali kalu* in Telegu.
[6] Village pound is *bandhala dhoddi*.

For the *herder*: (i) He must take the flock to the designated field by 6.30 p.m. and keep it there until 8 a.m. (ii) He must not allow the flock to graze standing crops. (iii) Half of the amount to be paid to the shepherd for the first 'turn' (four nights) must be put on deposit with the council; if the shepherd leaves before four turns have been completed he must forfeit this amount to the village fund. (This is to discourage herders from leaving inconveniently early, before farmers have their fields manured and cleared of stubble.) (iv) The herder must stay within village boundaries; if the farmer asks him to go to a field outside the village boundaries, he must refuse.

For the *farmer*: (i) He must keep the flock within the village boundaries. (This is to ensure that the farmers of Kottapalle village, rather than those of elsewhere, have their fields cleared of stubble; and also to reduce opportunities for conflict between villages, since if a farmer from Kottapalle brought a flock into another village where he owned land he might ignore that village's own implicit or explicit rules of grazing and be less subject to sanctions.) (ii) If he pays the fund or the herder in kind rather than cash he must make the conversion at the rate of Rs. 1.25 per measure of hybrid sorghum, or Rs. 1.50 per measure of 'local' sorghum (as of early 1980). (iii) He must send men to help the shepherd guard the flock at night, at the rate of two men per 2,000 head. Labourers must be paid Rs. 3 per night, or equivalent grain at the rate set in point (ii).

One other point is read out; if animals are stolen while they are in the village, the council will do its best to trace the culprits. And a further condition is implicit: that the group of herders has exclusive rights to village grazing for as long as it wants, other outside herders being allowed in only as flocks leave.

These rules were drawn up by the council many years ago, and are written into the notebook where details of the sheep-folding auction are recorded. While they may seem rudimentary in relation to the elaborate by-laws of open-field villages in medieval England (Ault 1972), they are remarkable against the conventional picture of village India. In particular, they show a surprisingly high degree of collective specification of activities; the collective entity makes decisions about such matters as how many labourers are to help the herder and even how much the labourers are to be paid (to ensure that the farmer does not send young children or the infirm, because at that wage able-bodied men will be available). These are matters that would ordinarily be within the scope of bargaining between each individual household and herder. Such tight specification of responsibilities by the council reflects the very real danger of loss to standing crops in unfenced fields.

The field guards' job, then, is to enforce these regulations and those on the cropping, and generally to see that livestock are kept under proper watch. They retain all the money they collect from small fines (Rs. 2 and Rs. 4 per animal, by day and night respectively). They keep 25 per cent of bigger fines, decided by the council, and are responsible for collection. They divide the fine money equally between themselves, regardless of who was involved in a particular case. In the late 1970s their income was about Rs. 60 to Rs. 80 a month (higher around harvest, lower at the start of the season). This works out at a daily rate rather less than the prevailing off-peak male agricultural wage rate (while the common irrigators get slightly more); and considerably less than the rate for farm servants on annual contract. Not only does a low salary ease the pressure on the village fund to raise very considerable amounts of money annually for the wages; it also gives the field guards an incentive to invigilate and be persistent in collecting fines – not infrequently a difficult and unpleasant task.

Field guarding: crop thefts

The other major function of the field guards is to guard against theft. (Even dung after sheep folding is at risk from people who come at night with baskets to carry it onto their nearby plots).[7] But crops are the main target. Groundnut, red gram, bengal gram and sorghum are particularly subject to frequent small-scale theft, because they are good to eat raw or feed to animals before being ready to harvest, while they are normally grown in large extensions and need infrequent attention once planting is finished. Paddy is less at risk from casual, day-time thefts, not only because it is of little use prior to harvest but also because by day during the growing season there are more people at work in the fields or routinely checking water levels.

The big crop thefts take place at night in groups organized for the purpose. It is said that such groups always come from other villages and that 'labourers' from Kottapalle will likewise go elsewhere, to reduce

---

[7] Michael Lipton comments on this part of the story:

> Of excremental crapital/output ratios
>
> For millet, the neighborhood baddy
> Abetted, I fear, by his daddy
> Steals the shit of the sheep
> While the field guard's asleep
> But pigshit is better for paddy.

Chapter 9, 'Sheep-shit economics', clarifies the connection between crop type and manure type.

risk of recognition. Paddy is at least as much the object of these groups' attention as the other food crops. Hence Kottapalle's veritable army of collectively provided harvest guards at the time of the first season paddy crop.

In 1976, more than an acre of grain was stolen in one night by men who were later identified as having come from a village five miles away. Fifty men from Kottapalle set out to attack the village and get revenge; but the 'labourers' presumed to have made the theft had advance warning, and fled. When the Kottapalle men arrived they were met by the 'big Reddys' of the village, who promised they would keep their labourers in better order in future. No clash occurred. In another case at about the same time, labourers from a village some six miles away were said to have stolen an acre of sorghum. They were brought before the council, it is said, and made to pay a fine of Rs. 600 (though there is no record of such a fine in the income accounts). Village justice can be much rougher. On one occasion a man who had come to Kottapalle to gamble tried to steal a ram as he set off home to his village six miles away. He was caught, beaten up, tied to a pole in the main meeting area, and abused for two days. Some threatened to break his arm or leg, to make sure he wouldn't do it again. The village council counselled that such action should be taken 'next time', and the man was released. Such small thefts of a sheep or two are quite common, and are often related, in retrospect, to the appearance in the village the previous day of two or three strange men passing through.

Note that in none of these cases was there any thought of making a complaint to the police or taking the presumed culprit to them. This would only be done if the theft was very big, because the costs of getting the police to act would be high. In other than big cases, the matter is settled – or not – within the village.

By mid-December 1980, with much of the harvest already in,[8] more than half an acre of that season's crops had been stolen at night: on one occasion three bags of sorghum, on another two bags of paddy, on a third half an acre of paddy. In all cases (private) harvest guards were sleeping in the very fields from where the grain was lifted. In the sorghum case the thieves stripped the harvest guard naked and made off with his clothes, presumably to delay him raising the alarm – 'if you are going to sleep by your crop in the fields don't take a good *dhoti* or blanket with you', – people wryly reminded each other. In the first paddy case, three guards were sleeping side by side, and the thieves beat them with a stick

[8] Mid-December, because I left the village then, not returning until the middle of the next year. The thefts continued up to the end of harvest.

to make them run away. In the second paddy case, two guards and the field owner were sleeping in the field but did not wake up – though the paddy was lifted from all around where they slept. It is cold at night during the paddy harvest, the middle of the South Indian winter; people wrap themselves tightly in a blanket and sleep deeply.

One can appreciate that from the perspective of a crop or animal owner, even occasional thefts give rise to almost panicky concern. There are a large number of people in all villages who have few crops or animals of their own; and who, by the time of the first paddy season, have exhausted whatever stores of grain they may have had. The temptation to steal from the abundance in the fields must be strong. This reinforces the wish of the owners of land and of animals to have village-provided field guards. The poor performance of the 1980 field guards in stopping crop thefts led them to be replaced in 1981, as we shall see.

The field guards

By day the field guards travel about village lands in ones or twos, on the lookout for straying cattle and thieves in the groundnut, sorghum, or gram. The danger of cattle straying comes mostly during the day because the animals are normally locked up at night inside or next to their owner's house. By night the field guards travel in groups of four or more, taking one or two of the field roads at random and walking up and down them, shouting periodically and flashing their torches to scare off thieves and animals. Bird damage is taken as a given; no special effort is made by field guards or owners to keep the birds off, though the rule on the start of the sorghum harvest helps protect those who might otherwise harvest late from birds displaced off the early harvested fields.

The four 'permanent' field guards are appointed each year after the start of the first season, as long after the rainfed crops and paddy seedbeds have been planted as is safe. The occasion for appointment is normally the general assembly meeting, when the accounts are read out and the council members affirmed. Notice of the general meeting is announced by village crier; those who want a field guard job indicate this at the meeting, and the council decides. The demand for the jobs is not high – less than for common irrigators. At the meeting the newly appointed field guards are admonished to be conscientious about their duties, which include not only guarding the fields and animals but also making light repairs to field roads and culverts (assisted during the first season by the common irrigators), arranging the sheep-folding auction, protecting the haystacks around the periphery of the village from thieves and cattle, collecting fines, helping with the organization of village festivals, and acting as an informal police force in the village itself as well as in the fields. Their presence is easily distinguished by the long pole they carry with the characteristic rope on the end, used for tying up straying cattle. They might also intervene in a quarrel which threatens to get out of hand, calming people down.

The 1980 permanent field guards had all done the job for at least the previous three years, one of them for the previous ten years. Three of them were Reddy caste, the fourth belonged to a Muslim sub-caste. The latter was the wealthiest, with between 20 and 30 acres of land and 1 pair of oxen, while the others had at least 5 acres each but no oxen. Field guards need to carry a certain respect, and accordingly are not drawn from the poorer sections of the village; a Harijan would not be appointed, even if of moderate means.

Other responses to open-field problems

There is, then, an elaborate organization for providing protection to crop growers and animal owners against animal damage and theft and to keep field access roads in repair. The same organization has addressed itself to several other crop-livestock problems. The council first rented a room in the village where sick animals could be treated, then financed the building of a new community-owned structure. It has also pressed the relevant government department to provide a veterinary assistant (Compounder) part-time for the village, and helps provide him with meals and other necessities when he is in the village. Without such pressure, it would be more difficult to get veterinary assistance to the village. And finally, the village council provides one stud buffalo to serve the village's stock of milk buffalo, so helping to reduce uncontrolled breeding.

As for the problem of excessive numbers of livestock, the council limits the number of small stock which can be brought into the village to graze the stubble, so as to balance the need of farmers for manure against the anxieties of those with standing crops and to minimize the danger of excessive soil compaction. But there is no collective regulation of the number of stock which a villager can graze in the village, as there often was in open-field villages of Europe. 'Stinting', in other words, is applied only to outside herders. For villagers, the decision about how many animals to own and graze is left to each individual.

Financing the field guards

The field guards must be paid. In the late 1970s, the bill came to some Rs. 3,500 to Rs. 4,000 a year. The council might lay down a flat rate – so much per cultivated acre – for each landowner to pay. But this arrangement is vulnerable to free riding. A farmer may delay payment indefinitely, hoping others' pay up more quickly; in this way he can expect to benefit from the general discipline of livestock which the field guards provide while not himself having to pay a part of their cost. So in most villages the arrangements for income raising do not depend on individual contributions.

The most common financial arrangement is based on sheep folding. Recall that the village's own stock of animals is adjusted to year-round grazing, which is much less than the grazing available after the harvest of (most of) the rainfed crops. This offers an opportunity for revenue to be raised by renting out the village's surplus grazing. In Kottapalle the arrangement is as follow.

In late February herders come to the village to inquire when they might bring their flocks and what numbers they might bring.[9] Some 8 to 10 flocks normally come, each from 800 to 4,000 head, some from villages as far as 50 miles away. The single small flock owned by a Kottapalle resident is too small to be useful as a folding unit on its own, so it is merged with other small flocks from outside.

Many farmers wish to have flocks folded on their rainfed and lightly irrigated fields. The sooner they get a flock on their land the more manure they will get – manure being a function of the amount and quality of stubble, which is best soon after the harvest. Hence there is a problem of allocating flocks to farmers, and this is settled by means of price. The allocation is made by auction.[10] On the first morning that the herders come, and on every fourth morning thereafter, each flock is put up for auction to decide on whose land it will be folded at night for the next four nights (one 'turn'). Half of the winning bid goes to the owner of the flock, and half to the village fund.

For the first auction of the year the farmers and the shepherds begin to assemble in the meeting area outside the accountant's house around about 10 a.m., in early March. The meeting starts as one of the village notables reads out the list of by-laws binding on herders and farmers. The bidders and interested onlookers sit tightly packed on the veranda of the accountant's house, and people come and go about the periphery; the herders sit together a little apart, marked by their long poles and

[9] I know little about the organization of herders. The herders who come to sound out the council and to judge the quality of the grazing represent several others, each with their own flocks. Each herder normally owns virtually all the animals in his flock; there is little 'tenancy' of animals. In Kottapalle, more than half of the herders who come in one year will have come in the previous year.

[10] The auction method is called *gorala savalu* (sheep auction).

shabby clothing. The auctioneer, one of the field guards, takes each flock in turn, announces its size and the opening bid. He begins to intone this number, again and again; the bidders look at the ground disinterestedly, carefully puffing on their beedies; then someone increases the bid, the auctioneer intones the new number, a few more bids are made and intoned and the auctioneer begins to close the bid by announcing first time of calling, intones the highest figure some more, second time of calling, third time of calling, then closes it. The name of the shepherd and the name of the farmer is then written down by the man who read out the by-laws. But the whole procedure is punctuated by bursts of discussion and laughter, which relieve a certain tension; and there might be a dispute between farmers and a herder about the *true* number of head in his flock. Auctioning 7 flocks in this way can take two hours. In 1980 12,500 head came in 7 flocks; and the average price per head per four-night turn at the first auction was Rs. 0.152 (with a range from 0.127 to 0.171). The total raised was Rs. 1,900, of which half went to the village fund, or Rs. 950 in four days. It is easy to see how the fund received about Rs. 5,500 during the sheep-folding auctions of 1980. The previous year the maximum number of sheep and goats had been 9,900, and the fund got Rs. 4,700.[11]

It would be interesting to know who bears the incidence of this payment to the fund. The herders can go to other villages, to be paid by farmers there who want dung and cleared fields. If the herders were indifferent as to where they grazed their herds, concerned only about the price, then the Kottapalle dung-users would contribute all of the payment to the village fund. It would be an intra-village transfer. To the extent that the herders are prepared to accept less per animal because of Kottapalle's other advantages, they in effect contribute to the village fund, and the income comes from outside the village. In fact, in comparison with many other villages (especially those near the head of the distributory) Kottapalle's supply of fodder is good; and from the herder's point of view, the supply of fodder and sufficient water is generally more important than the price he gets for the dung. But certainly there is an element of intra-village transfer – a payment from successful bidders, who are generally in the wealthiest half of cultivators, to the village fund.

But the implicit condition offered by the council to the herders, that they can stay for as long as they wish (in four-night 'turns'), that other

[11] The 1976/7 accounts should include income from two sets of auctions (because they cover more than one 12-month period), and it is not clear why such a small amount is shown (see table 6.3). Possibly some of the money is included in 'sales of grain', if the farmers paid in kind.

herders can come onto the village land for grazing and sale of dung only as some of them leave, brings an element of franchise rent. The herders obtain exclusive access rights, and are paid back by individual farmers bidding against each other. This is exactly how the matter is arranged in some villages: the herders contract, as a single unit, to pay the village fund a given amount as a condition of exclusive access, and then make their own individual deals with farmers, keeping the entire proceeds. We return to these matters in chapter 8 and 9.

5

The social response to irrigation

Problems of tail-end location

Any irrigation system that experiences water shortages contains inherent conflict between 'upstream' and 'downstream' farmers.[1] Upstream farmers have first access and can enjoy relatively abundant supplies, while their behaviour determines when and how much water the downstreamers will get. Without rules of restrained access conflict and crop loss are likely when water is scarce.

Kottapalle's land begins 15 miles down a 20-mile unlined distributary of the MN Canal. By the time water reaches Kottapalle, the distributary has fed the land of 11 villages. Only one more village below Kottapalle draws water from it (map 2.2, p. 21). The state Irrigation Department is responsible for regulating water allocation between each outlet from the canal (and so between each village: each village normally has several outlets, each of which normally supplies water to the land of that village alone). In practice the Irrigation Department is not strong enough to regulate effectively at this level of the network, and the farmers themselves intervene – illegally – to improve their own group or individual supply. The consequence of such intervention in upstream villages is that tail-end villages like Kottapalle experience a scarcer and more unreliable supply than the others, or than was planned for when the network was designed.

Paddy is the only significant first (wet) season crop. Kottapalle normally has about 1,000 to 1,200 acres under paddy in the first season. In the second season (December to early May) only about 50 to 150 acres are under paddy. Some 700 to 1,000 acres are under lightly irrigated crops like hybrid sorghum and groundnut.

On the paddy lands much is at stake. By harvest time the farmer will have incurred costs of around Rs. 1,000 per acre. With a good harvest he

---

[1] Downstream locations do not always experience greater water scarcity; they may get too much water when it is not wanted higher up. Also, the degree of locational disadvantage depends on the type of water control system: tail-end areas are less disadvantaged with a 'downstream controlled' system (found in France and French-influenced parts of Africa) than with the conventional 'upstream control'.

stands to make a net profit of over Rs. 1,200 per acre. Rainfed crops require less investment, but give much lower profits.[2] It is not just a matter of financial return, however. Paddy is strongly preferred as the basic subsistence food. Even wage labourers eat much more rice than one would expect from the price differential in favour of sorghum and from the fact that the calorific value of rice is marginally less than that of sorghum (Gopalan *et al.* 1978; Ryan *et al.* 1980).

If rice receives a supply of water from rain or irrigation less than potential evapotranspiration level[3] the effect on yields is much more drastic than for other crops (Levine 1977). In Kurnool district the heavy rains generally finish by late September, and from then on paddy is heavily dependent on canal water. Groundwater is little used.

In this situation, farmers are anxious to ensure that their paddy has a reliable water supply. This can be done (illegally) by enlarging the official canal outlets, by breaking off the gates so the outlets cannot be shut, by cutting extra outlets in the canal banks, by partially blocking the flow of water immediately downstream of an outlet to force more water through, or by bribing officials to force more water along the distributary. Use of some of these methods in upstream villages squeezes water supply to lower down villages, whose farmers have to exert themselves even more to protect their supply. But locational advantage is difficult to overcome, and scarcity is likely to persist beneath each outlet in lower villages. If farmers near the outlet have generous notions of how much water their paddy needs, farmers further down the same field channel may find that their crops get too little too late, and suffer yield reduction.

One response would be to shift out of paddy into less water-con-sumptive crops. Apart from prices, there are two main reasons for this shift not occurring. One is the strong preference for rice as the subsistence foodstuff, coupled with a strong preference for 'self-provisioning' (rather than relying on purchase of the subsistence crop from the sale of commercial crops). The second is that seepage water close to the distributary tends to put the immediately surrounding land out of production for any crop other than paddy (only paddy can grow in constantly saturated soil). So if paddy is grown close to the channel, it must also be grown lower down the same mini-catchment area, because drainage water from the rice paddies will saturate the lower lands.

The government has tried to regulate the cropping pattern under irrigation canals by means of a zoning system specifying which land may

---

[2] See chapter 3, p. 42.
[3] On potential evapotranspiration see table 3.1.

be irrigated and for what crops. A three-fold categorization is used, of: a paddy crop in the first season, two paddy crops, and a non-paddy crop in the second season. Land which is irrigated out of zone, or with the wrong type of crop, is meant to be subject to heavy financial penalties. In practice the penalties go mostly uncollected; partly because the zoning fails to take account of the realities of topography and soil type (Government of Andhra Pradesh, Andhra Pradesh Irrigation Committee, 1974:355). Farmers with land which is not zoned for paddy but which for seepage reasons is unable to grow anything else justifiably refuse to pay the fines, which encourages others to do likewise.

Since the water consumption of paddy is much greater than that of other crops, the existence of large unplanned paddy areas makes the demand for water much greater than expected. This causes problems for irrigation staff, and for lower villages which get only a fraction of their (zoned) entitlement. But even in tail-end villages many farmers are locked into paddy, because if farmers with land close to the distributary start to grow paddy then others lower down the same mini-catchment have to do the same. The existence of large extensions of water-consuming paddy even in tail-end villages heightens the need for an organization able to bring more water to the village, able to effect an equal distribution of water at times of shortage, and able also to repair the environmental damage that the large volume of paddy water causes.

Irrigation organization

We can distinguish four phases of irrigation: control of the water source (in this case, control of the outlets from the distributary), delivery from the source (outlet) to the fields, application from field boundary to crops, and drainage. At each phase, four tasks may have to be carried out: building of structures, maintaining structures, operating structures, and allocating water, and finally, resolving water conflicts (Kelly 1982).

The first phase of irrigation, 'control of water source', lies, in principle, wholly with the Irrigation Department. The last phase drainage, is relatively simple because there is no specific infrastructure or organization for drainage as such. The third phase, 'application to crops', is also straightforward in that what happens at this phase does not involve cooperation or coordination with other farmers. The social organization of irrigation is concentrated especially at the second phase, 'delivery from outlet to field' – though as we shall see, it is also much more involved in the first phase (control of the outlets and distribution within the main system) than government rules allow.

With respect to the second phase: construction of field channels below the outlet is the primary responsibility of farmers. In principle, the Irrigation Department is meant to construct a channel into the middle of the block, but the precise responsibility is not well defined. It appears that sometimes the Irrigation Department did construct the 'parent' field channel, and sometimes the work was left entirely to farmers. The work was done in the mid to late 1950s when the whole canal system was rehabilitated, and is not now a matter of easy recollection. (For details of the irrigation network within Kottapalle, see appendix, p. 218.)

Maintenance of field channels is the responsibility of farmers under each channel. The common irrigators have a role in prodding farmers to clear out their field channels if they have not already done so, by refusing to deliver water down an ill-kept channel. But the work itself must be organized by the farmers. The work is done as needed, not at a regular time (like just before irrigation begins). Normally some of the bigger farmers near the tail-end of the field channel take the initiative, approaching other farmers to say that Rs. X needs to be collected for the whole field channel. If top-enders are unwilling to contribute (being less affected by poor water supply), tail-enders can insist on taking water at the end of the season when top-enders are trying to let their fields dry out prior to harvest. This makes the harvest more difficult for them, and gives tail-enders bargaining power. Moreover, the scattering of holdings – which may result in a tail-ender and top-ender under one field channel being in opposite positions under another – keeps head/tail divergences in check. Each farmer contributes to total cost, in money or grain equivalent, in proportion to his land area under the channel. The job is then put out for (informal) tender with village-based labour contract gangs.

Collective control is concerned primarily with the tasks of (1) getting more water to the village, (2) distributing it within the village land, and (3) resolving water conflicts.

Common irrigators

The institution of common irrigators[4] requires individual households to relinquish some of the decisions on agricultural operations to agents appointed by and responsible to the village council.

Kottapalle normally has 12 or 13 common irrigators each year, depending on water supply conditions and the area planted in paddy.

---

[4] What I call 'common irrigators' are called *neeruganti* or *neerukuttu* in Telegu, meaning 'water men' and 'water dividers' respectively; the former term is used on the MN Canal side of the district, the latter on the TS Canal side.

The common irrigators are employed only in the first season, only for paddy. Common irrigators are normally hired sometime in October, depending on water supply, and are then employed up to harvest, a period of 60–90 days. Their job is to distribute water between the paddy fields, apply it to each field, and help bring more water down the distributary to the village. Indeed, two of them are stationed permanently at the fork two miles up the distributary from Kottapalle's boundary, to prevent irrigators who depend on the other branch of the fork from blocking up Kottapalle's branch in order to increase their own supplies. In addition to their primary duties, the common irrigators also make minor repairs to the field access roads and help the field guards protect crops from theft near harvest time.

Each common irrigator (excluding the pair at the fork) looks after about 100 acres on average. The common irrigators work in groups of 2 to 4, each with one to four designated outlets; no common irrigator works alone, both because 2 or more can organize the work more efficiently and also because violating the procedures for equitable distribution is more difficult with more than 1 common irrigator present. When a group has finished irrigating its designated area it will help some other group. The biggest paddy block, with roughly 700 acres under paddy in the first season, normally has 3 or 4 common irrigators working it, at times as many as 6. (This is block 3 in map A.1, p. 220).

They are paid in grain after the harvest is in, a single payment calculated on the basis of a daily rate roughly equal to what male agricultural labourers would earn at that time of the year – but the continuity of employment makes their income over the period somewhat larger and more secure than that of an agricultural labourer. The exact daily rate is decided by the council at the start of their employment; it was about 4.5 kilos of paddy (slightly more than 3 kilos of rice) per day per person in 1979, or between about 300 and 400 kilos per season.[5] At the end of the season the council divides the total payment due to the common irrigators between irrigating households according to their acreage, and the common irrigators collect it from each household (plus a per acre 'tip' for the field staff of the Irrigation Department). This works out at about 7–10 kilos of paddy per acre for the common irrigators, and another 2–3 kilos for the Irrigation Department and miscellaneous purposes.

---

[5] The common irrigators are paid according to a volumetric, not a weight measure of paddy, the *paddi* (plural, *pallu*). One *paddi* equals 1.1–1.2 kg. of paddy, and 1.5 kg of sorghum. The common irrigator payment in 1979 was expressed as 4 *pallu* a day of paddy. Its monetary value was about Rs. 4.5–5.5. The average male daily wage in agriculture at about this time was Rs. 4 per day, rising to Rs. 5 to 6 at seasonal peaks.

Benefits of common irrigators

(1) *More water to the village.* The employment of common irrigators permits a constant guard to be kept on the distributary upstream of the village land, to reduce the likelihood of water supplies being cut off by upstream irrigators. Without such a guard this likelihood would be high – for upstream irrigators are only a little less inclined to interfere with the main system than Kottapalle's irrigators are. And Kottapalle's guards can also take the opportunity to increase supplies to Kottapalle by cutting off supplies to other villages when the occasion safely presents itself. This is a considerable benefit for all of Kottapalle's irrigators.

(2) *Reduced drainage.* Individual irrigators have no particular incentive to prevent excess water from flowing to waste in the (natural) drains. Common irrigators, on the other hand, can manage the sequence and amount of irrigation to reduce the amount of waste, and also to channel it back for use within the village land. In other words, the common irrigators can ensure that more of the water reaching the boundary is put to use within the village.

(3) *Improved water supply to the more distant fields.*[6] As water supply becomes short in relation to irrigation requirements disputes over water increase, and crops on more distant land within any one block and in blocks lower down the distributary risk water stress as irrigators of land closer to or higher up the distributary take more of the available water. Removing water distribution decisions from the hands of individual irrigators and placing them in the hands of agents responsible to the whole 'community' of irrigators brings disproportionate advantages to the irrigators of more distant lands, both to big farmers and small.

Because common irrigators are able to institute a rotational irrigation schedule they can improve water supplies to the tail-ends. In its broader sense rotational irrigation is contrasted with continuous flow irrigation (both being rules of water delivery). Rotational irrigation is any set of procedures by which water is delivered in turn to parts of an area rather than to all parts simultaneously. However the particular principle of rotational delivery used in our villages differs significantly from the celebrated *warabandi* (water-turn) of Northwest India. By the latter rule, each field is given a fixed time of the week when all water in the field channel can be taken for that field (such as Monday from 5.21 to 8.47 a.m.), the length of time being proportional to field area. In our villages, by contrast, the criterion is not 'fixed time per field', but 'adequately

---

[6] 'More distant fields', 'land further from the outlets', 'lower down lands', 'tail-end lands' – these phrases refer both to the area beneath each outlet and, within the village area as a whole, to blocks lower down the distributary (such as blocks 10, 11 and 12).

ponded'; each field is irrigated until it has an 'adequate' depth of water standing in it, and cannot receive more water until all other fields under the same outlet have been similarly treated. This type of rotation requires superordinate irrigators to judge the adequacy; the *warabandi*, on the other hand, can be self-policing, with the Irrigation Department rather than a local authority ruling in case of breakdown (Wade 1982b).

Two levels of rotation are distinguished: between outlets, and between fields within outlet blocks. Between outlets, the procedure in all but severe drought is as follows. The largest outlet in Kottapalle's land (no. 2 in Appendix map A.1) is kept open continuously at maximum height. It addition, the distributary is sometimes cross-bunded for one or two days at a time, in order to raise the depth and drive more water through the outlet. But the cross-bund is not complete; most of the water continues to flow down the distributary to be sent through the remaining 10 outlets. Most of these lower outlets require some degree of cross-bunding (with stones, branches, and so on) even if water flows are at the rate warranted by the area to be irrigated, because the surrounding land is relatively high compared to the height of the outlets. When each outlet command has been adequately ponded the cross-bund in the channel will be removed, the depth of water will fall, less water will flow through the outlet, and more will be available downstream. When the bottom-most outlet within Kottapalle's land is reached, the procedure starts again.

In normal times there is considerable flexibility in these procedures. How long each cross-bund is maintained depends on balancing water need under the outlet with water need in lower blocks, as judged by the common irrigators. As water becomes scarcer, each outlet opening may be blocked with sticks and mud after its land has been adequately irrigated, to prevent water from getting through.

Within outlet commands, different procedures are used by the common irrigators for night and day irrigation. At night the common irrigators let the water flow into sectors of each outlet block, of roughly 60 acres in size, with cross-bunds and cuts in the paddy bunds placed in such a way that during the night the water will spread evenly over the whole sector. In the mornings the common irrigators inspect the area and make up shortages before sealing it off and switching over to the day-time rotation.[7] This rotation focuses on one 15-acre sector at a time, with 2 to 4 common irrigators working in close cooperation on this single subunit of land. They take a length of field channel, make four or five cuts in the bank, cross-bund the field channel at the lower end, and

---

[7] The day-time rotation is known as a *vanthu*, meaning 'share'.

force the water through the cuts onto the paddies; when the paddies are adequately filled, they move onto the next length of field channel in the same manner. With day-time rotation water supplies are more rushed than at night (discharge is higher). When water supply is normal it takes about 4 to 5 days, within the big 700 acre block, for the common irrigators to come back to the same holdings; [8] when water is scarce it may take 10 days or more.

(4) *Saving labour time.* The common irrigators save a great deal of labour time as well as improve water supplies. Let us take as an example the situation of one of the well-to-do households, with 3 acres of paddy land. The total area is divided into three fields. They are at widely scattered locations; it would take the best part of two hours to visit all three of them (on foot – bicycles are not used for travelling to and from the fields and in any case few households own a bicycle). The biggest field (1.5 acres) is several hundred yards from the distributary, and though a field channel runs down to it, its water supply – in the absence of common irrigators and a rotation – depends on the demand for water from farmers higher up the same field channel. If the upper farmers are taking water it may take 10 to 12 hours or more to give the field one irrigation; otherwise it requires 6 to 7 hours. The field's poor levelling makes water replenishment necessary relatively often, about once in 5 days. (This assumes little rainfall, as is normally the case during most of the period of the common irrigators' appointment.) The other fields each require about 7 to 8 hours per irrigation if water supply is good, more if it is bad, once every 6 to 7 days.

Clearly the employment of common irrigators to take charge of bringing the water to the fields and distributing it evenly saves this household a great deal of labour. Saved travelling time alone is considerable. More than that, if a man is not present someone higher up may take all the water, or someone lower down may block the cuts in the field channel so as to take water further down. It is often necessary to have a man (preferably two) at the field for the whole irrigation period, especially when the demand for water is strong. If so, the employment of common irrigators saves this household at least 30 work-hours a week.

Futhermore, this saving becomes especially important after the transplanting is over, because up to then irrigation is only a part of the work for which labour has to turn out anyway, while afterwards it may be the *only* job to be done. And since the application of water to bunded

---

[8] These figures were obtained directly from the common irrigators. To calculate what rate of flow they imply, assume (as is conventional) that one wetting of paddy consists of 1 acre inch, convert the area irrigated per day into square feet (say, 700 acres/4–5 days × 43,560), times 1/12, times 1/24 × 60 × 60, equals about 6–8 cubic feet per second.

paddy fields is not a skilled job (as it is for lightly irrigated crops) there is no need to have the work done by a household member or employee who cares about it being done well.

The saving of labour time is likely to benefit especially the bigger farmers, who are either already employing labourers full-time through the growing season or whose household labour resources are so stretched that in order to meet the post-transplantation labour time requirement of irrigation work they would have to employ labourers. For these bigger farmers, then, the collective employment of common irrigators represents an important financial saving.

(5) *Repair of field access roads.* With large areas under irrigation, roads and drainage culverts are subject to damage from water, even more than the roads and culverts of dry villages under the impact of monsoon rains. Once appointed, common irrigators are available at any time to undertake repairs. Without common irrigators, repairs beyond the limited capability of the field guards would require the council to hire labourers, or be left to the initiative of those inconvenienced by collapsed facilities. Either way, it is likely that action on repairs would be much slower than with the full-time common irrigator work group.

(6) *Extra crop guarding at harvest.* The risks of crop theft from unguarded areas are perceived to be high at the time of the first season harvest, because poor households' stores from the previous harvest are low while household need is high. We considered crop theft earlier. Here it is sufficient to recall that the use of common irrigators for full-time crop guarding after the last water is applied expands Kottapalle's corporate field guarding force at harvest time from about 7 to nearly 20.

These six kinds of benefits constitute important economies of scale. On the other hand, the costs to paddy growers are very small, no more than Rs. 18 per acre, in relation to a very poor yield of 8 bags (about 600 kilos) of paddy per acre (valued at about Rs. 850 in 1981 prices) or an average to good yield of 20 bags (or Rs. 2,100). Employing these services privately would cost individual farmers or small groups of farmers much more.

It is important to note that the common irrigators are only appointed – whatever the water supply conditions – once the main production decisions about where to grow paddy and how much to grow have been taken by individual households. Post-transplantation appointment means that the common irrigators do not have to mediate between sometimes conflicting and varying demands for irrigation water at the time of land preparation and transplanting, the time when the future demand schedule for the rest of the season's water is laid down. They are appointed once the demand schedule has become stable and the seasonal claims for a share of the water have been entered; their job is to make sure those claims are met as fully and equally as possible.[9] In other words, their job is less regulatory, the decisions they have to take are less important than if they were responsible for allocating water during transplantation, for then they might be able to influence the size and location of the lands sharing the available water later in the season. Moreover, hiring common irrigators post-transplantation means that the wages bill for the common irrigators is not inflated by the relatively high rates prevailing during transplantation for agricultural labourers.

It is worth noting again that they are not responsible for repair of the field channels or of field bunds; they draw the farmers' attention to defects and leave the action to them. And they are employed only for first season paddy. So even in Kottapalle much of the irrigation proceeds without any collective control. This is not to say that anarchy prevails. Activities are loosely structured, but there are recurrent patterns. Water is allocated mostly through casual contracts between individuals who depend on the same outlet or field channel, and between small informal groups defined by common water supply interests. Vigilance of water levels in the fields and distribution network, and of the activities of other irrigators, is done by the farmers themselves in ad hoc arrangements. In the case of big farmers (big enough to employ a labourer by the season or by the year) some of the irrigation work is done by the labourer, and some by members of the household. The practice of groups of farmers with contiguous landholdings employing their own private 'common irrigators' is known (the 'common irrigators' might double as private 'field guards'), but infrequent even amongst big farmers; if the work is not done by village-appointed common irrigators, it tends to be done by each household. But small groups of farmers may get together to walk up the distributary to the next village to see if supplies are being interrupted.

How contingent on water supply?

Common irrigators are principally a way of coping with water scarcity, particularly with the tendency for top-enders within the village to take a fixed quantity rather than a share of what is available. This is suggested by farmers' statements that common irrigators are employed 'when the farmers start quarrelling about water'. Pressure on the council to

---

[9] There is no explicit notion of 'sacrifice lands', lands which have only a secondary claim to irrigation. *De facto*, lands in the tail-end blocks – especially, for topographical reasons, block 11 – do get less water when overall supplies are short, and this is reflected in land prices in these blocks. Compare Maass and Anderson 1978, e.g. p. 35.

appoint them is likely to come first from farmers with land towards the tail end of the biggest paddy block. These farmers are the first to feel water shortages, as the upper farmers within the block adopt what seem to tail-enders to be overgenerous notions of how much water their paddy needs. In practice, of course the tail-end farmers do not wait until their crop actually experiences water shortage before they begin to press for common irrigators – they monitor the flows coming across the village boundary and they hear from the common irrigators at the fork two miles up about flows reaching that point, and by using both the volume of flow and time at that volume they can calculate when their crops might begin to suffer. The recruitment of common irrigators to match water supply can be seen from the events of 1980. Abundant rain at the time of transplanting, in August, led to an expansion of the paddy area from its norm of about 1,200 acres to 1,600 acres. Then the rains failed, leaving the paddy almost completely dependent on canal water. So the common irrigators were appointed on 13 September, a month or so earlier than usual, and 15 were appointed instead of the normal 12 or 13, plus (a month later) another 4 'common irrigator supervisors'.

The farmers' presentation of the institution as a purely contingent response to water supply reflects their views about what it should be as much as their perception of what it is: they want to employ common irrigators only when the advantages are great, for they are acutely aware that they are to pay for the common irrigators' services out of their own grain stores. In fact, however, the institution is both more and less than a contingent response. It is less, in that common irrigators are not appointed for all periods of water shortage – specifically, not for the second paddy crop even though water is often very scare towards the end of the second season. In the second season, with only about a tenth or so of the first season area normally under paddy, farmers either irrigate it themselves perhaps with a neighbour's help, or hire labourers to do it.

The institution is more than a response to water scarcity in that it allows a large saving of labour time even when water is not scarce, which benefits the bigger farmers who are short of household labour. In addition, the common irrigator role has become institutionalized. While there is some flexibility in numbers, timing, and period of appointment according to water supply, there are also customary expectations. In practice common irrigators are appointed every year by late October, even if (unusually) water is not short by then. And they continue to be employed near the time of harvest, even if there is no longer an excess demand for water.

In November 1979, for example, water supplies near harvest time were abundant in relation to demand and temperatures were cooler than usual. The village council, pressed by cost-conscious farmers, wanted to terminate the employment of common irrigators *before* the harvest. (If there had earlier been a rash of crop thefts they would have hesitated to give up the additional protection offered by the common irrigators as extra field guards, but in 1979 there had been hardly any.) The common irrigators, led by a young, assertive and moderately prosperous Reddy common irrigator in a kind of 'shop steward' role, at first objected, appealing to the custom of continuing their employment until after the harvest. Then he gave a tactical assent to the council – on condition that the farmers pay them when they stopped work. As he expected, the council declined, saying – grain stocks being low – that the common irrigators should wait until after the harvest to be paid. At which point the common irrigators said, in effect, 'We will wait until after the harvest to be paid, but you must employ us until then.' Which is what happened; faced with this resistance the councillors acknowledged the legitimacy of customary expectations.

Accountability

How are the common irrigators made accountable to the council and to the farmers they serve (Coward 1977)? Failure to do their job could, after all, be costly. They are appointed by the council a few days before the period of employment is to begin. The council decides to appoint them after pressure from interested farmers; then sends the village crier out to announce that all who wish to be considered should assemble with the council on a certain evening. At the meeting the candidates' names are written down on a list; and at the same meeting or the following evening after less public discussions, the names of those appointed are announced. Since there are normally a few more candidates than positions, one means of control is not to re-employ a common irrigator whose work was thought unsatisfactory in the past.

Next, the common irrigators are allocated to particular outlets, for which they will take primary responsibility. Two village elders are asked by the council to undertake this task to make sure no common irrigator is assigned responsibility for an outlet leading to his own land.

The common irrigators are paid by the farmers at a rate set by the council. After the harvest is in, the council totals the amount due to all the common irrigators (at the rate of so much paddy per day per common irrigator), adds on the amount to be given to the field staff of the Irrigation Department, divides this total in proportion to the paddy land of each household, writes the amount due from each household on a piece of paper, and asks the common irrigators jointly to collect the given amount from each household. The grain is kept in a storeroom hired by the council for the purpose. The common irrigators divide their portion equally amongst themselves.[10] Note that it is the common irrigators themselves who collect from the farmers, thus creating a further means of accountability; though each common irrigator work-group does not collect only from the farmers it serves.

In 1978 the council appointed a large number of 'weaker sections' people (as Reddy informants refer to them, using government terminology), on the assumption that they would be more controllable, would do more scrupulously what the council wanted. But while the grain was in the storeroom awaiting distribution a large quantity went missing, and it was said that the common irrigators themselves had stolen it. The council fined them the amount that had gone missing (about 10 bags of paddy, or 750 kilos), and refused to employ most of them the following year. (The council used the 10 bags' fine as part of its contribution to the construction of the animal clinic, see chapter 6.)

The following year, 1979, the council decided to have more 'financially independent' people as common irrigators. In that year, 7 out of 13 were of Reddy caste, the others being: 4 low caste, 1 Muslim, 1 Harijan. In age they covered the span from under 20 to over 50. In terms of productive assets they had more land and more oxen than one would expect in a group of village servants (though there was considerable variation within the group, moderately correlated with caste): 7 out of 13 owned between 10 and 20 acres of land, only 3 owned less than 2.5 acres and 10 out of 13 had at least 1 pair of oxen (one had 2 pairs). These people, then, were not from the poorest half of the village. The other characteristic worth noting is that 9 out of 13 had at least one other mature male worker in their household. Especially if the household owns oxen or buffalo, it is difficult to fit in household production tasks with being a common irrigator. A reputation for being hard-working and conscientious is important in their selection; faction allegiance is probably not.

The change in the composition of the common irrigators after the 'debacle' of 1978 was directly related to the problem of control. The council concluded that it could more easily control them if it chose farmers who were financially more secure, including a greater proportion of dominant caste people.

In 1979, 5 out of 13 had never worked as common irrigators before; another 5 had worked for more than 3 years (continuously), but only

---

[10] If a common irrigator has been sick and unable to work the whole period, he will have sent a replacement, e.g. his son.

one of these for more than about 7 years. Even before 1979, however, turnover from one year to the next seems to have been fairly high; certainly there is no hereditary lifetime attachment to the job.

Although more than a third of the 1979 common irrigators were inexperienced, a sense of solidarity developed amongst them, which later helped their challenge of the council's wish to terminate their jobs before the harvest. After the harvest it was found that, allegedly because of a defect in the measure used, the common irrigators had collected 3.5 bags of paddy more than they were meant to. The common irrigators pressed the council for permission to share out the extra amongst themselves; but the council refused, saying they could keep only 1.5 bags, the rest to go to the village fund. The common irrigators decided it was scarcely worth dividing up 1.5 bags, and resolved – citing the Telegu proverb, 'Next year there's no telling who will be king and who will be peasant' – to blow it all on a night out together in Nowk. They feasted, they went to the cinema, and they capped it all by crowding into a photographer's studio for a group picture. (It was the first time a common irrigator group had been photographed as far as anyone can remember.)

In 1980 the rains early in the season were abundant, a much larger area than usual was transplanted, and then the rains failed; with the consequence, already noted, that farmers pressed the council to appoint common irrigators in mid-September, a month or so earlier than usual. However, because of the longer period of employment, the council also wanted to reduce the daily wage from the previous season's 4.5 kilos of paddy per day, to 3.9 kilos per day in the first half of their employment and 4.5 kilos in the second;[11] and also insisted that if rainfall were abundant later in the season, their employment would be terminated. To neither point would the 1979 common irrigators agree, coming as they did from relatively high up the village social hierarchy and self-confident in light of their bargaining success the previous year. The council and other farmers impressed upon them the enormity of the cost that would be incurred: '100 days times 4.5 kilos times 16 equals over 7,000 kilos,'[12] they kept repeating out loud, exclaiming in indignation at the final figure.

However, farmers were probably reacting not so much because the additional cost of common irrigators at the old rate would make a serious difference to their income and expenditure balance, but because

---

[11] Or in the terms which are actually used, 3.5 *pallu* per day in the first half and 4 *pallu* in the second half.

[12] Times 16 because 16 common irrigators were to be appointed, but one of those appointed failed to turn up for work and only 15 were in fact employed.

of a general uncertainty, as the drought gathered, about how much more they might have to pay out for all purposes (including extra weeding labour which would not have to be incurred if the paddies were kept under water), and about how much yield they would get at the end of it all. This general uncertainty made them more than usually anxious to minimize all further outlay.

The council therefore refused to re-employ the 1979 common irrigators for the 1980 season, and selected, instead, men from the 'weaker sections', as in 1978, who were prepared both to work for less and to have their employment terminated when the council chose. Whereas in 1979, 7 out of the 13 common irrigators were Reddys, in 1980 only 1 out of 15 was a Reddy. In 1979 Harijan or low caste people numbered only 5 out of 13; in 1980, 12 out of 15. In 1979, 7 out of 13 owned between 10 and 20 acres of land; in 1980, only 2 out of 15 owned this much. The 1980 common irrigators were also less experienced: 9 out of 15 had not worked as common irrigators before, compared to only 5 out of 13 who were new in 1979.

As the 1980 drought got worse, the council also took the step of appointing four men to be 'supervisors' of the common irrigators. Out of these 4, 3 were Reddys. It is not surprising that the council, 8 of whose 9 members are Reddys, should have chosen fellow castemen to fill supervisory roles.

The council

Once water becomes scarce in the first season irrigation roles become centralized and water distribution is made the responsibility of a village-wide political authority. But that authority still faces the problem of getting the water distribution agents to comply with its instructions. The changing composition of the common irrigators over 1978, 1979, and 1980 shows that the council actively manages the selection of common irrigators in the interests of maintaining its own control.

As well as being responsible for the common irrigators, the village council also has a role in getting more water to the village and in resolving conflicts over water within the village.

There is little village to village contact over water, in the sense that members of Kottapalle's council do not go to the village four miles upstream and speak to some of its influential farmers about letting more water down to Kottapalle. Only once in recent memory have farmers from the village downstream of Kottapalle come to talk to the council about letting more water downstream. The reason in both cases is probably the low chances of improvement, because neither the upstream village in relation to Kottapalle, nor Kottapalle in relation to the downstream village, would be prepared to make more than a token adjustment; and there is no pattern of village to village cooperation in any field of activity. Rather, villages rely for defence of or improvement in water supply both on non-institutionalized patrolling of the distributary upstream to remove upper villages' cross-bunds and on contacts with the Irrigation staff. Kottapalle, in addition, posts 2 of its common irrigators full time at the fork 2 miles up the channel.

Whenever the Irrigation Department's Supervisor or Assistant Engineer[13] comes to a village he will be told about its water problems. In Kottapalle's case, however, there is not today, nor has there been in the past, anything like a 'council with engineer' meeting; indeed the Irrigation officers scarcely know of the council's existence, let alone what it does.[14] Rather, the engineer will be approached by influential farmers individually, and discussions may take place with whoever is around when he arrives in the village or on the canal. However, the main contact between village and engineers is through a particular local man, the only contractor in the village working regularly for the Irrigation Department.[15] When the Supervisor or Assistant Engineer comes to the village he goes to his contractor's house for meals and relaxation. The contractor is close to, and in most years a member of, the council.

As the main intermediary, the contractor normally negotiates with the engineers on the bribe to be paid for assured supplies in the first season. How much is paid depends on how plausibly the Supervisor or Assistant Engineer can argue that water supplies will be inadequate in the coming season. That depends partly on what the newspapers have been saying about the state of water supply in the reservoir. In normal years the amount paid for an assurance is small, not more than Rs. 500 for the whole village, and if water supplies are expected to be good, nothing at all.

In a first season drought, however, when the engineers can plead that they cannot meet their assurances, the amount paid rises sharply and payments are made wetting by wetting. The total may run into several

---

[13] The hierarchy of Irrigation Department ranks is as follows: The MN canal as a whole is in the charge of an Executive Engineer; below him are four Assistant Engineers, each in charge of a sub-division; below them come Supervisors, of which there are 20 for the whole canal; then foremen, of which there are 73; then 258 channel men (or *lascars*). Foremen and channel men are 'field staff' (Wade 1982c).

[14] This statement would not be wholly true, for I have told some of the Irrigation staff about the village's corporate organization in response to their increasing anxiety about why I was showing so much interest in their canal.

[15] Like most village-based contractors he works on a small scale, mostly on maintenance contracts, which the Irrigation Department divides into very small units.

thousand rupees. In the first season drought of 1980, for example, the village paid out at least Rs. 10,000 to the irrigation staff to get better supplies, some of it for expenses, some for bribes.

First season bribe money is collected under the auspices of the council at a flat rate per irrigated acre, determined by the total to be collected. The council also arranges the use of village fund money to pay for hospitality when the engineers visit the village, and for the expenses of a jeep to take the engineers up the distributary on patrol or for a tractor to take village labourers up the distributary so that they can remove upper villages' cross-bunds.

In addition to money payments, the village also gives grain to the irrigation staff. Grain gifts are made after the harvest, usually in paddy; they are more regularized than money payments, less subject to bargaining, less dependent on the degree of water scarcity. They are seen by villagers as a tip rather than as a price. One farmer remarked that the grain is meant to ensure that 'the field staff will be good and faithful, and obedient to the farmers' wishes'. In Kottapalle, the common irrigators collect the grain from farmers along with their own payment. In villages without common irrigators the field staff themselves may collect from each household. In Kottapalle, about 1 kilogram per acre is collected from the first season paddy area. About a third is milled in the village and handed over to the Supervisor in the form of rice rather than paddy (the difference signalling the Supervisor's superior status). Part of this third the Supervisor gives to the Assistant Engineer. The unmilled two-thirds is given to the three field staff – two channel men and one foreman – who are responsible for the fork which feeds Kottapalle's land. This gives them roughly the equivalent of an extra month's salary. Grain gifts are their main source of extra income. There are no rags-to-riches stories among field staff.

In the second season Kottapalle village normally has an area of only about 100 acres under paddy, all of it out of zone, for which the cultivators pay at the start of the season an amount which has varied in recent years between Rs. 15 and Rs. 20 per acre. (This is recognized on all sides to be an illegal payment, quite separate from the official water rate of Rs. 41 per acre.) The payment is to assure that the irrigation staff will not try to cut off water to the out-of-zone paddy. In addition, the paddy growers pay at the end of the season some 5–10 kilos of paddy per acre, which is collected by the field staff themselves. If there is a general and acute water shortage during the second season, the irrigators will have to pay wetting by wetting to induce the irrigation staff to make the special effort required to get water down to them; and these payments may have to be made for the lightly irrigated crops as well as for the paddy.

In addition to its various water-assuring activities, the council also arranges representational action on bigger matters which are outside the power of local irrigation staff. In 1973, for example, a group of three village notables, all on or close to the council,[16] went to the state capital twice to press the relevant authorities to modify their existing water rights. They wanted some zoned land, which for topographical reasons could not be irrigated, to be excluded from zoning (so its owners would not be liable to Betterment Levy); and to change the zoning of block 8. Block 8 has been growing paddy at least since the 1930s, yet the zoning carried out in the 1950s demarcated it for lightly irrigated (second season) crops, and the council wanted it rezoned for paddy because seepage from the distributary made it difficult to grow anything else. The group of notables also wanted to obtain a one year's authorization to grow a second irrigated crop on land zoned only for a single paddy crop. With such an authorization from high up in the Irrigation Department they would have a stronger bargaining claim to water from the MN Canal staff and would have to pay them less. Finally, the group also lobbied to have a link channel cut from the main canal directly to the village. They went first to see their local representative in the state parliament, who took them to see the Deputy Chief Minister, a man from their own district. They failed on all counts except the one-year temporary authorization, despite spending a lot of money.

The travel, accommodation and eating expenses of the village representatives, in this case as in others, were paid from the village fund, as were hospitality expenses for those whom they contacted. But any outright bribe payments are shared out on a per acre basis amongst the potential beneficiaries.

Occasionally over the last 20 years representatives of Kottapalle have come together with representatives from other villages to exert concerted pressure on the Irrigation Department. On one such occasion representatives from Kottapalle and the nearby villages 3, 5, 6 and 7 (map 2.2) lobbied the Irrigation Department to send more water down the V Distributary and less down the main canal. The results were negligible. Generally, Kottapalle deals with the Irrigation Department on its own, not in cooperation with other villages on the same distributary. The

---

[16] These three will feature in chapter 7. They included the accountant, Venkat Swamy Reddy (the village's first university student, and leader of one of its factions), and M. Busi Reddy, the village's contractor for the Irrigation Department.

layout of the distributary and its 20-mile length make it too easy for upper villages with which Kottapalle might cooperate to cheat it of its share of any extra water the cooperating group of villages obtains. On shorter, non-branching distributaries, however, two or three villages may get together to deal with the department, and in particular, buy water jointly.[17]

On matters of water distribution *within* the village land during the first season, the council leaves the common irrigators to make decisions (except in a severe drought). Its role is limited to issuing warnings from time to time that farmers are not to interfere with the common irrigators' work; and occasionally, in cases where farmers fail to heed common irrigators' warnings not to interfere, the council acts as a judicial body with powers of fining. In cases of dispute between farmers over water, which do not infringe common irrigator authority, the common irrigators themselves may attempt to intervene, or the dispute may be settled by an informal *panchayat* of a few influentials (who may or may not be formally on the council) back in the village. The council rarely intervenes *as a body* in water disputes between farmers that do not involve the common irrigators.

For example, disputes over field channels may take place when land sales occur. Agreements made between the previous owner and the owners of lower down fields may not be honoured by the new owner, who may try to block up the field channel that the previous owner allowed to be run across his land. A new agreement must be made, or the field channel re-routed. If the elder who witnessed the agreement with the previous owner is still alive, the aggrieved party will try to take the matter to him, while the party which wants to deny the agreement may try to take the matter to government court. Either way, the council itself will not become involved. And it would certainly be very difficult for the council to orchestrate agreement on such a basic, difficult-to-reverse decision as putting in a more elaborate drainage network in places where the existing field channel network is insufficient for good drainage.

Managing a drought

The drought of 1980 provides an opportunity to see how the council attempts to protect the rule of restrained access to water when water becomes exceptionally scarce, and how it attempts to alleviate the scarcity. Heavy rains up to the beginning of September 1980 allowed an

---

[17] For further details on the 'corrupt' system of water allocation and canal maintenance, see Wade 1982a; 1982e; 1985b.

extra 400 to 500 acres to be planted to paddy; then no rain fell until early November, two months later. Normally over September and October rainfall provides more than half of the total water supply to the crops. Yet over the canal network as a whole, total production turned out to be little less than normal; and the same applies specifically to Kottapalle (Wade 1984c).

We noted that the common irrigators were appointed about a month earlier than usual, in mid-September, and three more than normal were appointed. Two or three cases of farmers taking water out of turn were reported to the council each day. The common irrigators, especially because they were mostly poor and of subordinate caste (for reasons explained earlier), were sometimes afraid to report cases against big farmers. The council met nearly every evening to hear the cases, the accused and the concerned common irrigators in attendance. Generally the council would decide a fine on the spot, but occasionally, if the farmer insisted that the common irrigator was not telling the truth and refused to pay, two or three of their number would be asked to inspect the point of contention the next day and report at the next meeting. The fines were normally of the order of Rs. 20 to 30.

A fine of Rs. 20 to Rs. 30 was regarded by many big farmers as an unimportant amount compared to the value of extra water. Some rationalized it as trivial in relation to the cost of diesel fuel they would have had to pay if they had been using groundwater (not that the groundwater option is open to them, but they are aware that in other parts of the state, farmers' input costs are much higher than theirs because of the cost of diesel). But even they were sensitive to the condemnation of the council and onlookers at the village council meeting, and to the gossip and face-to-face rebukes – 'you are making us suffer' – that spoilt their good name.

How were the fines enforced? Collection is in the hands of the field guards, who have an incentive to make sure the fine is paid because they receive a portion as commission. More importantly, the councillors kept repeating to each other the importance of council unity. 'All must agree to make person pay.' And scrupulous attention was given to making sure that anyone who might be considered an 'influential' in village matters (whether on the council or not) was invited, by word of the field guards, to attend all council meetings during this period, so that the widest possible number of potential dissidents would be party to the council's decision. For if, as the accountant explained, an influential person refuses to pay, others may follow him; but an influential person will not refuse to pay if all other influentials agree that he should pay. 'Ultimately', said the accountant with a smile, 'we will beat him', but added that there had never been cases of physical punishment – the threat was enough.

In 1980 two council members were fined. One was among the least influential members of the council; he took water out of turn and was fined Rs. 20. The second was one of the more influential members, who put a cross-bund at the outlet above his land when it was not the turn of that outlet, and then did so a second time without heeding the common irrigators' request not to; he was fined Rs. 30.

Another councillor, brother of the village's main link man with the Irrigation Department, created ill-will among those who thought he had broken the rules with impunity. He took what he claimed was excess water in his paddy field to another of his fields on the other side of the boundary road. With this alleged 'drainage' water he planted a crop of hybrid sorghum; so too did the owners of the land on either side of his sorghum field. The two common irrigators responsible for that part of the block thought the man had deliberately taken more water into his field while they were not looking so as to build up enough for it to flow to the sorghum field, and they reported the matter to the man's brother, the contractor. The contractor gave them short shrift: his brother, he said, was using only drainage water, and in any case, he himself was working hard for the whole village trying to get more water down the channel (through his contacts with the Irrigation Department). He wouldn't hear of action being taken against his brother.

Fortunately the rains came before the sorghum needed another wetting, and the incident blew over. But not before some people began muttering that if he had not been on the council, and had not been the brother of the contractor, he would have been fined, because 'at that time they (the common irrigators) were spreading water like money', and there would have been no drainage water in the paddy field had not the man engineered it.

At the beginning of October, more than a fortnight after the common irrigators started work, the council decided that the demand for water was too strong for the common irrigators to control water distribution properly without giving way to personal pressures. There was already gossip about one or two big farmers who had taken water out of turn but not been reported by the common irrigators, out of fear. The council proposed a supervision arrangement which required two village influentials, plus one field guard, to take a turn for one day touring the village's irrigated area to check that the common irrigators were doing their work properly, without interference from farmers. In practice, however, the village influentials tended to make only two tours a day, spending the rest of the time in the village or attending to their own fields. Infringements continued, especially at night.

By mid-October it was clear that the rainfed sorghum would fail, and many farmers wanted to take water to plant irrigated hybrid sorghum, which would require one wetting only. They were all the more anxious to do so because of the uncertainty about whether the paddy crop, their main subsistence, would come to successful harvest. So the demand for water shot up. But the council took the view that water should be used only to save the standing crop, not to plant a new one, since the investment had already been made in the standing crop.

With an anarchic scrambling for water threatening the council decided that stronger supervisory arrangements would have to be made, even though this would cost the farmers more money. In early November four supervisors of common irrigators were appointed, three of them Reddys, all of them middle landowners. They were paid cash of Rs. 6 per 24 hours, a little more than the common irrigator wage. At night they slept by the distributary. After the full-time supervisors were introduced there was only one big fine case, involving a man of low caste who restored a cross-bund three times after the common irrigator removed it, and was fined Rs. 50. One common irrigator was fined for negligence.

Getting more water to the village

It was not until a month after the last rains that the Irrigation Department staff began to use special procedures for coping with the drought – a slowness of response which is indicative of poor main system management generally (Wade 1980a; 1982a; 1982c). In early October, the village leaders persuaded the Supervisor of the V Distributary to come on a trip up the channel with them, in a jeep hired at the expense of the village fund. (Only the Executive Engineer in charge of the whole canal, and the Assistant Engineers in charge of its four subdivisions, have jeeps provided by the government. Consequently, the Supervisors normally go along the canal only in emergencies or when the weather is dry and not too hot.) After this trip the Supervisor introduced a rotational schedule for the whole distributary. During the times when the outlets upstream of the fork were meant to be partially closed, Kottapalle's village council hired a jeep from Nowk for him to use in patrolling the upper reaches. This was very costly: the jeep and diesel cost about Rs. 250 per day for a total of about 30 days, making a total of Rs. 7,500.

However, the cost of the jeep was only the beginning. The Supervisor required suitable hospitality in return for working hard for the village. His expensive tastes for up-market cigarettes and liquor became well known on the gossip networks. Whenever he came to the village he would be given an expensive meal, always at the house of the Irrigation Department contractor but with expenses covered by the village fund. Occasionally the Assistant Engineer would accompany him and they would both have to be fed. The council did try to get irrigators of Eramala village, the next village down the channel, to contribute to the cost of the jeep hire. The council representative who went to Eramala got a frosty reception, however, because Eramala people doubted, with good reason, that Kottapalle's irrigators would abide by any agreement to let them have water if they contributed. They preferred to exert influence on the Supervisor and Assistant Engineer directly in order to induce them to make sure that Kottapalle did release enough water, though without much success.

By late October the village fund was exhausted, and the council decided that a flat rate levy of Rs. 6 per acre would have to be raised. The total was divided into ten parts, each part assigned to a volunteer collector (not council member) to collect without commission.

Shortly after, one of the two village leaders (leaders of the two factional groups described in chapter 7) reported at a council meeting that one of the council members, not present, had announced he would not pay the flat rate levy. (The same man had earlier been fined by the council for water infringements.) This was a serious threat, for although the man was one of the less influential councillors his refusal might provide others with a justification also to refuse. The village leader raised the question of what should be done. He emphasized that the whole village, and specifically the council, must be united on the question of the contribution, so that the refuser would be isolated. If the man were allowed to get away with not paying, all the others who did pay would be shown up as weak and he as strong; if this happened the council's control would be lost. It was vital that everyone should be agreed on the matter of the contribution, so that potential dissidents would not be able to hold out. The man paid up.

All told, the village spent at least Rs. 10,000 on managing the drought, including as major items the jeep hire (Rs. 7,500), the cost of common irrigator supervisors (Rs. 600 plus), and hospitality costs (Rs. 2,000). These are the accountant's figures. Other voices mentioned a total of about Rs. 14,000, the difference being a bribe payment to the Supervisor and higher officers, which the accountant did not disclose.

We have seen Kottapalle's water organization managing a severe drought with considerable success. It is worth drawing attention again to the fact that the council was able, collectively, to discipline two of its own members for water offences by levying substantial fines on them. Yet the strains and antagonisms generated as the council tried to impose a collective interest in water distribution were to reinforce other strains which were being generated by quite different problems at more or less the same time. With several crises in the council's jurisdiction coinciding, discontent with the council and its activities became so great as to lead to an open questioning of the whole pattern of corporate organization. But that is running ahead of the story.

6

The range of council activities

Once in existence to handle the externalities of open-field husbandry and irrigation the council can extend its range to cover other activities. To the extent that these involve financial expenditure, extra revenue can be raised by applying the same principle used for sheep folding–the creation of a council-backed franchise – to other profitable activities. In Kottapalle the village fund is used to finance public goods and services as far from field guarding and water distribution as ridding the village of monkeys, repairing wells, and fireworks for the Ugadi festival.

The council has kept written accounts of village fund expenditure and income for most of the period between 1969 and 1978, from which one can get a more precise idea of the range and monetary significance of its activities. These accounts are no models of book-keeping – they merely record each item of fund expenditure and some items of fund income, more or less specifically described and dated. They cover irregular periods, depending on when each balance happened to be made. Some years, several councillors signed them; other years, only one or even none. Before 1969, the accounts were kept in flimsy books, thrown away once filled. The innovation in that year was to buy a massively bound ledger book, in which from time to time the items scribbled in the notebooks would be written up and a balance struck. It is titled, at the head of page 1, 'Om Sri Rama (an invocation to the god Rama), 1969, July, on this date onwards, Kottapalle village credit and debit book.' From mid-1978 to mid-1981, this consolidation was not made.[1] Other villages with a fund also keep written accounts, but in the impermanent way Kottapalle did before 1969. Kottapalle is unusual in attempting to maintain permanent records – in a cultural context where record keeping has been poorly developed outside government, and where the written word has not commanded much authority, being, as often as

---

[1] I suspect that consolidation of the accounts was not made after early 1980 partly because the council did not wish me to get details on, or hints about, its less legal activities in the very recent past. The village accountant, who also kept the ledger book for the council, was willing enough for me to look at the accounts up to 1978 but none too keen to provide up-to-date ones.

Table 6.1 *Village fund expenditure accounts, various years*

1-6-1971 to 1-8-1972 (14 months)

		Rs.
Within village		
Production	FG's salaries (@ Rs. 30, then 50/mo.)	2,515
	FGs' & CIs' batteries	109
	Wages for miscellaneous tasks	107
	Purchase of he-buffalo	60
	Construction of (illegal) sluice	728
	Field road repairs	694
	PWD auction of right to cut canal grass	15
	Sheep auction booklet	1
		4,229
Social	Entertainments, festivals (e.g. puppeteers, 'colour' for Ugadi)	190
	Donation to Muslim festival	60
	Temple (Brahmin services)	30
	Newspaper	16
	Electricity poles for village	15
		311
Other	Village crier	48
	Dispute over Muslim habitation next to Hindu temple – costs of 3–4 men to go 3 times to Nowk and Kurnool to present petitions to government	75
	Fire engine called from Nowk	21
		144
Village – government relations	Hospitality and gifts to, expenses of going to see, government officials or politicians	
	—PWD specified	85
	—'V. Rami Reddy to Koilkuntla to see B.V. Subba Reddy' (Deputy Chief Minister)	140
	—Other (purpose not specified, '3 members gone to Kurnool')	60
	Expenses of going to liquor licence auction	4
		289
Other		40
Total		5,013

1-1-1976 to 27-6-1977 (18 months)

		Rs.
Within village		
Production	FGs' salaries (@ Rs. 60/mo.)	3,701
	FGs' batteries	27
	Field road repairs	744
	Canal work	15
	PWD auction of right to cut canal grass	15
	Veterinary 'hospital' (partial construction cost)	880
		5,382
Social	School building (partial construction cost)	3,749
	Roof thatch for old school building	561
	Temple (repair, offering, etc.)	87

Table 6.1 *(cont.)*

	Donation to Muslim festival	100
	Entertainments (puppeteers, donation of liquor, 'colour')	683
		5,180
Other	Monkey catcher	150
	Expenses of well repairer	35
	Newspaper	104
	Village crier	33
	He-buffalo (purchase, veterinary treatment, repair of vet's bike tire)	211
	Utensils for village (e.g. when food taken to men posted higher up canal)	4
	FGs' fine commission	20
	Charity	15
		572
Village – government relations	Expenses for named persons going to see government officers	
	—PWD specified (including meals, transport of rice to PWD staff)	2,535
	—Not specified	613
	Meals to Agricultural Extension officer on village visit, to Electricity worker sent to repair cable	57
	Petition to government	6
		3,211
Other	Expenses for named persons on unidentified business (quite possible PWD)	2,470
	'School, sugar'	1,200
		3,670
Total		18,015

27-6-1977 to 10-3-1978 (8.5 months)

Within village		Rs.
Production	FGs' salaries (@ Rs. 60 then 70/mo.) plus incidentals	2,192
	Other wages for miscell. Tasks and repair of field roads	80
	Animal clinic (rental of temporary accommodation, & light bulbs)	303
	Expenses for going to contact outside herders	10
		2,585
Social	School (donation for prizes, etc.)	150
	Entertainments (e.g. liquor for labourers erecting temporary shelter, honorarium to visiting School Inspector who gave recital of mythological stories, puppeteers)	516
	Temple (Brahmin services, God's cow, repair, electricity)	237
		903

Table 6.1 *(cont.)*

Village – government *relations*	Gifts identified as to PWD (e.g. clarified butter, hire of bullock cart to take wood to Supervisor)	276
	Gifts and hospitality to other named departments (e.g. dinner for Rev. Dept. official who came to collect for Cyclone Relief Fund), and to unspecified depts.	903
	Expenses to named village elder, for going to see officials, some specified, some unspecified	138
	Cyclone Relief Fund	30
	Expenses for going to government liquor licence auction	272
	Payment to accountant of statutory *Panchayat*'s books (who makes a living from keeping accounts for several *Panchayats*)	400
		2,019
Other		20
Total		5,527

Note: The expenditure categories are the author's

not, something to be changed or avoided to suit local or personal convenience.

A classification of the expenditure items for periods in 1971/2, 1976/7 and 1977/8 is given in table 6.1, and table 6.2 presents a financial summary. Reading the expenditure items gives a more exact idea of the range of the council's activities. One should not use the accounts, though, to measure how frequent particular activities have been – some years the payment for well repairs, for example, might be specified as such, other years it may be lumped with a more general item, or described merely as 'payment to Dalenna' (the person who did the work).

What is common to all the items is that the benefits of the expenditure are not privatizable. They are 'public' goods, which if provided at all must be provided for many. There are only three partial exceptions: the distribution of rationed sugar, which became a cause of major conflict (chapter 7); money for high-school prizes; and donations to itinerant beggars, who are always from *outside* the village and are generally 'deserving poor' (perhaps a man who had a clerk's job in the railways, lost his arm in an accident, and was dismissed – he may be given Rs. 10 from the fund and sent on his way). But in no case is the village fund used for insurance or welfare assistance to villagers.

The hiring of a monkey catcher when monkeys become a nuisance (see

Table 6.2 *Summary of expenditure accounts*

		Within village					Average rate of expenditure per 12 months (approx.)
		Production		Social	Village government relations	Total	
Year	Months	Total	Field guards				
1971/2	14	4,229	2,515	311	285	5,013	5,000
%		84	50	6	6	100	
1976/7	18	5,382	3,728	6,060	3,211	18,015	12,000
%		30	21	34	18	100	
1977/8	8.5	2,585	2,192	903	2,019	5,526	8,000
%		47	40	16	36	100	

Note: If most of the Rs. 2,470 under 'expenses for named persons on unidentified business' in the 1976/7 accounts, were put under 'village–government relations,' this heading would account for about 30% of total expenditure.

1976/7 accounts) is just one example of a quantitatively trivial but sociologically significant public good. It is likely that no single individual or group of individuals would take the initiative in collecting money for that purpose, unless the monkeys became intolerable. Similarly for well repairs or field road maintenance. The fund pays the Irrigation Department for the right to cut a certain type of canal reed grass within the village boundaries so that whoever likes may use the grass for thatch – whereas in villages without a fluid fund individuals compete to buy the rights from the Irrigation Department and then sell the grass privately. Wandering troupes of players and puppeteers do not have to go from house to house collecting donations for their performance; the village fund pays, they get on with the performance, and don't loiter afterwards. (The more outsiders hanging about the village the greater the risk of thefts and quarrels, it is believed.)

Representatives who go to the Irrigation Department to get more water for the village can have their own expenses paid from the fund, as well as the expenses of the irrigation officers (such as jeep hire and the cost of liquor and cigarettes). Normally, though, the bribe payments, as distinct from 'expenses', are collected from individual households, not from the standing fund. The village fund can make a donation to the various Government Subscription Funds, to the benefit both of the officer sent to collect donations and of the wealthier households on whose doors he would otherwise have to go knocking. If he is a man of some seniority he will be given a good meal and will go away favourably impressed by the warm-hearted generosity of the villagers. The agricultural extension officer, too, or a worker sent to repair an electricity cable, can have his creature comforts cared for, and will more gladly return.

This is not to say that the benefits accrue to everyone in the village, that they are 'functionally identical' good for all. The money spent to get more water from the Irrigation Department benefits the owners of irrigated land (and mainly, paddy land). The money spent to construct an animal clinic benefits animal owners. That spent for helping the construction of a new primary school building benefits those who have children in school – in the school to which most Harijans do *not* go. Village fund money has sometimes been used to finance repairs to the Harijans' wells; but getting the council to release money for this purpose is more difficult than for repairs of 'clean caste' wells. Therefore, when we say that the goods provided are public goods, this should be taken to mean that if provided at all they benefit many, but certainly not all.

The council is also involved in regulatory activities which, having no financial cost, do not show up in the accounts. We have already noticed the regulation of harvesting practices, of sheep folding, of the grazing of big stock. It hears cases of alleged crop theft, and of water disputes which infringe the common irrigator's authority. The sanction for this regulatory activity is a fine, in money or grain. The small fines on individual trespassing animals which the field guards keep for themselves are not recorded in the accounts. A quarter of the bigger fines goes to the field guards, while the balance goes to the village fund. At least in the early 1970s fine money was a not insignificant element of the fund's recorded income (table 6.3). The accounts are unfortunately not at all specific about the nature of the offences for which fines have been levied. But it is clear that most of the fine money that gets into the accounts is for crop thefts or interference with the work of the common irrigators. While fines in the late 1970s were small compared to those of the early 1970s, the amount raised for the village fund in fines during the drought of 1980 came to several hundred rupees (chapter 7).

In any case, it is clear that within the recent past the council has been able to wield enough authority to levy very substantial fines on individuals – mostly individuals from the same village (though in the early 1970s are recorded several cases of fine payments by people from nearby villages for infringements within Kottapalle's land – perhaps they owned land within the village boundaries). This is an important point, because the ability to levy fines against one's own 'members' is a good indicator of the strength of collective action. The fines do not, it should be noted, go to the aggrieved party as compensation; the fine is intended to deter, not to compensate, because (a council member explained) to judge relative compensation would invite recurrent disputes, as each damaged party claimed he had been undercompensated. The council has tried to avoid exposing its authority to such challenge.[2]

The council also intervenes in a more ad hoc fashion to lay down what cannot be done in the village. A recent example concerns the gambling game called *matka*. Each day people throughout India place bets on a number from 0 to 9 by 7 p.m.; and again on a second number by 10 p.m. If they win on either number they normally recover about 4 times their bet, if both, about 80 times. The smallest bid is a fraction of a rupee, so the gamble is within reach of virtually anyone. The Indian telephone system demonstrates extraordinary efficiency in allowing information about the bets placed on different numbers to be aggregated from thousands upon thousands of dealers across the country, so that the '*matka* king' in Bombay can know in advance which number has the maximum money on it and therefore which number he must not choose from a pack of cards; and similar efficiency is shown in sending back the winning number to those thousands of dealers by 8 p.m. and 11 p.m. respectively. The special telephone system installed by the State Electricity Boards is said to be used in order to speed things up. With the possibility of getting back 80 times the bet, the game has for many an irresistible attraction; devotees spend hours studying past trends and deriving formulas for predicting the winning number, associations are formed to pool bets and expertise, and in Kottapalle people who don't know the name of the Chief Minister know of the *matka* king in Bombay and his extravagant ways. In 1980 the game began to be highly organized in Batampur, the big village three miles away. A schoolteacher at the local high school hired someone else to do his teaching and devoted himself to organizing *matka* full-time, in return, of course, for a sizeable commission on the business. He wanted to appoint sub-dealers in the surrounding villages. The Kottapalle council, though it includes some devoted gamblers, was worried collectively that *matka*, if made more accessible to the men of Kottapalle, would be the undoing of the whole village. People who lose, it was pointed out over and over, are likely to steal to recoup their losses. So the council decided to announce (via the village crier) that no-one in the village was allowed to become a sub-dealer, on pain of a heavy fine. We shall see a number of other cases where the council has intervened in similar fashion to stipulate what can and cannot be done.

However the council does *not* have the kind of judicial role which is

[2] See (Wade 1982d) for a case where compensation is paid.

thought to have been a normal function of 'the Indian village *panchayat*'. It enters disputes only where its own authority or that of its agents is infringed. Even for water disputes in connection with lightly irrigated crops or second season irrigated paddy (for which no common irrigators are employed), the council as such is not involved: still less in connection with boundary disputes, or family quarrels; nor even with intercaste relations, except in very particular circumstances.[3] For such disputes there is no permanently existing machinery. The disputants may take the case to a third person or a set of three persons, agreeing in advance to abide by the arbitrator's decision. The arbitrator(s) may be a caste elder, if the disputants are of the same caste; or more commonly, will be drawn from amongst those recognized as 'village elders' and widely respected for being able to settle such matters. All the persons with this reputation are Reddys, with the addition of the village accountant, a Brahmin, who is reputed to be especially good for settling boundary disputes. The two parties will argue their case before the arbitrator(s), probably in the street outside the house of one of them, shouting and gesticulating, appealing to bystanders, until they get too weary to continue and some sort of settlement is made. But there is not much compunction, these days, about taking a case to the government court in Nowk.

Raising income for the village fund

With regard to income the village fund accounts are very incomplete. For one thing, income from the auction of the liquor licence was not recorded before 1976, because Prohibition was in force throughout the state. The village council still arranged an auction within the village for the exclusive right to sell illicit liquor; but it was thought unsafe to record the sale in the accounts ledger, in case some day the ledger was seen by someone from government. Since 1976 the sheep-folding auction receipts have not been entered, for no apparent reason. Nevertheless, for what they are worth (and they do indicate minimums), income details from the fund accounts are given for several years in table 6.3.

The two main sources of income are the sheep-folding auctions, already described, and the sale of the liquor licence. In 1980 the village

---

[3] One occasion when the council and fund became involved in an intercaste dispute concerned an incident when the *tahsildar* (senior government official in a subdivision of a district) gave a Muslim family permission to live in a house adjoining a Hindu temple, and the council organized representatives to go to Nowk and Kurnool to petition against the decision, the fund paying their expenses (see table 6.1, 1971/2).

Table 6.3 *Village fund income account, various years*

1-7-1969 to 16-6-1970 (11.5 months)	Rs.
Sale of grain	3,971
Fines (net of 25% collection commission)	399
	4,370
1-6-1971 to 1-8-1972 (14 months)	
Sheep-folding auction	3,234
Fines (net)	338
Paddy sale	303
Sale of he-buffalo	306
Sale of big stones	100
	4,281
1-1-1976 to 27-6-1977 (18 months)	
Liquor franchise	5,880
Sale of grain	3,410
Payment from persons holding fund money	1,910
Sheep-folding auction	1,832
Sugar	550
Fines (net)	60
Miscellaneous	50
	13,692
27-6-1977 to 10-3-1978 (8.5 months)	
Liquor franchise	2,270
Payment from person holding fund money	30
	2,300

Note: The income accounts are incomplete.

fund got Rs. 5,500 from the sheep folding and Rs. 4,500 from the sale of the liquor licence.

The method of raising village fund revenue from liquor changed over the 1970s. Until 1978 the government auctioned the liquor licence village-by-village. Bidders from each village were meant to attend the auction and bid against each other, the profit going to the government. Kottapalle, however, sent only one person to the auction. That person got the licence at minimum price; the council then re-auctioned it within the village, with the balance going to the fund. Or sometimes the village auction was held before the government auction and the winner went to the government auction alone to get the licence for as little as he could. During Prohibition, in force for some years before 1976, the system was little different, except that the auction in the village came to be for the council-backed right of exclusive sale of *illicit* liquor. (In similar fashion, the council has arranged that only one person should go to the Irrigation Department's auction of the right to cut the valuable type of canal reed grass within each village so it can be obtained at minimum cost; but in this case, the reed grass is then free for anyone in the village to take as they wish.)

However, in 1978 the basis of the government liquor auction was changed. Instead of being village by village, it became possible for individuals to buy up the licence for a whole sub-district, and put sales within the sub-district into the hands of agents. The big Reddy who got the licence for Nowk sub-district came to Kottapalle to discuss with the village council how much to pay the fund. The councillors said they had been getting Rs. 6,000 per year in the past, and wanted this amount to continue. He offered Rs. 3,000. The councillors were worried that if they accepted his offer not only would they lose money that year, but the next year's licensee would not hesitate to refuse to offer any more than Rs. 3,000; and so on. They refused. He went ahead and appointed as agent for Kottapalle a man from a nearby village, not from the village itself. The agent confirmed he would not pay the village fund anything. He came to begin business just before an important festival, when he might expect to turn over Rs. 2,000 in two days. The council announced by village crier that nobody was to buy liquor from him, under threat of a heavy fine; the populace should go to other villages to drink (the nearest being three miles away). Not only the council, but the maximum number of 'influentials' took part in the decision and agreed to it. The liquor seller had no customers. Then the big Reddy divided up his franchise into sub-units, and sold the one covering Kottapalle (and 20 to 30 nearby villages) to another man, who appointed his own agent in Kottapalle (a local man) and agreed to the agent's paying the fund about Rs. 450 a month, or Rs. 5,400 for a full year; but already two months of fund income had been lost. (In the auction towards the end of 1980 the situation changed again; but it is convenient to leave this till the discussion of factions in chapter 7.)

The council as a centre of village management

The village fund is effectively the only locally-controlled source of common finance for village activities, and the council is the only centre of village-wide coordination. The fund was spending about Rs. 10,000 a year in the late 1970s. The income of the statutory village council, the *Panchayat* (also known as 'the government *Panchayat*'), is about Rs. 4,000 a year. It should be higher, but as in virtually all villages below a certain large size there is no professional tax collector and the house tax goes uncollected. (In Nowk sub-district the model *Panchayat* income in 1979 was Rs. 3,000 to 5,000; virtually no village had as much as Rs. 10,000.) In any case, the *Panchayat's* income is – not only in Kottapalle but in the whole region – popularly, if cynically, believed to be for the disposal of the village president for his own private ends. In practice, very little is spent on 'village' matters, other than for scattered street lighting. As a deliberating body the *Panchayat* is defunct. Indeed, young people of Kottapalle too young to remember the last election in 1970 generally do not know there is such a thing as a *Panchayat*; they know only of the president. (In 1981 local government elections, including those for village *Panchayats*, were held throughout the state for the first time since 1970. The *Panchayat* election in Kottapalle was not contested.)

The disproportion between council and *Panchayat* in control over resources is greater than the comparison of their budgets – Rs. 10,000 against Rs. 4,000 – indicates. For at times when Food for Work money becomes available, it is possible for the village council to make decisions about much larger amounts of resources by means of the matching grant principle. With the new school building, for example, the council provided Rs. 7,000 from the fund and secured through a 10:1 matching grant an additional Rs. 70,000 from the government's Food for Work budget. It was the village council, not the *Panchayat*, which decided to put in an application and provide the village's 1/11 share. But the council did not decide who should do the work; that was decided by the sub-division office. If the council had had to decide it, disputes would have arisen over its discretionary allocations of privatizable benefits.

People make a sharp distinction between the sphere of the *Panchayat* and that of the council. As the accountant said, 'The *Panchayat* is only concerned with government and the *Samiti*, it is only concerned with government-approved works. The council is concerned with village betterment.' Said another notable, 'When villagers face difficulties they (the council) will solve and punish the persons responsible' – this version greatly overstates its juridical role but does reveal one of the axioms of the world view, that the difficulties people face are generally caused by other people, and that punishment of those others is the solution. Another notable said, 'For proper maintenance of the village the council will prescribe rules and conditions.' When discussing a matter like the construction of the new primary school building or the financing of festivals, people use the phrase, 'The village made a contribution', meaning the village fund.

In principle, the council does not discuss matters which belong to the world of government and *Panchayat*. It has, for example, not discussed the matter of the school teachers' lax attendance (most of the teachers are outsiders, and live outside), although this worries many parents; for the school teachers are part of the world of government. (Rather, the accountant has recently started an evening coaching school for those whose parents can pay, partly to compensate for the lax school teachers.) On the other hand, practical exigencies often force the council to move beyond the village/government dividing line. We have already noted that it discussed and made a contribution to the construction by the state of a new school building, because a contribution was a condition for a matching government grant. We have seen the council being continuously involved in the operation of what is, in principle, the state's irrigation system within the village's own land – and even upstream of its own land. It has also been heavily involved in the government's allocation of licences to distribute rationed sugar and to sell liquor. But while the line is often crossed, the council does not present itself as a unit in dealings with the government. Individuals are empowered by the council to deal with the government on its behalf, and in the eyes of the government officials those individuals are no more than village 'elders' or 'influentials', no different from the dozens of elders and influentials from other villages who daily ask their favour. They do not know about, and would care still less about, their role as representatives of a village council; because that council is empowered not by the state but by the villagers themselves. To the state the council is invisible.

Conclusion

This chapter has reviewed the kinds of activities which are the subject of a steady, long-term pattern of collective control. It is clear that the council is engaged in providing public goods, in the sense that if they are provided to one they must be provided to many. These include not only field guarding, but also such quantitatively unimportant but sociologically significant services as employment of a specialist monkey catcher, or of well repairers. Most items benefit more specifically defined groups than the 'whole village' – a donation towards the cost of construction of a new primary school building or replacing the thatch on the old building, benefits those whose children go to that school (but little fund money is spent on the Harijan school). The money spent on festivals is mostly for Hindu festivals; a donation is made to the Muslim festival, but nothing is given for the Christian festival of the Harijan Christian converts.

As these examples make clear, most of the benefits mean little to the very poor, especially the Harijans. It is significant that 'charity' is not given to people within the village; and is given only to 'deserving' itinerant beggars, people who have fallen on misfortune but are clearly of 'respectable caste', rather than to the many low-caste beggars who pass through the village and have to rely on door-to-door donations. The point is clearest in the two main services the council is concerned to provide: common irrigators and field guards, who benefit crop and animal owners. Many households in the village own no crops or animals.

While this shows that the council and the fund are institutions of and for the landed, this does not mean that they are against the interests of the landless. The lot of the landless would certainly not be improved if the village had none of these corporate institutions, as many other villages in the area do not.

The benefits provided by the council and fund, and the means of raising income to provide them, are also 'organizational goods', in the sense that people must organize to get the collective benefit. No outside agency will do it; and provision by private individuals, given the collective nature of the benefits, is unlikely. The pay-off to such organization can be high, as seen in the case of field guards and common irrigators. On the income side, means have been found to break the link between the provision of collective benefits and contributions from benefiting households. In a sense, contributions are not voluntary, but coerced; no individual has the right to say, for example, that he will not pay any sheep-folding money into the village fund and in return cease to get the help of the field guard's protection – not only does he not have a choice about paying half his bid to the fund, but there is no tight link between sheep-folding payments and any specific service provided from the fund which would allow him to claim the matter as a cost foregone in return for a benefit foregone. The coercion, of course, is derived from a central, but local, authority – the council acting as a single body.

Thus, the goods provided have the characteristics of public goods; both they and the income-raising arrangements are organizational goods; and the pay-off to individuals is high in the case of the two central services. Further, the goods are 'functionally identical' goods within the specific groups of beneficiaries. All animal owners may potentially benefit from the animal clinic and the availability of the vet, school children and their parents all benefit from the new school building or the improved roofing over the old one. All owners of crop land are at risk of theft, and benefit proportionately to area from field guard protection. Owners of paddy land all benefit from the common irrigators' services.

The fact that the common irrigators work only on paddy land is a striking illustration of the principle of functional identity. If they worked also on feeding lightly irrigated crops they could not treat each field as identical, for the amounts of water required by lightly irrigated crops as well as the timing vary considerably from crop to crop. Confining the common irrigators to paddy means that their job is to treat each acre equally (subject to differences in soil type). This in turn means that the category of paddy growers have a stronger common interest than the category of growers of lightly irrigated crops, and maintenance of the common irrigator system is easier than it would be if applied to lightly irrigated crops.

On the other hand, the principle of individual benefit is very much preserved in the sense that individuals, outside the specific restrictions of the council and fund, can use their profits as they wish, except to change the rules of the system.

The council is also careful to avoid activities which do not have a large element of publicness. In particular, it adjudicates rival claims between individuals only when its own authority is in question. This is because it could not get enough 'distance' from the parties for adjudication not to threaten the council's ability to reach consensus on matters of common interest. It would be threatened by the potential politicization of the case, as the loser attempted to enlist factional support within and outside the council to get a more favourable judgement. If it were seen to give differential treatment according to the status of the accused, disputes might arise within the council. In adjudication of disputes such as boundary quarrels between individuals, on the other hand, the dominant concern is to find a solution which is acceptable to all parties and will thereby prevent the dispute from disrupting social relations; for which purpose the disputants choose as arbitrators men who are skilled at just these kinds of social compromise, according to the status of the participants.

Equally, the council and village fund are not involved in distributing welfare benefits within the village. So there is a sharp difference between Kottapalle and the image of the 'peasant village' common in much of the literature on (precapitalist) peasantry: as a collectivity which, in Scott's terms (1976), operates to assure a minimum income to its inhabitants, to equalize the life chances and life risks of its members. Other than the equalization which is inherent in the notion of public goods and services, Kottapalle shows no sign of such mechanisms; for the reason that its collective organization deals only with the provision of public goods and services, whose distribution is therefore less open to conflict between competing individuals and households.

Partly for the same reason, the council has shown no interest in the sort of activities which the community development movement hoped would be ignited in India's villages, such as promoting acceptance of agricultural innovations, literacy, mass innoculations, and so on. It is partly that these are seen as pertaining to the world of government officials; and partly that their benefits are privatizable. If the council were to request the agricultural extension officer to set up some demonstration plots in Kottapalle's land, the immediate and potentially conflict-laden question would be, on whose land?

These restrictions on the content of what is allowed to enter the public realm are one part of the answer to the question of how Kottapalle politics are kept relatively 'civil'.

7

The mode of public choice

Open debate, stated grounds, standard ways of setting the boundaries of rule: these are indicators of the civilizing of the political process in Kottapalle. They put it far from the extreme alternative of straightforward aggression, usurpation or repression such as Sharma, for one, shows to be almost routine in her North Indian village (1978). One reason politics is kept relatively civil is that the net benefits of abiding by the rules of grazing and irrigation are seen to be high. A second is that all the activities that are allowed to enter the public domain are – with one exception to be described – characterized by a high degree of publicness, in that if undertaken at all their benefits are available to many at the same time. Both reasons have been considered at length in earlier chapters. Now we examine several other factors that influence the civility of politics, including leadership, factions, procedures of compromise and accountability, and crisis management.

Who is on the council?

The village council normally has 9 members plus the village accountant. The latter is a kind of *ex officio* member who undertakes a role resembling that of 'honorary secretary', and the meetings always take place on the veranda of his house. Of the nominated members, 8 are Reddys and 1 is low caste (of Shepherd caste). What is striking is not the predominance of Reddys, but the fact that a low caste person is included at all. This composition of the council has been stable for as long as records go, back to 1969, though the individuals have changed.

Of the 1980 council, all the members show a certain solid comfort. All have electricity to their houses, along with about 50 others. All own at least one pair of oxen (but only 4 have more than 1 pair, against a total of about 20 households with more than one). Six have at least 1 farm labourer on annual contract. This last, the employment of an annual labourer, is a clearer indication of a tendency to withdraw from the manual labour of cultivation than is the number of oxen, and it is significant that over half the council employ one or more. Seven out of 10 own more than 30 acres of land. However, it can be misleading to take each household as a separate unit, because some of them are closely related to households with equal or more land and wealth (brothers or son-in-law/father-in-law, for example), and this gives them more economic weight than their landownership alone might suggest.

In age, they average about 50, with three aged 60 or more and three less than 40. They are all literate, but only 5 went to high school. Their wives all come from within a 60-kilometre radius. Out of 10, 7 have been at least once to Hyderabad, the state capital, the best part of a day's journey away; but only the accountant has been there more than a few times in his life. Most of them will browse over the daily (Telegu) newspaper which the accountant has delivered to his house, but they do not follow state politics. On the whole, their attitude to state politics and political parties is one of scorn, and none of them is actively involved in a party. They have not invested in their children's education any more than other households of roughly comparable economic position in the village. Of the village's 12 university graduates since the mid-1960s, only 2 are sons of 1980 councillors.

It is then, a council of the landed, with enough land to be net buyers of labour and net sellers of food; of active farmers; and of older men. It is also a council of household representatives, in the sense that there can be only one representative per household, and 'household' includes brothers who may have quite separate households. On top of that, nomination to the council depends on force of personality, on savoir-faire in the world of officials, on a quality of gravitas in bearing. But the Kottapalle councillors are, to repeat, working farmers; there is no hint in their demeanour that leadership, the exercise of rule, is for them the original vocation, the focus of their mode of life. Ancestry has little to do with it, except that the family's standing in the village influences the self-confidence of its young men as they grow up and their ability to give an impression of wisdom and strength; and of course its standing reflects land ownership, and how much is bequeathed to the next generation.

Plenty of other households are at least as wealthy and as 'cosmopolitan' as these, but do not have a member on the 1980 council. For reasons we shall come to, many householders which have the solid economic security that seems a necessary condition for council membership prefer, most of the time, not to be a member; though some of these exert considerable influence on the council's decisions without formal membership. The three primary school teachers who reside in the village, all men, take no part in any of its activities – even though Kottapalle is their native village, where they were born and brought up. They appertain to the world of government, not to the world of village and fields. Nor are the village's priests involved in it. Women are completely excluded from the public domain.

About 17 per cent of Kottapalle's 575 households derive a solid surplus from their land, and 23 per cent of the 575 households are Reddys. About 10 to 15 per cent meet both criteria, or 60 to 90 households. This is Kottapalle's 'power elite', the pool from which come active participants in council decisionmaking.

The councillors could be characterized as locally-oriented conservors, not nationally-oriented innovators. They give little value to popular participation as such, but will promote whatever degree seems necessary both to reduce conflict and to have the council's decisions obeyed. They are not in the least interested in promoting economic equality, and the idea that their stewardship of the village entails obligations to provide a minimum income to all its inhabitants would strike them as utterly foreign. Their concern to avoid conflict and their lack of interest in egalitarian measures help to circumscribe the public realm.

Factions[1]

There are, people say, two 'fractions' in the village, one called 'Pulla Linga Reddy's group', the other, 'Venkat Swamy Reddy's group'. Pulla Linga Reddy is the biggest landowner, with 120 acres of land and the village's only tractor. He also runs three pairs of oxen, and employs four full-time farm labourers (p. 48). His house is one of only two in the village to have some hint of grandeur; a fine, two storied, white-washed building, with arches instead of simple pillars on the veranda contributing to the impression of solidity and power. He is an old man of over 80, and effective management of the household is now in the hands of his four sons. They are the leaders of 'Pulla Linga Reddy's group'.

Venkat Swamy Reddy, leader of the other faction, is the village's first university student, and still introduces himself as 'Venkat Swamy Reddy, BA Failed', for at the time when he went to university in the 1950s even to get into a university was a rare achievement.

He has about 40 acres of land, most of it inherited; he employs 2 full-time farm labourers, and owns 1 pair of oxen. He also owns a one-third share in a truck, which is kept by the other partners in Nowk. His house is modest, on one floor only. While Pulla Linga Reddy and his sons are loud and aggresive, Venkat Swamy Reddy is quiet and retiring, with an air of shrewd wisdom. His number-one supporter and co-leader of the

---

[1] Faction is used in a generic sense, without implying that alignments are shifting and unstable; compare Beals 1969:35.

'group' is G. Siva Reddy, a man with 50 acres of land, 2 full-time labourers and 1 pair of big oxen (for his other requirements he borrows from his brother's 2 pairs). G. Siva Reddy lives in the other grand house of the village, and is more disengaged from cultivation work than any of the other big men. He dresses in elegant, well-ironed (but traditional) clothes, and shows, more than the other leaders, the insouciance of power. He is one of the treasurers of the village fund, along with one of Pulla Linga Reddy's sons.

However, while people talk of two 'groups', there are only a few other men who are clearly identified as belonging to one side or the other, though others may be identified as inclining more or less towards one or the other. In everyday life, in terms of who mixes with whom, factional identity makes little difference. Half-way between the houses of Pulla Linga Reddy and Venkat Swamy Reddy is the accountant's house with its ample veranda, and here anyone who is anyone gathers or pauses while going somewhere else (it is on the main thoroughfare through the Reddy quarter). Opposite the accountant's house is his walled farm-yard, where safely out of sight but conveniently close at hand the men gamble away the afternoons and evenings. Here faction is irrelevant. So it is in marriage.

People don't like to speak about factions; 'village politics' are not thought to be the dignified face of the village that the outsider should see. They like to say that factions operate only in elections, not in 'village matters'. They may go on to speak of two kinds of factions: one where there are quarrels between the parties, perhaps over land, and fights with sticks or agricultural implements break out periodically; the other, where the groups mobilize only at election times. It is the second kind, they say, that exists in Kottapalle. The same point is sometimes made by saying that while Kottapalle has 'litigations' – quarrels between two opposed groups over small matters, in a restrained way – it does not have 'parties', the quarrels between which often involve fighting, rioting and even murder. There is indeed some truth in these accounts, though it is a partial truth.

The two groups often, but not always, divide at elections if there are rival candidates. In the last five (state) Assembly elections, and the last four (national) parliamentary elections, the two groups have *not* split their support on four occasions. On the five occasions when they have split, Venkat Swamy Reddy's candidate has won.[2] Elections for the

---

[2] For example, in the election following Sanjeeva Reddy's elevation to the Presidency of India, Venkat Swamy Reddy's group backed the winning Congress (I) party, the other group backed the Janata loser.

village president have always been contested, except in 1981, with one of the two candidates getting support from one group, the other from the other group. More of the 1981 election later.

At elections, other castes are brought into the contest because their votes are needed – this is about as far as the development of universal suffrage has established a basic equality of citizenship in the villages. Customarily, Venkat Swamy Reddy's group has got support of the Shepherd caste and a Harijan sub-caste; Pulla Linga Reddy's group has been supported by the Warrior caste and another Harijan sub-caste. The Muslims have tended to divide rather than vote solidly for one group or the other. But such support is not automatic; it has to be paid for. For Assembly or parliamentary elections the outside candidates pay their local agents in the villages to procure votes; and/or they may promise specific public works projects in return for pledges of support – a bore well in the Shepherd caste's quarter, for example, or more ambitiously, tarring of the road from the village to the main road. Whether money is paid out directly in return for votes varies from election to election depending on the state of the contest between the candidates and their electoral strategy (the closer the contest, the more likely votes are purchased). In the *Panchayat* elections, however, purchase of votes by candidates for president is common. In the 1970 *Panchayat* elections, the last to be held before those of 1981, the president was elected indirectly by the successful candidates from each of the 9 wards into which the village was divided, from amongst themselves. One of the two candidates for president spent Rs. 1,500 in each of at least two low-caste wards to buy votes for his nominees (between one and two weeks' wages for a male agricultural labourer, per vote);[3] and spent at least Rs. 15,000 in total. But he lost, and had to sell half his land to meet his debts. (With this and later gambling debts he was been reduced from a sizeable landowner to a modest one with ten acres. He now depends heavily on contracting work from the Irrigation Department – he is the contractor we met in chapter 5, and appears here later in this chapter.) The 1981 election for president was not contested in Kottapalle due partly to the fact that no one was keen to lay out the estimated Rs. 40–50,000 it would cost to win. In the big village three miles away (population over 5,000), the losing side in 1981 spent some Rs. 60,000; in another village, a hamlet with 150 voters held out till the last minute and received Rs. 35,000 from the eventual winner for its crucial votes. Some of the money to finance vote purchases comes from above, from candidates for the presidency of

---

[3] Much less than Wurfel's figure for the Philippines (Scott 1972:97), much more than Harriss' indicators for Randam (1982:275).

the next higher level local council the *Panchayat Samiti*, whose president is elected by members of the council, including all village presidents; they in turn may get finance from still higher up, from representatives in the state or federal assemblies who are battling to have their candidate made president of the district council, the *Zilla Parishad*. But each village president also expects to recoup his election expenses from the *Panchayat*'s budget and from rake-offs on public works contracts (Wade 1982). Within the village the vote money is not always paid out household by household or voter by voter; it is given to the 'group leader' – the organizer of the vote bank – who may distribute the money to the voters against carbon copies of their ballot, or supply them with liquor, or he may simply rely on his orders to bring out the vote keeping the money for himself (Bailey 1963).

There have been two 'groups' in Kottapalle for as long as anyone can remember, one group being Pulla Linga Reddy's or his father's before him, the other for which various families have provided the leader and core members. 'Party' conflict, marked by 'fights, sickles, bombs, and murders also', has occurred between them twice in living memory, both periods coinciding with the arrival of new contenders for village leadership. One period was around 1925–7. The leaders were the young Pulla Linga Reddy and the grandfather of the defeated candidate for president in 1970 (the Irrigation Department contractor), on one side; and on the other, the grandfather of G. Siva Reddy (the main supporter of Venkat Swamy Reddy today) and the grandfather's brothers. One can draw straight descent lines, then, from the leaders of that time to the present day leaders – though in the 1970 elections the defeated candidate – the above-mentioned contractor – had the support not of Pulla Linga Reddy (as did his grandfather) but of the other side. In 1927, after at least one person had been killed, 'peace' was declared, and a special ritual 'for the village goodness' was held.

One generation later, in about 1952, came another period of conflict lasting two years. It was triggered by an inheritance dispute between two leading brothers – one of them the father of G. Siva Reddy – and rapidly escalated to the 'party' stage, with Pulla Linga Reddy leading one side supporting G. Siva Reddy's father, and with the other side being led by a young man who was then a substantial landowner but is no more a force in village politics (he sold off most of his lands after competing unsuccessfully for president in the 1950s). Here too there was a murder. The present accountant, who had just taken up his office, remembers as one of his first official duties having to walk the 14 miles to Nowk to give evidence in court. The special ritual was not repeated nor has it been subsequently, partly because the custom is dying out everywhere, partly because it is expensive, and partly because it requires agreement on the rank order of families.

But peace was declared, and 'Then this village was a compromised village', said the accountant in English, meaning that people were ready to make compromises and avoid open conflict. As far as can be remembered, the council and common irrigator/field guard organization endured through both periods of intense factionalism.

The normative distinction which villagers make between 'elections' and 'village matters', with factions today pertaining to the former, is considerably overdrawn, even if there are no longer sharp cleavages between the sides. The line of cleavage may again appear when crises occur in the public realm.

Managing crises

By the late 1970s Pulla Linga Reddy had withdrawn from active leadership in the village, and his eldest son was asserting himself as his father's successor. This in itself raised the salience of factional identity in village life, one generation after the last period of high tension. Then in 1980–1 a series of crises occurred which all impinged on the council. At any time these crises would have imposed strain, but their effect was amplified by coincidence with the conflictual stage of a generational cycle of conflict. The upshot was a decision at the 1981 general assembly meeting to confine the scope of the organization to field guarding alone. This constituted a drastic curtailment of the council's role. Let us follow the events which led to this decision – and to the twist at the end of the story.

The sugar crisis

For a short time in the mid-1970s, and again in early 1980, the state government of the day introduced a scheme to distribute a certain amount of sugar at subsidized rates. Each village was allocated a quota according to its population, and authorized dealers then sold the sugar at the subsidized price within the village. Villagers quickly learned that the dealership could be very profitable. In 1980 the subsidized price was Rs. 3 or Rs. 4 per kilo, below the open market price, so that if the dealer (illegally) sold four 50 kilo bags on the open market he stood to make Rs. 600 to Rs. 800. If he did this with every month's quota he made a very tidy income (equivalent to the official income of an Irrigation Department foreman). So people were prepared to pay the issuing authority (the Revenue Department's sub-divisional officer) substantial illicit amounts for the dealership and the latter was prepared to oblige competitors from the same village by splitting its dealership in two. In villages with factions such an arrangement might be deliberately sought as the basis for a compromise with each side having one dealership at its disposal.

The struggle for the dealership in Kottapalle began almost immediately after the scheme was re-introduced in 1980. The first month the man who had last held the dealership when the mid-1970s scheme was discontinued went to Nowk and collected all of Kottapalle's allocated nine bags. But when his supply ran out before the month finished complaints began to be heard that he had sold half the quota on the open market for his own profit. The next month, the Irrigation Department contractor managed to persuade the issuing authority to divide the dealership in two and assign the second half to his own client. This was in line with factional balance. He and his client supported Pulla Linga Reddy's group, while the first dealer supported Venkat Swamy Reddy's group. For simplicity let us call the first dealer A, the second B.

Still the complaints continued, though now directed against both dealers. In July 1980 the complaints reached a crescendo, because July is a festival month when the demand for sugar skyrockets, yet little sugar could be found in the village despite an increase in the village's allocation. At a certain point one of the councillors, affronted at being told by B that he should obtain his sugar from 'his' dealer, A, decided that the council would have to do something about the situation.

He asked the field guards to call the council to discuss the problem the following morning. By 10 a.m. some 15 men were present, seated or squatting on the veranda of the accountant's house. They included some councillors and some others. One or two people aired their opinions from time to time – 'shouted' rather than spoke, for this was a high tension matter. P. Adinarayana Reddy, son of Pulla Linga Reddy and member of the council, was present, together with B, 'his' dealer, standing by his side. Three field guards stood apart with their long poles. One of them went off to try to find the other sugar dealer but returned saying he was not in the village. More people continued to arrive, until more than 50 were present. There was no clear start to the meeting; the declamations gradually grew louder and louder as more people started to speak simultaneously, some to a specific intended listener whose eye happened to have been caught, others to no one in particular. They gesticulated, stood up, sat down, elbowed to face the man whose point they were opposing, walked back, approached again. Then they subsided, and soon only one or two would be speaking while the others puffed on their beedies. Then others would begin to interject, and the volume of sound would swell again to a deafening point. Occasionally this display of passionate anger was punctuated by general laughter.

The argument was about the specific behaviour of the dealers, about whether they should be changed, and about what role the council should have in the distribution of sugar. 'If the village council is responsible for sugar', said several people, 'it must manage it *fairly*.' Everyone agreed with that; the problem was, how. Some said it would be better for the village to give up getting fair price sugar altogether, because it caused so much conflict. Others said the dealers should be changed. P. Adin-arayana Reddy argued aggressively that instead of changing the dealers they – the council – should see that the dealers distributed it properly; all the sugar, all 12 bags for this month's quota, should be brought before the council and distributed to whoever wanted it under the council's supervision. Still others argued for a ration card system by which each household would be entitled to buy up to a certain amount depending on its size. The arguments went on and on, and the crowd only began to ebb away after more than two hours of debate. Nothing was agreed. Afterwards, the sugar continued to be distributed by the same dealers, and people continued to complain about not getting enough because the dealers were selling too much on the open market outside the village. But the council was unwilling to intervene directly because the whole issue of sugar distribution was so fraught with conflict; and also because two of the leading councillors were (it was said) getting a good share of B's profits, which they would lose if the council itself were to hold the dealership.

A week later, with nothing changed, the council held another meeting, which again swelled to a kind of general meeting. Here one of the village notables, not on the council, argued passionately that if the council could not ensure the fair distribution of sugar it was not competent to organize field guards either. He urged that the field guards be immediately suspended for five days, in which time the council would have to come up with a way of distributing all the sugar itself. The general consensus of the meeting was in favour, to the disgust of some of the councillors. One commented the following morning, 'It is a doomsday for the village, after nearly three or four decades of an effectively operating village committee.'

During the five days in which the field guards were suspended people drove their cattle with almost festive abandon to graze on the field around the village, unattended crops and all. The bigger landowners were of course most disadvantaged, for they had the most land to protect. And it seems to have been explicitly calculated that threats to their crops would shake the big men to their senses, and make them reach agreement on the sugar issue.

At the end of the fifth day, as planned, a general assembly meeting was held. Well over 100 people came, and discussion went on into the small hours. The meeting agreed that the field guards should be reinstated immediately – and that henceforth no village dispute, whether about sugar or anything else, should interfere with the council's provision of field guards, which were agreed to be a permanent necessity; and it agreed, contrary to the conclusion of the meeting five days before, that henceforth the council should have nothing to do with the distribution of sugar. For if it did, conflict would never cease. People were aware that in the not distant future the selection of common irrigators for the forthcoming irrigation season would have to be made, which could not also be jeopardized by such extraneous matters as sugar.

The liquor crisis

In the meantime dealer A had found a job in Nowk, and someone else had used this as a pretext to get the issuing authority to reallocate his half of the dealership to himself. A was upset at being deprived of his dealership and so were some of A's friends, one of whom was the new liquor agent.

It will be recalled (chapter 6) that for the previous two years the liquor licence had been allocated for a much bigger unit than the single village, and the licensee had then appointed his own agent in each village. The previous year, after the successful boycott of the agent who had refused to pay the fund, the new agent agreed to pay at a rate about equal to what the fund had got when the licence had been re-auctioned in the village. But the licence for the bigger area went in 1980 to another man, and he supported his Kottapalle agent's refusal to give money to the fund.

The new Kottapalle liquor agent had for a long time been critical of the way the council was handling – or not handling – the distribution of sugar. When he got the liquor agency he said at a meeting of the council, in September 1980, that he would give the council six weeks to find a satisfactory arrangement for the sugar distribution, and if it had not done so by then he would refuse to pay any money to the fund on behalf of the liquor agency. He was incensed that *liquor* had to make a contribution to the village fund when *sugar* did not; the council should sell *all* the sugar on the open market, he argued, then the village fund would not need more money from any other source, including liquor. His discontent multiplied when he learned that his friend, A, had been stripped of the sugar dealership without his knowledge.

He duly refused to pay any money to the fund. The previous year the council had broken the resistance of his predecessor by mounting a successful boycott. This year, however, the water crisis was on, and the council was having a hard enough time enforcing its authority over the distribution of water. It did not want to risk having its authority called into question by asking for, but not getting, another liquor boycott. If the liquor boycott failed, people might start taking water whenever they could. And the boycott might fail because the present agent (unlike the last) was known as an 'influential' man – not in the sense of elder or notable but in the sense of, 'some think on his side he's got mob – mob means labour class'.

The liquor agent was known to lean rather more to Venkat Swamy Reddy's side than to the other, and both Venkat Swamy Reddy and G. Siva Reddy tried hard to persuade him to pay over, to no avail. G. Siva Reddy said to him at a council meeting, 'If that's your attitude, we will have to cancel *all* village committee's activities (including field guards, etc.).' To which the liquor man retorted, 'Who are you? If *you* are not interested then let others take charge. If the village fund does not have enough money for field guards' salaries, *I* will collect from each household.'

Faced with his refusal, the council sent a number of men (some on the council, some not, including G. Siva Reddy and P. Adinarayana Reddy, principal protagonists in the sugar dispute) to Nowk to meet with the licence holder for the Kottapalle area, to persuade him to withdraw the franchise from his agent in Kottapalle and give it to someone else. The licence holder declined. He did not need the council's protection in Kottapalle, he said, because if anyone started harrassing his agent or selling liquor 'illicitly' he had very good connections in the police force, and they would certainly take stern action. He in any case had his own worries, because the drought was affecting sales badly. (Later, the Rayalseema Arrack [Liquor] Contractor's Association would petition the government for relief in terms of reduced taxes and rentals, on the grounds that their earnings in 1980 dropped by more than half the normal year's revenue. They solicited the government to 'take a compassionate view' [*The Hindu*, Hyderabad, July 3, 1981].)

The water crisis

The situation had become extremely serious. The village fund was exhausted by late October 1980 in meeting 'water expenses', and a per acre levy had to be made to cover additional expenses to bring the crop to harvest. There was talk of having to stop the employment of field guards from the end of December, because no money was left.

In the second season of 1980–1 (January to April 1981), a larger than normal area of paddy was planted after assurances from the Irrigation Department Supervisor that water would be sufficient. In the event water again became extremely scarce. The council took the almost unprecedented step in the second season of appointing 6 common irrigators for the area of some 300 acres of paddy (compared with a second-season norm of only 50 to 150 acres). As water supply continued to be very insufficient a levy of Rs. 30 per paddy acre had to be raised to hire a jeep for the Supervisor and to meet his other expenses. All the same, the crop failed on almost the whole 300 acres. People who had paid out so much – not only for Supervisor's costs but also for the common irrigators' payment – were extremely angry, and focused their resentment on the council. They said it was the council's fault.

To all the resentment aroused by the sugar crisis, the liquor crisis, and by the council's imposition of stiff fines and a levy during the first season drought, was added the total failure of the crop in the second season of 1980–1, which the council had been heavily involved in trying to protect. And it was not only resentment expressed towards the council by non-members; within the council, too, recriminations flew back and forth – within as well as between the conventional factional groupings. Furthermore, the generally restraining presence of Venkat Swamy Reddy was no longer there; he had been killed in a road accident in January 1981.

Response to the crises

Then came the 1981 *Panchayat* elections, in May. People were worried that this might provide a further occasion for the open expression of conflict, reviving unpleasant memories of the 1952 bout of 'party' conflict. It had been known for some time that P. Adinarayana Reddy, Pulla Linga Reddy's son, wanted to be the next president. Two other men were also interested. But without much difficulty they were persuaded not to stand, not least because neither of them looked at all plausible against the already established figure of P. Adinarayana Reddy. On the village council the argument was that they – the villagers – had already lost a lot of money because of the droughts, why should they – the candidates – each waste another Rs. 40,000? P. Adinarayana Reddy agreed to give six out of twelve seats to Venkat Swamy Reddy's group (which used his name as a term of reference even after his death), in return for their support for him as president. Each side appointed its own people – none, with the exception of P. Adinarayana Reddy himself and one man for Venkat Swamy Reddy's group, of the men of influence, but two of them were women, as required by regulation.

The field guards, as usual, were not employed after the harvest in April and early May. Normally they would be re-employed for the next season in late June, with the planting of the rainfed crops and paddy seedbeds. In 1981 the general assembly meeting to reaffirm the council, look at the accounts and appoint field guards, was delayed into the middle of July, by which time the planting was already well under way and the risk of having new fields and seedbeds damaged by straying cattle materialized.

When the meeting was eventually held, with over 100 people present, it was stormy. The council came in for all manner of criticism from all sides, including from among themselves. In the event, it was decided that henceforth the village council should concern itself only with 'fields' – only with the appointment, salary, and monitoring of field guards. Matters like sugar, approaching the Irrigation Department for water and appointing common irrigators, should not be its concern. It was not even discussed how approaches to the Irrigation Department or appointment of common irrigators were to be organized; that was something to be decided later, in October, when the time came. Nor should the council be concerned with entertainments (like paying for puppet shows); nor anything else other than 'fields'. The Irrigation Department contractor later began to talk of forming a separate 'water committee', but others immediately countered (behind his back) by saying that he had a strong personal interest in a separate water committee, since, given his good connections with the Irrigation Department, he would have to be head of it; and probably a water committee would be more powerful, control more money with greater discretion, than the old village council if the latter were confined to fields.

Behind the sharp curtailment of the council's scope lay the financial crisis caused by the withdrawal of the liquor money. It meant that the village fund did not have enough money to do more than cover the cost of the field guards' salaries. There was no question of paying the field guards with a per acre levy and using the fund money for sustaining the fund's other activities, because people will reliably pay acreage contributions only in an emergency when they themselves risk a sizable loss.

But the financial situation looked to be even worse in future. For the fund could no longer count on getting as much from its one remaining big source, the sheep-folding auction, as in the past. At the annual assembly in July 1981 many farmers of second season lightly irrigated and paddy crops complained that their standing crops were being damaged, despite all the elaborate field guarding instituted by the council, by the 10,000 or so sheep and goats brought into the village in March and April. They urged that the sheep and goats should only come in late April, after all their crops had been safely harvested. This would mean much less income from sheep folding for the village fund: because the amount farmers are prepared to bid per night per 1,000 head depends on how much manure they expect to get, which depends in turn on how ample and green the vegetation is. The sooner after the harvest the animals are let in the more abundant and the greener is the fodder. If the animals did not come till late April the fund might not have enough money even to pay field guards' salaries without a per acre levy, let alone do the wide range of other things it has normally financed. A fiscal crisis threatened.

The new council

Reflecting its narrower scope and limited financial power, the social composition of the new council changed. The new council contained only one member of the old one, P. Adinarayana Reddy, the new president. It was expanded from ten to fourteen members, including the accountant. Only four out of fourteen had ever been on the council before. It contained *two* low caste members. The new council members tended to be younger than their predecessors, and to be from less well-off households; all owned at least 1 pair of oxen but only 5 owned 2 pairs and, more significantly, only 3 had 2 or more full-time farm labourers (compared to 4 out of 10 on the old council). In terms of factional identity (bearing in mind that in the case of most men their identification with one side or the other is not sharp), four were identified as Pulla Linga Reddy's group, 4 to 6 as Venkat Swamy Reddy's group, and 4 to 6 as neutral. So it is not the case that with Venkat Swamy Reddy out of the way, Pulla Linga Reddy's group swept the board on the new council, even though since Venkat Swamy Reddy's death no clear leader had emerged in his place.

The new council's first job was to appoint field guards for the new year, but on this they could not agree. The previous year's field guards wanted to be reappointed; some on the new council wanted to reappoint them, others wanted to reappoint some but not all, and others, the majority, wanted to replace the whole lot – saying that if the previous group had been more vigilant the crop thefts and livestock damage would not have happened. A week or so later, long after field guards are normally appointed, the council agreed on a set of four new people. So field guards as well as council personnel were changed drastically.

Interest and honour

What is striking about the radical change in the composition and scope of the council is the absence of a sense of regret, or loss, at the council's proposed withdrawal from a wide range of village initiatives. If other villages manage without all the other things, went the argument, why shouldn't we? If in other villages the troupes of players and puppeteers first give their show and then have to solicit donations, why shouldn't they do the same in Kottapalle?

There is at most a very thin sense that a collective approach to such matters is a morally superior way of doing things compared to the alternative of individual household initiative. It is mainly the accountant and his ex-headmaster brother, Brahmins and educated, who articulate this kind of notion of Kottapalle as a 'community', as a 'cooperative' village. When others speak of it as a 'cooperative village' they mean it is one where the factions don't fight physically, where quarrels are relatively restrained. For most people, including the well-to-do, living in Kottapalle is mainly just a matter of residence and livelihood. The living realities for them are less the 'community', than the household, the caste and sub-caste, the loose circle of neighbours. (Whatever other merits or demerits this approach may have, at least discussion of the council and its activities is generally down to earth, quite free of sententious generalities.)

There remains, however, a distinct notion of the council as a mutual interest association. People take part, either as members or as non-member participants, not out of a sense of duty or devotion to the unity and purpose of the village, but because it deals with matters which affect their household more or less directly, and because there is honour to be got from recognition that one's household is sufficiently important to share in the determination of that mutual interest. When mutual interest does not seem to be served, as in the events of 1980–1, then there is talk of a complete change of personnel, or even ending the whole council, with no regrets.

But the matter is more complex than that. Honour comes not only from recognition of economic importance. The word for an 'honourable' man is *peddamanshi*, from the Telegu for 'elder' (*pedda*) and 'man' (*manshi*). And *peddamanshi* is used more or less interchangeably with the English word 'elder' (even by speakers who know little English). For in Indian culture generally, ideas of honour and respect are closely associated with the idea of mature age (Hofstede 1980:117; Triandis *et al.* 1972:248). So the term *peddamanshi* has connotations of mature age, of worthy background ('only certain kinds of families, by tradition'), of experience with local problems; but not necessarily of wealth. What matters most is recognition of a quality of wisdom and gravitas. For a *peddamanshi*, said an informant about the term in general, 'his character is the most important thing, he can guide others, he will not have prejudices, whoever a person is [who comes for help or arbitration] the decisions will be the same'. The main contrast is with *nayakudo*, which carries the connotations of: a rich man; perhaps young, certainly aggressive, arrogant, emotional, 'he may beat people up', 'selfish', 'his own people should benefit from his actions'. Anyone who stands for elective political office is veering towards *nayakudo* classification.[4] The liquor man in Kottapalle (of whom it was said, 'some say on his side he's got mob') is a *nayakudo*, though not rich. But notice that the connotations of *peddamanshi* have little to do with the idea of 'public' service, of serving 'village' welfare; it is his ability to help individuals or settle quarrels between groups which is highlighted in the general term. This is the second component of honour for which men seek recognition on the council, in addition to economic importance.

The word for council member is *peddamanshi*; or the English 'elder' or 'committee member' may also be used. The council itself is called by the plural form, namely *peddamanshulu*; and sometimes the English phrase, 'the village elders' is used to refer to the council. Whether *peddamanshulu* or 'village elders', the council is here being denoted as an aggregate of individuals. But even in the middle of Telegu speech, the council will often be referred to by the English phrase, 'village committee', or a hybrid phrase, '*grama* committee' (*grama* meaning village). These latter terms speak of the council as an entity.

Of course, in villages without a council some men will normally be recognized as *peddamanshulu*. But the council does provide an explicit locus for such recognition. As long as it is seen as the natural place for those who are so recognized, men will wish to be associated with it, in addition to the strictly mutual (material) interest aspect of their concern. On the council, they can see more clearly the reflection of their own worth in the eyes of their neighbours.

If this is the case, many men will continue to want to be associated with the council's deliberations, even though being associated with the council not infrequently brings 'lots of botheration, nuisance, criticism'.

---

[4] For historical background on the term *nayaka*, from which *nayakudo* comes, see Stein 1980:407.

People who have been associated with it tend to express acute sensitivity to the criticism to which it exposes them. Venkat Swamy Reddy explained why he refused to be a member any more some years ago (though he remained involved, at his own discretion, especially in keeping and scrutinizing accounts): 'There may be so many problems in the village. Why to take risk? And better to give chances to the others.' Another well-to-do man who had also remained in the periphery for many years said, 'I am not interested. It is a risk. You have to settle village problems, some people are mischievous.'

In 1981 this criticism became very sharp, and while there is no doubt that the renovation of the council came mainly because large numbers of people not on the council wanted a complete change, it is also true that many council members were fed-up, after the running disputes over sugar, liquor, the strains of the 1980 first season drought, and the even worse water shortage in the following dry season.

It might be expected, however, that the composition of the new 1981 council would not be stable. It was a significantly less 'elite' council than all the previous ones (as far as records tell). So one might expect that the elite associated with the old council would either distance themselves from the new council by way of asserting their superiority, or would simply take it over again and restore its wide range of functions. The permeability of the member/non-member boundary would facilitate this take-over.

It might be expected, too, that a separate 'water committee' would not be viable. In no other village in the sample is there a distinct water organization. Many people in Kottapalle said that with a separate water committee 'fractions' would soon arise between it and the village council; better to have only one organization, they said. Many, especially on Venkat Swamy Reddy's side, saw the idea of a water committee as being too obviously to the advantage of its proposer, the Irrigation Department contractor, who would be its obvious leader because of his close relations with the Irrigation Department. And it was remarked by some that he had not shown much respect for the wider interest when he prompted the sugar crisis by getting the Kottapalle dealership split into two, with one half going to his own man, to his own presumed handsome profit. It is one thing for the president to use the *Panchayat*'s income as his own – for that is not really 'of the village' anyway; it is altogether different for someone to deflect the mutual interest in sugar, or water, to his own profit. Having the water work done by the village council would at least provide better checks on such behaviour than in small 'water committee' dominated by the contractor. Here, in other words, people were saying that in the village context, as distinct from the *Panchayat* context, the distinction between public responsibility – in the sense of respect for mutual interest – and personal aggrandizement, can be blurred only so far and no further. For it is the villagers themselves, and the other members of the elite most especially, that personal aggrandizement is at the expense of. The protection of mutual interest rather than pursuit of public duty is the check.

The council and its organizations are therefore vulnerable to scepticism and withdrawal of participation because it is not underwritten by a faith in the essential rightness of the institutions. Without the protection of a sense of civic duty or devotion, it is more vulnerable than otherwise to the temptation to gain advantage by breaking the rules or refusing to take the risks entailed in defending them. But on the other hand, it *is* widely recognized that there is a big net benefit to be derived, by individuals, from the organization. This acts as a check on individuals trying to 'free ride', because it is apparent that without *continuous* organized effort the supply of public goods is at risk. There is, then, a basic, rational, self-interested calculation behind the collective organization.

That calculation resulted in the reestablishment of the normal pattern of control in the months after July 1981. What have been presented as predictions came to pass.

Reestablishment of the normal pattern

After the general assembly meeting in July 1981 the future of the whole pattern of corporate organization looked bleak. The council's scope was restricted to providing field guards; its size was expanded; its social composition was made less elite; the sheep folding in the following year was not to begin until late April after all standing crops had been harvested, which would mean a sharp reduction in income for the standing fund. Just how common irrigators were to be provided remained unclear.

Then two things happened which removed much of the strain on the council's finances and organizing authority. First, rainfall in the 1981 season, including the often difficult months of September and October, was far above average;[5] so much so that even tail-end fields at no time experienced water difficulties. This permitted the whole question of who was to appoint and supervise common irrigators to be temporarily

---

[5] In 1981 September had 359 mm, October 141, compared with the long-term average of 181 and 89, respectively, and 1980's 100 and 0.

shelved; with no water difficulties even in tail-end plots no common irrigators needed to be employed, for the first time anyone could remember. The second happy coincidence was a sharp rise in the rationed price of sugar to near the open market price, so that it was no longer very advantageous to have the sugar dealership. This removed one of the chronic sources of disaffection with and within the council.

New field guards were appointed in July 1981 for the whole year, as normal. But because the council saw fit – given the parlous state of the village fund – to offer them a lower salary than in recent years (Rs. 70 per month, rising to Rs. 80 at harvest time) they included none who had done the job the previous year, and were of distinctly lower caste than normal. To help compensate for the low salary, however, the council made a remarkable pledge: that its members would pay a much higher fine than everyone else for each animal of *theirs* caught straying (Rs. 15 per head, against the normal rate of Rs. 2 during the day and Rs. 4 at night). In effect, the councillors made themselves liable to meet some of the difference between the new field guards' salary and the normal field guard salary. This is another indication of the strength of the organization, even if by taking extra care with their animals the councillors could ensure that the gesture was more symbolic than substantive.

In February 1982 the outside herders sent their representatives as usual to inquire about when they could enter the village. A long debate ensued on and around the council between those who argued the herders should come in early March as usual so that the village fund could get a good income, and those who, with standing crops to protect, wanted the sheep to be kept out till late April, even at the cost of less income to the village fund (which had been the resolution of the general assembly meeting in July 1981). In the end a compromise was reached, by which the shepherds were allowed into the village in late rather than early March. So the threatened fiscal crisis was eased. By late February 1982 the village fund ledger book, into which entries had not been made during the crisis of 1981, was written up. At the July 1982 general assembly meeting the new council resumed its normal size of nine members plus village accountant; it took up its former irrigation functions; and its members had virtually all been on the council prior to 1981. So one year after the crisis the pre-crisis roles and responsibilities had been largely restored.

This series of events suggests a conclusion about leadership. Kottapalle's leaders are certainly worried by the criticism to which they are exposed. But the pursuit of mutual economic interest and the achievement of social honour seem to be sufficient to prompt many to take part in the council. The supply of leadership, in other words, is not a problem. On the other hand, the present leaders are harmonizers, conservers, risk-averters, not innovators. If the council were to try to undertake more ambitious, developmental activities, especially those that require an investment of tangible resources, leadership might be more of a constraint.

The council as decisionmaker

We can see from the events of 1980–1 how responsive is the council to changes in the demand for public goods. The change of field guards in 1981 in response to the perceived poor performance of the previous year's, the addition of extra common irrigators in the 1981 drought, the provision of *second* season common irrigators in 1981–2; these changes show the equilibrating mechanism to bring supply in line with changed demand. And the best example is the change in the composition of the council by the 1981 annual general meeting.

The organization could not have survived over the past several decades had it not developed techniques for remaining accountable to a wider public, and for balancing conflicting interests. The factional conflicts and the suspicions of authority have been held in check by being given institutionalized expression.

In several ways care is taken to balance the factions' power within the council. When discussing prospective members for the next year's council, the village notables aim at roughly equal representation. In the 1980 council, for example, three out of ten were clearly identified as Pulla Linga Reddy's group (one of the three being his son). Two were clearly identified with the other group. Four others were placed by some informants as leaning to one side or the other, by some as neutral. The tenth, the accountant, was seen as neutral.

Control over the village fund is also shared when factional tensions become more pronounced. In peaceful times most of the handling and accounting for money is done by the village accountant on his own. But in periods of tension, two councillors share control of the village fund. In 1980–1 one was P. Adinarayana Reddy, Pulla Linga Reddy's son, the other was G. Siva Reddy, the insouciant co-leader of the other group. Between the periodic consolidations of the accounts, people who owed the fund or were owed from it dealt with either of the two treasurers, each of whom kept accounts of his fund income and expenditure. The choice of which treasurer to deal with was normally taken to indicate which side one was on.

Consolidations were needed only when one of the treasurers ran out of money; and hence occurred at irregular intervals. On one occasion during the drought of late 1980, about 12 men were gathered on the veranda of the accountant's house while the accounts were being settled. The two treasurers had their notebooks open, and surrounded by onlookers and helpful advisers, were adding up their amounts. People moved between the two sides, inspecting what was going on; passers-by came to watch for a while and then went on with their business. At the end, one of the treasurers said to the other, 'This is our balance. What's yours?' One said he had a surplus of Rs. 857, the other, a surplus of Rs. 3,814. The reason for the settlement, in this case, was not that one side had run out of money, but that the council needed to know what the total credit in the fund was, so as to estimate how much was available for further expenditure on jeep and Supervisor for getting more water if the drought continued.

Having two treasurers helps to provide a check on each. Likewise, it is not accidental that *two* notables always accompanied the Supervisor when he travelled up the channel in Kottapalle's hired jeep during the 1980 drought: one from each group, and usually, the two treasurers themselves. In this way they could not only check the Supervisor's good use of their funds, but also keep check on each other. Yet they behaved to each other like bosom friends, and as the jeep progressed up the channel the atmosphere became increasingly festive as they all shared in the up-market drink and cigarettes which the council calculated were necessary to maintain the Supervisor's interest. Back in the village there was some grumbling at the way the two treasurers were obviously benefiting from the hospitality lavished on the Supervisor. The jeep trips illustrate both the balancing and the limits of village factions.

The need to institutionalize better controls over the village fund received tangible expression in 1969 when the village ledger book was purchased, and the village accounts permanently entered. In the same year, Rs. 300 was spent on buying a massive steel safe, to be used for keeping big amounts of money ready for quick disposition (to the Irrigation Department Supervisor, for example). With the safe, it would not be necessary for individuals to hold onto temptingly large amounts of cash. The alternative of putting the money in a bank account was ruled out not only for reasons of difficulty in getting quickly to a bank, but also because, 'In whose name would the deposit be?' meaning that to register it in any individual's name would invite abuse. Almost certainly the new keeping of accounts and the steel safe of 1969 were a response to conflict over the use and accounting of village money. The elaborateness of these checks contrasts sharply with the absence, in practice, of checks on how the village president uses the statutory *Panchayat's* income.

A more general check on the council comes from the public nature of its discussions. The council meetings are always held on the veranda of the accountant's house, and whoever happens to be passing may stop to listen, and if self-confident enough, speak. The accountant's house is neutral territory, where a great deal of socializing takes place quite apart from the business of the council.

But an equally important aspect is this: the distinction between council member and non-member is by no means as sharp in practice as it is in theory. It is true that at the annual meeting the council is reaffirmed name by name, or some people are changed name by name, so there is no ambiguity at the end of the meeting who is and who is not on the council for that year. Yet because the meetings are in public, whoever wants to come and is informed in advance or happens to be passing can come. Several people who are not officially on the council nevertheless take an active part in its affairs (though brothers, even if in separate households, are not normally active together in the council's business, because of the rule of one representative per household). For instance, the accountant avows that his position as a government servant precludes him from being on the council and his name is not on the 1980 list. But most people think he is on the council because he is virtually always present and active in the discussions. He is one of the signatories in all years between 1969 and 1978 when the accounts were signed; and in most years he kept the accounts. Venkat Swamy Reddy had not been a member for several years before his death; but he was often present – indeed, in the settling of accounts just described, it was he, not G. Siva Reddy, the official treasurer for 'his' group, who was adding up the items, because the other man was absent from the village.

In any case, the council is well aware that on important issues, such as boycotting the liquor agent or raising a per acre levy to pay for getting more water, it is important to widen the circle of participants to include all those who could conceivably have 'influence' (including, in such circumstances, brothers of active participants). Their involvement in the decisionmaking is sought out because otherwise, so past experience teaches, it may be difficult to enforce the decision. Then there is the normal general meeting, near the start of the planting season, announced throughout the village by village crier, attended by fifty to a hundred men or more. At this meeting the accounts of the village fund are read out, the field guards appointed, and the new council ratified.

The modality of decisionmaking is one of almost endless ad hoc, often public negotiation, coupled with a rule of consensus. Frequently meetings end without a decision for unified action, because of the failure to reach a stage where no one disagrees with the proposal. The failure is never acknowledged; the meeting simply ebbs away. Voting to settle issues or select councillors is inconceivable.

These are the various ways the council is kept accountable to a wider public. They express a relation of representation between a diffusely conceptualized, but nonetheless real, notion of a general assembly of the landed and a smaller body acting on its behalf. Equally the procedures are the means by which the two factional groupings within the council, as within the general assembly, can check each other. The very diffuseness of the boundary between member and non-member helps this process of scrutiny and accountability, at the same time as it indicates a low degree of formalization of 'legal-rational' procedures.

But the idea of the council's accountability to a wider public should not be exaggerated. The council most of the time acts like a superordinate authority, not like a committee whose members are steered by opinions and cleavages in the wider public. The upheaval of 1981 in the council membership is quite exceptional. It is to emphasize this superordinate aspect that I have used the word 'council' rather than the English word 'committee' which the villagers themselves use. The council's superordinate position is seen in the fact that it both makes policies and enforces them, wielding substantial and specific sanctions in support of its decisions once arrived at.

8

Variation between villages (1): social structure

The 41 villages are located in an area small enough for technology, tastes, and general social norms to be constant, while resources of soil and water vary. Details on village organization are given in table 8.1 for the irrigated villages. The table uses a simple 'present or absent' measure for each of the four key components – common irrigators, field guards, village council, and village standing fund.

Eight of 31 irrigated villages (a quarter) have all four core institutions. Nine have some but not all. Fourteen out of 31 show no trace of them (but two of these have *sub*-village common irrigators or field guards appointed by farmers in a specific segment of the village's land). Only one of the four core institutions, field guards, is found in a majority of cases (17 out of 31).

The sample was not chosen randomly,[1] however, so not much significance can be attached to the proportions of the total which do or do not have corporate institutions – except to say the corporate forms are clearly not rare. It is nevertheless likely that out of all the villages irrigated from the MN Canal and the TS Canal, those with all four core components are fewer in number than those with none, for reasons suggested in the next chapter.

Table 8.2 gives details on corporate institutions in 10 dry villages, 8 of which are on the MN Canal side of the district, 2 on the (drier) TS Canal side (map 2.1, p. 20). Of the 10 dry villages, 8 have field guards, 6 have a village council, 6 have a village fund. While our interest is primarily in the irrigated villages, it is clear that, as one would expect from the argument about common stubble pasturage (but contrary to the initial expectation of this study, formulated in Wade, 1979), the four corporate institutions cannot be understood simply as a response to irrigation.

We are, of course, interested in more than just the presence or absence of the institutions. Resource mobilization, supply of public goods and services, and popular involvement should be treated as three separate dimensions of 'public activeness'. However, evidence on popular involvement is difficult to get without participant observation, which means that usable data cannot be obtained for more than a few cases. And difficulties of access to the accounts mean that evidence on resource mobilization has to be indirect, in terms of the approximate cost and scope of activities financed from the village fund. (Account books are generally not kept from one year to the next, the treasurer may be out of the village at the time of one's visit, and in any case villagers are understandably wary of allowing outsiders to see the accounts.) But by and large there is a close connection between presence or absence of the institutions and 'public activeness' as a composite of all three dimensions: if all four components are present, there is a good chance that the level of activeness will be markedly higher than if only two are present.

The 'activeness' index shown in table 8.1 uses a combination of

---

[1] The initial intention of the research was to see how and why corporate organization varied with water supply. For this purpose it was important to be able to make comparative statements about water supply. This was made easier by the fact that groundwater and tank irrigation is little developed in this area – the main source of water is the canal. But it was made difficult because we had no means of measuring absolute flows (other than by very rough estimate), and in any case flow measurement over a period of time is a very time-consuming business. (The Irrigation Department does not measure flows to each outlet or village.) So between two villages at the tail-ends of two different distributaries, it was often difficult to say which had the better or worse water supply. One step was to take a long distributary. The nearest accessible long distributary to Nowk was the V Distributary System. Hence the villages of V Distributary System became the core of the sample.

The second step was to choose small clusters of villages, within which it was possible to rank them more or less unambiguously in terms of location (e.g. TSC–2 and TSC–7; MNC–17 and MNC–22; MNC–18, MNC–20, MNC–19). And the third step was to use a crude location scale – 'top-third', 'middle third', and 'bottom third' – putting villages watered directly from the main canal (e.g. MNC–23, MNC–24, MNC–21, MNC–22) in the 'top third' category.

Twenty-four of the 31 irrigated villages were visited in 1977, and 8 of the 10 dry villages (Wade 1979). In 1980–1 another 7 irrigated and 2 dry villages were added (all on the MNC side of the district); and 13 of the original 24 irrigated villages were revisited (all on the MNC side). These revisits led to a few small modifications of the 1977 results village by village, but not to any major changes. Table 8.1 includes more reliable data on population and irrigated area than was available in 1977.

The need to include a range of water supply conditions in the sample was one major criterion of selection. The second was the more mundane one of access. Travel is slow and difficult. In 1977 I had the use of a jeep for a short period, whose value only became fully clear in the 1980–1 field work when the budget stretched only to a small motorcycle. All but the biggest motorcycles are at risk of potholes, and ours had more than its share of punctures and other failures. In these circumstances I was even less inclined than in 1977 to go chasing randomly selected villages.

In the 1977 study one, or occasionally two, visits were made to each village in the sample. Each visit took two to three hours. I had two Telegu-speaking research assistants with me, one of whom talked independently with small farmers to check the information I was getting from members of the village elite. In addition, some of the discussions were followed up with farmers when they visited the market town, and these follow-ups were often more useful than the original more public discussion in the village. In 1980–1 Jeremy and Rosemary Jackson, Lakshmi Reddy and I lived in Kottapalle village, and made visits to accessible villages from there. Some villages, like MNC–5, MNC–7 and MNC–4, we visited several times. A few Lakshmi Reddy visited on his own, with a prepared set of questions.

Table 8.1 *Village organization, sample of irrigated villages*

														MN Ca
Canal^a						V Channel								
Village^b	1	2	3	4	5	6	7	8	9	10	11	12	13	
Common irrigators^c	−	+	+	+	−	−	−	−	−	−	−	+	−	
Field guards^d	+	+	+	+	+	+	−	−	+	−	+	+	−	
Council^e	+	+	+	+	+	+	−	−	−	−	+	+	−	
Fund^f	+	+	+	+	+	+	−	−	+	−	+	+	−	
Activeness index^g	1	2	2	2	2	1	0	0	1	0	2	2	0	
Water location^h	III	III	III	III	III	III	II	II	II	II	II	II + I	I	
Population (ooo)^i														
1981	2.0	3.1	1.1	1.0	1.4	2.7	2.4	1.3	3.0	0.8	4.4	3.0	2.7	3
1961	1.6	2.6	0.9	0.6	1.1	2.0	1.5	0.7	2.1	0.5	2.2	1.3	1.1	1
Irrigated area (ac)^j														
first season	146	1,221	98	609	515	577	1,093	775	596	987	705	1,639	1,792	1,5
second season	65	1,002	123	376	395	430	1,180	895	638	539	1,095	2,244	2,626	1,6
Population per														
irrigated acre	9.5	1.4	5.0	1.0	1.5	2.7	1.1	0.8	2.4	0.5	2.4	0.8	0.6	•
Geographic area														
(sq. km.)	10.2	19.5	8.5	7.4	30.5	20.6	14.7	11.5	16.5	15.0	12.0	17.8	23.5	1
Tractors^k	0	0/1	1	0	0/1/0	0	3	1	1	0/1	3/5	0	1	
Landowners with														
> 100 acres^l	0	1	3 − 4	3	4	0	3 − 4	1	1	2	4 − 5	2	2	
Electricity by 1971^m	No	Yes	Yes	No	No	No	Yes	No	No	No	No	No	No	Y
Distance to														
nearest town														
(km.)^n	13	19	22	21	19	21	22	24	26	28	27	20	?	

Notes:
^a For the location of the canals, distributaries and villages, see maps 2.1 and 2.2
^b The table is to be read village by village (column by column).
^c Common irrigators: indicated as present (+) if (a) they are employed by a village-based council, rather than by outlet-defined group, and (b) their employment is a regular feature of either crop season. Indicated as = if they a employed by farmers under each separate outlet acting collectively.
^d Field guards: as for common irrigators, except that the relevant alternative to a village-based council is the group landowners in a defined segment of the village land (rather than specifically a water outlet group).
^e Village council: indicated as present if there is a recognized council, separate from *panchayat* board and from vill officers (*karnam, munsif, sarpanch*), which deals with cultivation and irrigation problems.
^f Village fund: indicated as present if there is a standing fund. Not simply *ad hoc* collections for specific purpos
^g Activeness index: 0 − not active (no corporate organization); 1 − active (village fund big enough for at most sm surplus above field guards' salaries; or village-wide field guards and common irrigators without council or fun 2 − highly active (village fund in substantial yearly surplus above field guards' salaries, and used for wide range village initiatives).

resource mobilization and supply of public goods to make a slightly different measure. (Popular involvement cannot be included because of lack of comparative data.) On a scale from 0 to 2 a village can be ranked as 0 if it has no corporate village-based organization, 1 if the village fund is big enough to provide at most a small surplus above field guards' salaries or if there are village-wide field guards and common irrigators without a fund or council, and 2 if the village fund is used for a wide range of village initiatives. In terms, 10 of the 31 villages are 'highly range of village initiatives. In these terms, 10 of the 31 irrigated villages

MN Canal										TS Canal						
				Other MNC												
15	16	17	18	19	20	21	22	23	24	1	2	3	4	5	6	7
−	+	+	+	=	−	=	−	−	−	+	+	+	=	−	−	−
−	+	+	+	+	−	−	−	+	−	+	+	+	=	−	−	−
−	+	+	+	+	−	−	−	−	−	+	−	−	−	−	−	−
−	+	+	+	+	−	−	−	+	−	+	−	−	−	−	−	−
0	2	2	1	2	0	0	0	1	0	2	1	1	0	0	0	0
I	III	III	III	I + II	I	I	I	I	I	III	III	III	II	I	I	I
2.5	1.6	3.0	1.6	5.3	1.1	4.6		2.3	2.4	1.4	2.4	4.3	3.1	2.1	1.9	1.6
1.9	1.3	2.0	1.2	3.6	1.0	2.2		1.3	1.0	1.0	2.0	2.8	2.6	?	1.5	0.9
913	(400)	?	265	930	232	(2,000)		(1,000)	(1,000)	73	377	350	349	(300)	235	−
1,114	(100)	?	116	627	158	(2,000)		(800)	(800)	88	442	334	490	(200)	228	181
1.2	3.2	?	4.2	3.4	2.8	1.2		1.3	1.3	8.7	2.9	6.3	3.7	4.2	4.1	8.8
24.4	12.9	13.7	9.9	20.3	7.2	24.3		19.0	13.7	8.2	18.5	7.7	5.6	?	26.1	3.8
2	1	?	0	0/1	?	8	6	0	1	0	2	0	0	0	0	0
10	3	?	0	1	2	1	10	0	1	0	6	6	4			
No	Yes	No	Yes	No	No	Yes	Yes	Yes	Yes	Yes	Yes	Yes	Yes	Yes	Yes	No
17	19	20	6	13	14	10	10	9	9	13	20	40	35	35	18	4

Water location: III – bottom third of a distributary; II – middle third; I – top third, or fed directly from (non-tail-end portion of) main canal.

Population: 1981 figures from preliminary census returns; 1961 from census, rounded to nearest hundred. MNC–22 is a large hamlet of MNC–21.

Irrigated area: from Irrigation Department records, except where figures bracketed, in which case from village informants. Irrigation Department figures average 1978/9 to 1980/1, except MNC–18, MNC–19, MNC–20, which average latter two years.

Tractors: 0/1 means that in 1977, no tractors; 1 tractor. 0/1/0 means no tractors in 1977, 1 bought between 1977 and 1980, sold again by 1980.

Landowners: village informants.

Electricity: from 1971 census.

Distance to nearest town: 1971 census; 'town' has more than 5,000 population, of whom 3/4 or more are not cultivators or agricultural labourers.

are 'highly active' (have a score of 2), seven are 'active', and 14 are 'not active'. Of the ten dry villages, seven are 'active', but none are highly active. So none of the dry villages is as active as some of the irrigated villages; but many of the dry villages are more active than some of the irrigated villages.

A second set of conclusions has to do with how the four core institutions are associated with each other. Field guards are clearly likely to be associated with both a standing fund and a village council. Of the 17 irrigated villages with field guards, all but 4 have both fund and council. In the 4 cases without a council, the field guards are appointed either by a 'general meeting' of all farmers (in small villages such as dry

Table 8.2 *Village organization, sample of dry villages*

Village	D1	D2	D3	D4	D5	D6	D7	D8	D9	D10
	Dry villages									
	MNC side of district							TSC side		
Field guards	+	+	+	+	+	+	+	−	+	−
Council	+	+	+	+	+	+	−	−	−	−
Fund	+	+	−	+	+	+	+	−	−	−
Activeness index	1	1	1	1	1	1	1	0	0	0
Population 1981	0.8	1.2	1.6	3.5	1.8	1.5	0.4	1.5	2.0	3.7
(000) 1961	0.7	0.9	1.3	2.8	1.5	1.2	?	1.3	1.3	2.7
Geographic area (sq. km.)	7.3	9.8	12.5	15.5	12.4	9.5	2.7	11.4	11.1	18.3
Tractors	0	0	0	1	0	0	0	0	0	0
Landowners with > 100 acres	0	1	0	3	0	0	0	1	0	2
Electricity by 1971	No	No	Yes	Yes	No	Yes	No	Yes	Yes	Yes
Distance to nearest town (km.)	16	14	8	11	18	14	35	21	11	18

village D–7) or more usually by the village officers acting on their own or together with the dominant farmer of the village (e.g. TSC–2 and TSC–3). In the two cases where field guards are present without a fund they are paid by a per acre levy (TSC–2 and TSC–3). As for common irrigators, they are very likely to be associated with a council (again, TSC–2 and TSC–3 are the exceptions, making 2 out of 10 cases where common irrigators are not associated with a council). They are not associated with a fund (though this cannot be inferred from the table) because in no case are common irrigators paid from a standing fund rather than by benefiting farmers through an acreage levy. Where common irrigators are present, field guards are also present. On the other hand, field guards may be present without common irrigators (true in 6 cases out of 17). Finally, the council and fund are only present where there are either or both field guards and common irrigators; in no case is there a council and/or fund in the absence of both work groups, whereas both work groups can be present without either council or fund. So there is a strong tendency for field guards to be associated with a council and standing fund, and for common irrigators to be associated with a council.

The third set of conclusions has to do with how the four institutions vary with respect to location of the village along an irrigation distributary. A three-fold classification of locations has been used, of 'top third' (I), 'middle third' (II), and 'bottom third' (III). Along an 18 mile distributary, villages whose land falls mostly in the first 6 miles are 'top third', while those from 12 to 18 miles are 'bottom third' or tail end.

Table 8.3 *Frequency of village corporate institutions in sample of irri-gated villages (from table 8.1)*

Location of village	Number of villages	Number of villages with			
		Common irrigators	Field guards	Council	Fund
III	12	9	12	10	10
II	6	0	2	1	2
I	11	0	1	1	1
I & II	2	1	2	2	2
Total	31	10	17	14	15

Note: Table reads: of the 12 villages out of 31 in a III (bottom third of the distributary) location 9 have common irrigators, 12 have field guards, etc. For further details, see table 8.1.

Villages irrigated from outlets which take directly off the main canal are classed as 'top third' (e.g. MNC–21, MNC–24, map 2.1, p. 20).[2]

The results show a clear tendency for corporate organization to be concentrated in villages of 'tail-end' location (table 8.3). Villages outside a tail-end location are likely to have rather little.

We take up this set of conclusions in the following chapter. Here the intention is to show something of the similarity and variation within the 'highly active', 'active' and 'non-active' patterns. Then we shall look briefly backwards in time, at admittedly fragmentary evidence which suggests that a pattern of village organization similar to that found today was known in Kurnool district in the nineteenth century. Finally we examine how activeness today is affected by the system of social relations within the community, notably by patterns of cleavage and conflict.

The 'highly active' pattern

The following thumb-nail sketches of highly active villages will serve to illustrate the similarity and variation between them.

Padu village (MNC–16)

Padu village has a population of about 1,600, half Kottapalle's. In terms of level of development, inequality of living standards, agricultural

---

[2] This would obviously have to be qualified towards the tail-end of the main canal system itself.

technology and social relations of production it is much the same. (The two villages are about 50 kilometres apart as the crow flies.) It too is a Reddy village, with the Reddy caste dominant in land-holding and political power though in a numerical minority. My information is for 1977 and again for 1980, and part of the interest of this account lies in the changes during that period.[3]

It has a village council, of 6 members in 1977, 5 in 1980. Such variation over time in the size of the village council is common in all villages which have them. But informants who follow the affairs of the council will be able to say how many members it has for that year – even though in practice, as we have seen in Kottapalle, the boundary between member and non-member is not sharp. A Padu informant said that what matters is not the number of council members, but that however many they are they must be 'strict men, they must command, the entire village must be commanded by these people. If I cannot command, I will step down. If I can command, I will continue.' All the members, in both years, were Reddys.

The village is located at the tail-end of an 8-mile distributary, which takes off half-way down another 8-mile distributary, which in turn leaves the main canal at mile 120. Below Padu is one other village which is entitled to get water but never gets any. Until 1978 Padu had some 400 acres under first season paddy, and the council appointed 8 common irrigators to administer the irrigation. But in 1978 it was decided at the general meeting that nobody should grow paddy any more, because of the chronic difficulties all had been experiencing in getting enough water (caused in part by the much larger than planned area under paddy in the next village up). Most former paddy farmers switched to cotton or hybrid sorghum, both of which require much less intensive irrigation. Now common irrigators are still employed for getting more water to the village. They arrange to bribe the Irrigation field staff and officers, especially to persuade them to release more water into the distributary at night (when no one is around to see and when demands from higher villages are much lower), and they also patrol higher up the distributary to make sure the upper villages are not taking too much water. Within the village land, the common irrigators now bring the water only up to each field boundary, its application to the field being the farmer's responsibility. For with paddy the common irrigators had applied the water to the fields.

The council also appoints field guards, 4 full-time (i.e. about 10

---

[3] I came to learn of Padu by a chance encounter with an agricultural extension officer in Nowk who was a native of the village.

months of the year) rising to 7 in the latter half of the growth cycle of the rainfed crops. They are paid from the standing fund. The council regulates the date of the sorghum harvest, as in Kottapalle. The starting day is announced by village crier.

The village fund was spending about Rs. 10,000 a year in the late 1970s (about the same amount as Kottapalle's but twice as much per capita). One major income source is the sheep folding, as in Kottapalle, but the 'leasing' method rather than the 'auction' method is used in Padu village. Four to five herders approach the village council in late February or March and bargain as a unit for the rights to graze their flocks over the village land. The price depends particularly on the area under groundnut, sorghum and cotton, for these crops give good fodder. The herders themselves then arrange a periodic auction within the village to decide whose land they will fold each flock on at night. They pocket what is bid at these auctions, their profit being the difference between what they pay to get the lease-hold and what they receive for folding. The village fund gets about Rs. 3,000 a year this way.

A more important source of income, which is not used in Kottapalle, is the auction of the franchise to collect a commission on the purchase of crops.[4] The council sets a levy on outside purchasers of the village's crops. It auctions the right to collect this amount, and the village fund gets the franchise money while the successful bidder keeps as profit the difference between what he pays and what he collects. Potential bidders will watch carefully the state of the crops and the area ready to harvest; and the successful bidder will keep a close eye on who comes to the village to buy. The normal amount received by the fund in the late 1970s was about Rs. 4,500.[5]

In 1977 the auction of the liquor franchise was another important source of fund money. But when the arrangements for the liquor franchise were changed (state-wide) in 1978, so that a whole sub-district or large parts of it were auctioned as a unit, the franchise holder for the Padu area refused to pay anything to the fund; no attempt was made, as in Kottapalle, to boycott his local agent in order to force him to pay over. So the council looked for another source of income, and found it in the dung auction. The council now auctions the right to collect animal dung dropped on village roads and at the village's animal watering

---

[4] This franchise is called *kata kuli*.

[5] I was told the levy is Rs. 0.03 per quintal. But the value of the franchise payment alone (Rs. 4,500) is equivalent (at Rs. 0.03/qu.) to about 15,000 m tons, which from a cultivated area probably not greater than 3,000 acres is excessive. I do not know the answer. I did not see written accounts for Padu (nor for any village other than Kottapalle). The figures come from oral estimates by usually well-informed villagers.

place. The successful bidder employs people to collect the dung, which he sells. From this the fund receives another Rs. 2,000 per year.

Finally, the fund gets most of the fine money in cases where big fines are levied for sheep and goat damage. As in Kottapalle the field guards keep (and divide equally amongst themselves) the fines for the odd straying ox or buffalo. But when flocks of sheep and goats commit substantial damage the fine may run to several hundred rupees, and this money goes to the village fund, minus a commission to the field guards for collection. As in Kottapalle, the fine is to deter, not to compensate.

In addition, for specific common irrigation expenses the council may decide on an acreage levy, usually of Rs. 10 in the first season, for meeting bribe costs, renting a jeep to take villagers and/or the supervisor up the distributary. Because, as one person put it simply, 'If we don't pay (the Irrigation Department), we don't get water.' But this money is kept quite separate from the village fund.

Nayaka (MNC–5)

About 4 miles up from Kottapalle's boundary the distributary forks, one side coming down to Kottapalle, the other going down to a village I call Nayaka (map 2.2). Like Kottapalle, Nayaka is the tail-end village (the village below it, though having water rights, gets scarcely any water). Its population is about 1,400. In 1980 it had a first season irrigated area of about 450 acres, including about 100 acres of paddy and 350 acres of cotton (the final pickings of which come well into the second season, in March). It had a second season irrigated area of about 260 acres, including 10 acres of paddy, 50 acres of groundnut, and 200 acres of hybrid sorghum (planted in November and harvested in late February). So compared to Kottapalle it has much less area under irrigation, and much less of that area is under paddy. The village also has a substantial area of rainfed crops, mainly groundnut and sorghum. It is a Reddy village, with rather more inequality in the distribution of wealth than Kottapalle, as we shall see.

The village council has seven members (1980), all but one are Reddys. It appoints 2 full-time field guards, supplementing them near the time of harvest to make 5 or 6 in all, and pays them rather more than in Kottapalle, Rs. 90–100/month compared to Rs. 60–80/month in Kottapalle (late 1970s). There are no common irrigators because there is too little paddy. So irrigation is arranged wholly by each farmer and his labourers, reaching agreements (or not) with other involved farmers as to when they will take water. However, one important function which Kottapalle's common irrigators perform – watching the dividing point at the fork to make sure people from the other side do not cut off their water – is performed (intermittently) in Nayaka by the field guards. The field guards also help the Irrigation Department's channel men keep the channel upstream free of obstructions.

The main source of income for the village fund is the auction of the franchise to catch and sell the fish in the village's small tank. The village fund pays for fish with which to stock the tank each year, and later the council auctions the right to catch the fish. This brings in about Rs. 3,000 a year, and has been a big source of income for a long time. The franchise holder is responsible for defending his exclusive right to fish. The second source is a variant of the leasing' method of sheep folding. Five herders, between them owning over 2,000 head, lease the lands of the village after the harvest for about Rs. 2,600, and themselves arrange an auction every second day to determine who gets the flocks for the following two nights. Once they recoup the expense of leasing the lands they take a fixed rate of grain per night. But in this case the herders belong to Nayaka village. Nayaka is unusual in having a very large area of 'waste' land suitable for sheep and goat grazing. Until 1978 the auction of the liquor license brought in another Rs. 200 or so a month.

Accounts of fund income and expenditure are kept – but in flimsy notebooks thrown away once filled (as in Padu). The village fund largely paid for the construction of a (one-roomed) animal clinic in 1977, at a cost of about Rs. 11,000. It also helps meet expenses of a veterinary assistant, to make veterinary help more readily available in the village. As in Padu, the fund also finances a wide range of 'social' activities, including contributions to festivals and donations to the primary school.

The 'active' pattern

Villages within the 'active' category are those with a village fund sufficient to pay for field guards but for a much less substantial range of other activities than in 'highly active' villages.[6]

Eramala village (MNC–1)

Eramala village is of particular interest, being the next village down the distributary from Kottapalle. Because of water shortage it has only a small area under irrigation (table 8.1 and chapter 5, p. 94), too small to support common irrigators. It does, however, have village field guards: 4

---

[6] I have also included in this category the few cases where field guards are paid by a levy, but are appointed by a village council or general assembly.

from August to the end of January (six months), and one for most of the remainder of the year. During the crop-growing period the salary is high compared to Kottapalle's – Rs. 110 per month; then the salary drops to Rs. 80 per month. Fines for cattle trespass are also relatively high: Rs. 5 by day, Rs. 10 by night (compared to Rs. 2 and Rs. 4 respectively in Kottapalle); they go to the field guards.

About Rs. 3,000 a year is needed to pay for the field guards. The village fund has only one main source of income, the sheep-folding auction. Some 2,000 to 3,000 head come into the village, and the village fund gets about Rs. 200 per day from the auction (held every second day).[7] All told, the fund gets about Rs. 3,200–3,600 in this way. As in the other villages, re-auction of the liquor licence used to be another source of income, till 1978. Most of the balance has been used to establish unusually generous prizes for competitions to find the strongest oxen teams, for which this village is noted. The fund is clearly much less important as a means of financing public goods and services in Eramala than it is in Kottapalle or the other two villages just described. The village council has 5 members, who do not include the village officers. As in most of the other villages, the council decides the date on which the sorghum harvest is allowed to begin.

So in the village next down the distributary from Kottapalle, the level of public activeness is much reduced; and this goes with a much smaller area under irrigation. We shall see shortly that in the next village *upstream* of Kottapalle the level of public activeness is still less than in Eramala.

A dry village

D-7 village has 60 households and 425 people, and is located about 80 kilometres south of Kottapalle, 25 kilometres away from the canal. Until a few years ago things were arranged as follows: At the Ugadi festival in April, on the first day of the Telegu New Year, the farmers of the village would meet together to discuss common cultivation matters. There was no council as such. At this meeting they re-appointed the village's single field guard for the following year – the same rather elderly man did the job for many years, at the rate of about 2.5 kilos of sorghum per day. They also listened as the man who kept the accounts of the village fund read them out. The main source of income to the fund

---

[7] It may be that the length of the folding 'turn' is inversely related to the importance of small farmers as a source of demand for folding: small farmers would not be able to afford, nor need, a turn of, say, one week. Notice that Kottapalle's turn period is four days, Eramala's and Nayaka's, two days.

was an acreage levy in grain with which to pay the field guard's salary and secondarily the auction of the franchise to collect dung from the village's animal watering place.

There are a few herders in this village, with some 1,200–1,500 head of sheep and goats between them. Until a few years ago, the herders paid nothing for using the village land and that of the bigger adjoining village. Rather, in exchange for exclusive grazing rights the herders gave one night's free folding for each pair of oxen – so that each of the village's 35 households with one pair got one night's free folding, and the five with two pairs each got two free nights. Then the herders bargained with individual farmers for each subsequent night. They did the same in the adjoining big village, which had no herders of its own. But when some farmers began to try to avoid paying the acreage levy for the field guard's salary, the 'leasing' system was introduced. Now the village fund gets some Rs. 650 a year from the franchise for the grazing of its 600 acres. This plus the dung auction gives a total of about Rs. 1,000 a year, more than sufficient to pay the field guard's salary (he is employed for only 7 to 8 months). The field guard also keeps fines for catching trespassing animals; the fine is paid in kind, 1.5 kilos of sorghum per animal.[8]

As well as paying the field guard's salary, the fund has also over the past several years helped to pay for construction of accommodation for the primary schoolmaster (a private donation paid the balance). The fund has covered the cost of whitewashing the school building and the temple; of utensils to be used at marriage feasts which the villagers can use free (in Kottapalle these are hired along with the service of the marriage cook); of a metal weighing scale to replace the village's broken, wooden one; and of expenses for government officials who come on business. For a few years the fund gave Rs. 300–400 a year to the local Member of the Legislative Assembly; but then some farmers objected because the money did not benefit the village directly, they said, and the donation was stopped.

This village has had a standing fund of Rs. 1,000 in recent years. No dry village has a standing fund of more than Rs. 5,000 per year. In all the

---

[8] However in a recent case in this village the herders were fined Rs. 250 for allowing their sheep to damage some groundnut fields. A meeting of the village assembly was called by the aggrieved farmers; a couple of men were nominated to investigate their complaints; two weeks later the assembly met again and decided that the shepherds should be fined Rs. 100 for breaking village regulations, plus Rs. 150 to compensate the three farmers who suffered the major losses. The three farmers each received Rs. 50 – their losses were not equal, but equal payment avoided disputes about the judgement of relative compensation. Of the Rs. 100, Rs. 20 went to the field guard for collecting it and the balance went to the village fund.

dry villages the fund is used mostly for field guard's salaries. In terms of simple 'present or absent' measures one cannot differentiate between a village with a council, a single field guard and a standing fund just big enough to pay his salary and, say, Nayaka. Yet in Nayaka, and still more so in Kottapalle and Padu, the council and fund are much stronger influences in village life.

The 'non-active' pattern

Twelve of the 31 irrigated villages show no trace of field guards or common irrigators, not even for sub-sectors of the village's land, and no trace, either, of a village council or fund. What arrangements are made in these villages for irrigation, field guarding, and the other public goods and services provided in the more active villages?

Irrigation

In canal irrigated villages without common irrigators farmers either do the irrigation work using household labour or they 'send coolies', the coolies being either daily wage labourers or labourers on annual contract. Each household normally arranges its irrigation labour individually. The practice of several households getting together to employ a man to do their (paddy) irrigation is known, but is not usual. Villages without common irrigators have no 'turn system', no schedule of turns for taking irrigation water. The farmers take water when they want it and can get it. A big farmer with land several hundred yards from an outlet may have to employ several labourers to guard the field channel above his fields to stop other people from blocking it while his fields are taking water, and to maintain a cross-bund in the main channel to divert more water through the outlet. Small farmers may solve the same problem by entering highly localized exchange relations, in which two or three small farmers with nearby land help each other patrol the field channel higher up while all of them are trying to take water. But normally they simply wait till the water arrives of its own accord. In these villages the field channel network is less dense than in villages with common irrigators.[9]

Coordination between irrigators is low in absolute terms, and is confined to relatively small sections of the distribution network below the outlet. People in the upstream villages of the MNC sample (such as MNC–13, MNC–14, MNC–23, MNC–24) know little about the

---

[9] Based on impressionistic evidence.

phenomenon of common irrigators. Indeed, in MNC–23 and MNC–24 informants expressed surprise that such things as common irrigators, a village council and village fund could exist, although they had heard of field guards. In these villages, when (unusually) water does become scarce, the big farmers can keep labourers on their land 24 hours a day to take and apply water–an important advantage over small farmers, not least because the big farmers can thus irrigate at night with no disruption to their daily routine.

Field guarding

Field guarding without village-appointed field guards again tends to be done by each landowning household or by labourers (often old men) hired by the household. Any one household is assisted by the argus-eye of communal surveillance; whoever sees animals grazing on standing crops will scare them away if he is close by, and the mere presence of passers-by or workers in neighbouring fields makes crop or dung theft more difficult to get away with. The man whose crops are damaged by a straying animal will 'use harsh words' to the animal's owner, unless the latter is very powerful; and the owner of damaged crops may insist on a fine by way of compensation, either on the strength of his own right arm or through an informal *panchayat*.

So while both irrigation and field guarding are done mainly by each household using its own or hired labour, there is some informal cooperation – or at least mutual restraint – between holders of nearby plots in the open fields.

Council

Where there is no village council its substitute – to the extent that there is one – is not the statutory *Panchayat* board (which in all villages is inactive) but one or more of the village officers – the accountant or the magistrate, generally together with the head of the dominant family of the village.

Fund

Where there is no village fund ad hoc collections may be made for particular purposes (such as repair of field access roads). Or the village president may doctor the *Panchayat* books to take money from the *Panchayat*'s income for, say, festival expenses. Where levies are made, they are almost always per acre; though there is one case in the dry village sample (D–3) where money for field guards' salaries is raised by a levy on each pair of oxen. Another common method for raising money for 'village' purposes is simply to rely on donations from rich farmers.

The supply of public goods and services

Let us take some of the uses of the village fund in Kottapalle, and see how, if at all, those purposes are met in villages without a fund. Take the auction of the right to cut a certain valuable type of canal reed, for a start. In Kottapalle the council sends a man to the Irrigation Department's auction who, being the only bidder, gets it at a low price; the fund pays the price; and then anyone in the village can help themselves. In other villages without fund and council, one individual may buy the right and sell the reed grass privately; or he may even divide up the area into smaller areas and sell rights to cut them; or the low level Irrigation Department staff themselves may buy the right within their jurisdiction and sell the reeds in the villages, for roofing. All these variations occur within the sample.

For removing monkeys, there may be a levy on each household as the need to hire a monkey catcher arises; or a few big farmers may meet the whole cost; or as in one case, the villagers themselves may cooperate to catch the monkeys rather than hire a specialist. Or the monkeys do not get caught and remain a nuisance for all.

For well repairs, the *Panchayat*'s income may be used, or big farmers may meet the cost. Field access roads may be maintained by 'farmers' contributions'; but in non-active villages there tends to be no ready way of arranging such contributions, and in practice roads are commonly left to deteriorate until they become impassable (for instance where a culvert breaks), and it is left to the next several farmers who pass along the road to improvise some repairs. There are no by-laws which say that adjoining farmers must repair the roads.

Many villages do not have an animal clinic; where a non-active village has one, it has usually been built by donations from big farmers, or, in one case, by the president himself with his own money.

Non-active villages have no collective regulation of the data of sorghum harvesting, unlike most of the villages with a council. So one might find an active village where heavy fines are levied on people who attempt to harvest sorghum before a stipulated date, next to a non-active village where there is no such regulation. Similarly for the groundnut harvest: reliance is placed in non-active villages on neighbourly restraint and communal surveillance.

When government officers come to a non-active village or when government labourers come to work on something which benefits the village (like electricity supply) they will be given meals by 'concerned people', notably the president, who provides the meals out of his own pocket (and probably indirectly out of *Panchayat* income).

As for the primary school building, whose cost in active villages may be met partly out of the village fund and partly out of a matching government grant, its cost in non-active villages may be met wholly out of government (*Samiti*) funds; or the land may be donated by a private individual (but never with a plaque to commemorate his gift); in one case, the village president donated both land and building – a conditional donation, it turned out, because when he refused to repair it and the Block Development Officer wanted to use government funds to do the same, he refused permission. In some villages there is no separate school building, and the premises are either rented or the *Panchayat* building is used.

For bringing electricity to the village, Kottapalle's fund spent some Rs. 3,200 in the late 1960s, and electricity came in 1968. Some non-active villages near Kottapalle have not paid money, waiting rather for the supply to arrive according to the due process of the Electricity Board; and have waited ten more years.

Finally, a few villages have amply endowed temples and all money for temple repairs, temple cow, and extras to help finance festivals come from temple funds. In other villages temple maintenance is, again, a matter of 'donations' from the wealthy; as are performances by travelling troupes of players.

Nineteenth-century corporate organization

The old men of Kottapalle say that its corporate organization goes back to their grandfathers' time and before. As far as I am aware there is no documentary evidence to support this, for Kottapalle or for other corporate villages. However it is known that the practice of sheep folding was common in South India (outside the paddy tracts), and that there were some village-wide arrangements for field guarding. The accounts of these practices and arrangements in Kurnool district given by Gopalakrishnamah Chetty and C.H. Benson in the later part of the nineteenth century hint at a larger form of organization with a family resemblance to Kottapalle's – and since the Kottapalle type of organization is invisible to the eyes of the state today it is hardly surprising that they give no more than hints.

C.H. Benson, writing in the 1880s, reports that '[the ryot] supplements his meagre supply of farm-yard manure by hiring sheep and having them folded on his fields' (1889:73). He quotes farmers' proverbs:

The tread of the sheep is enough.
The foot of the sheep is gold (1889:73).

The Kurnool *Manual* elaborates:

The practice of folding sheep at nights is another method of manuring. A few wealthy ryots maintain flocks for this purpose but the generality of the ryots get the village shepherd who breeds for the purpose of trade, to pen his flock for a night in his fields for a trifling consideration and one pan-supari (watchman) to help him watch his flocks for the night. After the cotton harvest large flocks are occasionally brought from *distant villages or adjoining taluks* and penned in the fields; but in such cases the shepherds' consideration is increased by two meals per diem. In some cases, however, the shepherds *rent the fields for large sums*, from Rs. 20–100, which *the village by common consent*, deposit with the *headman or other respectable men and spend it for Jatra* [festival] *or other like public purpose* (Gopalakrishnamah Chetty 1886:164, emphasis added).[10]

Three points should be noticed about this account. First, the *Manual* suggests that bringing in large numbers of outside flocks was not the norm, that generally each village had enough sheep of its own, which is consistent with a population density much lower than today's. With lower population density the pressure to expand the arable was less acute and more land remained in waste and fallow, so more livestock could be supported within the village.

Second, the *Manual* implies that when outside shepherds did come into villages a version of the 'leasing' method was used, as in many villages (but not Kottapalle) today: in which instead of auctioning the folding rights by turns the shepherds pay a lump sum for exclusive rights to the village's grazing, and then make their own deals with farmers to determine whose fields they go to and in what order.

Thirdly, the quotation hints that in the villages to which outside flocks came, some degree of 'public activeness' was generated by that fact namely, resource mobilization ('large sums' as rental of the fields), popular involvement ('the village by common consent'), and provision of public goods ('for Jatra or other like public purpose').

Benson adds further details. Fifteen hundred sheep were considered sufficient to manure an acre in a night (Kerridge reports that 1,000 sheep were judged sufficient to fold one acre a night in lowland England of the early modern period [1953–4:282]). For this number,

He [the farmer] pays the shepherd little or nothing, but feeds him and his dogs during such period as the sheep are penned on the land. One shepherd may be

---

[10] In 1911 *tehsildars* and high-grade clerks received a salary of somewhat more than Rs. 100 per year (Washbrook 1977:57).

allowed to every 150 sheep, and the cost of feeding him and giving him the usual allowance of betel-nut and tobacco for ten days will amount to about one rupee (1889:76).

Benson concludes that although this form of manuring went on over large areas its value must be small – otherwise the shepherd would be paid more than this low amount. He also calculates that given the number of sheep and assuming a very small allowance of 1.5 tons of manure per acre, it would take between 7 and 20 years for the whole of the district's cropped area to be manured; and that, in fact, 'a great deal of land is never manured at all'. Finally, he says that the period within which sheep folding is done 'is short, and the flocks are, during long periods of the year, driven off to distant hills and grazing grounds' (76) – a practice which is less feasible today because those distant hills and grazing grounds have become, under the pressure of population, more firmly incorporated within the boundaries of settlements within those tracts.

What about routine village-provided field guarding? The only reference is in the *Manual*:

In several villages, for the protection of crops from cattle-trespass, a man, called poundman, is employed *by common consent of the ryots* and paid in grain for the purpose of seizing cattle that might trespass on to the fields and convey them to the pound. The cattle so taken are, however, released upon payment, generally of a seer or two of grain by the owner of the animal (171, emphasis added).[11]

He does not say what happened to the fine, but it presumably went, as today, to supplement the poundman's income. He also does not indicate how the poundman's non-fine income was raised. Again, the reference to 'common consent of the ryots' hints at some joint decisionmaking capacity. There is no way of knowing how frequent villages with poundmen were (but the *Manual*'s phrase, 'In several villages', implies not all villages had one); nor of knowing how usual was the practice of renting stubble grazing to outside herders.

The conclusion, then, is that something bearing a family resemblance to Kottapalle's type of corporate organization may have existed even in the late nineteenth century. It is possible that some of the ideas embodied in the colonial government's administrative models for local government (chapter 2) were themselves taken from 'autonomous' institutions whose existence colonial administrators came to know of. It is also possible that causality worked the other way as well, with 'autonomous' elaborations on the basic pattern being guided by ideas

---

[11] A seer weighed about two pounds.

embodied in the administrative models proposed by the colonial government. At any rate, it seems clear enough that the Kottapalle type of organization is not a recent phenomenon, not a precipitate of post-colonial development effort. If so, this would seem to strengthen the argument that 'local' factors, whether sociological or ecological, are the major elements in an explanation of variation, rather than, for example, the terms of power between the local community and outside elites.

The structure of wealth and power

How important in explaining the variation between villages is the pattern of human relations within the community? In particular, how relevant are the structures of power and wealth, and the lines of cleavage and conflict?

One might perhaps expect that highly unequal villages, with power and wealth concentrated in the hands of a few households, would show little village-wide corporate organization, for the reason that such organization could not be sustained without the support of (some of) the dominant households, yet those households might be sufficiently wealthy and powerful to be able to arrange their own supply of the goods and services which in more equal villages give an impetus to 'public' provision. That is, they might be able to finance ample field guarding for themselves (and other villagers would in any case be fearful of allowing their animals to damage the crops of the dominant households); and they could employ enough labourers and pay enough in bribes to ensure themselves enough irrigation water. Can this account for variation in the degree of corporate organization?

The two indicators of elite inequality in table 8.1 – tractors and landowners with 100 acres or more – certainly show no correlation with variables of corporate organization. But these are very crude indicators, and it is sensible to examine the relationship by taking a smaller number of cases and treating them in more detail. For this purpose it is useful to compare Kottapalle with Nayaka (MNC–5) and Polur (MNC–6). All three are irrigated from the V Distributary System. Kottapalle and Nayaka are both tail-end villages, while Polur, the next village upstream from Kottapalle, is mostly in the middle-third.

Nayaka's corporate organization has already been described. Its fund is smaller than Kottapalle's in absolute amount (Rs. 8,000 or so a year in the mid-1970s), but bigger per capita. Nayaka does not have common irrigators, which is surprising for a village in a tail-end location. Polur, four miles upstream from Kottapalle village, has no corporate organization. So Kottapalle and Nayaka are about the same in terms of public activeness, with the major qualification that Nayaka does not provide common irrigator services to its irrigators; and both are much more active than Polur.

Nayaka and Polur are both substantially more unequal villages than Kottapalle, and Polur is more unequal than Nayaka (referring now to elite inequality). Both Nayaka and Polur display some large and imposing houses, grander than anything in Kottapalle. Both show sizable extensions of high technology cotton, with wide spacing between rows, frequent sprayings and careful irrigation, while Kottapalle has little. Indicators such as number of tractors, number of households with more than two pairs of oxen confirm the picture.[12] Evidence on land ownership in 1907 suggests that the same was true at that time; that Kottapalle then had a larger number of solidly surplus farmers, but fewer very large landlords.[13]

The structure of wealth and power in Nayaka and Polur does seem to be relevant to why Nayaka does not have common irrigators, and why Polur has no corporate organization at all. Take Nayaka and its common irrigators first.

---

[12] See table 8.1, MNC–2, MNC–5, MNC–7.
[13] Indicators of inequality of land ownership, 1907 Settlement:

	Kottapalle	Nayaka	Polur
Population (1901)	1,637	754	1,127
% *ryotwari* land held by top 10% of *ryotwari* owners	43	58	47
% *ryotwari* land held by bottom 50% of *ryotwari* owners	14	9	11
No. of owners paying Rs. 10–50 in land tax on *ryotwari* land (% of area owned)	87(39)	42(32)	53(42)
Ditto Rs. 50–250	24(41)	11(40)	9(26)
Total *ryotwari* area (acres)	2,940	2,529	2,212
Total *inam* area (acres)	1,606	975	1,265
Total geographic area (acres)	4,546	3,504	3,477
Total geographic area (sq. km.)	18.6	14.4	14.3

Source: Settlement Registers, 1907, elaborated by Jeremy Jackson and G. Vittal Rao.

Note: Inam land paid a reduced tax assessment – 1/8 to 1/2 of the assessment of equivalent *ryotwari* land. In 21 villages of V Distributary (including some which the channel is meant to reach but does not – such as the dry villages below MNC–5 in map 2.1), the Settlement Registers for 1907 show a total of 31,417 acres of *ryotwari* land. Eight owners, in 6 villages, paid more than Rs. 250 in land tax (no one paid more than Rs. 500), and held a total of 1687 acres (average of 211 acres), or 5% of the *ryotwari* area.

Nayaka's water organization

Nayaka is dominated by two lineages, one of which is stronger and wealthier than the other. The first, which we shall refer to as the MLA's lineage, includes some 18 households in the village whose heads are the sons or grandsons of 5 brothers. One of the sons is the local MLA (Member of the State Legislative Assembly). The MLA's sister is married to the brother of a senior figure in national politics. These 18 households account for about 7 per cent of the cultivating households, and 18 per cent of the village's land (about 640 acres). The second lineage, of 5 brothers, controls 220 acres. Together, the two lineages make up 9 per cent of landowning households and own 24 per cent of village land. The figures of owned area should be taken as minimums.[14]

The simple area figures are misleading, however, because of a pronounced spatial concentration of ownership of irrigated land close to the distributary. Land close to the distributary tends to be owned by members of the MLA's lineage, and they refuse to allow field channels to be taken all the way across their lands so that the fields lower down can be irrigated. Or more precisely, they have allowed field channels to go to one or two fields below their lands but no further – if the owner of the field where the field channel now stops were to sell to the next owner down the right-of-way between the present end of the field channel and the boundary of the next owner's field, the last member of the MLA's lineage would simply plough up the field channel before it reaches its present end-point, saying that he had sold the right-of-way on condition that the field channel went no further. (Only in 1982 has the Andhra Pradesh government introduced legislation governing such matters as field channel right-of-way.)[15]

In this way, the area of land actually irrigated is kept to much less than the area zoned for irrigation (the ratio of paddy irrigated land to paddy zoned land in Nayaka is about 23 per cent, compared to 102 per cent in Kottapalle).[16] Hence the water supply is much more abundant than if all the zoned area could claim its share.

So water supply is not inadequate or unreliable for this much reduced area; and common irrigators are less necessary. In Kottapalle, on the other hand, the only constraint on irrigated area is water supply and

---

[14] These figures were calculated by Jeremy Jackson, on the basis of a lengthy poring over the land records with the village accountant.

[15] Andhra Pradesh Command Area Development Act, 1982.

[16] The reasons for this dramatic difference in the ratio of actual paddy irrigated area to zoned paddy area are (i) the field channel restriction in Nayaka, and (ii) the fact that many Nayaka cultivators have switched from paddy – only 31 per cent of the first season irrigated area is paddy, compared with 95 per cent in Kottapalle.

how far that supply can reliably be stretched. This is a clear illustration of how a sharp concentration of wealth and power can negatively affect the provision of public goods. But no other village in the sample has a similar situation, in which one or two lineages monopolize land in strategic locations and restrict water supply to the rest of the village's potentially irrigable area.

Polur's corporate organization

Three or four households in Polur have a clear predominance over the rest. For example, two of them have land on the opposite side of the village from the distributary, and are so powerful as to get away with diverting water from one of the main field channels and directing it through the center of the village to their (out-of-zone) lands, using the main street as a water course. For days on end during the irrigation season the village populace has to splash through water up and down the main street, and those whose houses border the street are put to chronic inconvenience.

It is said that until 10 to 15 years ago Polur had a village council, fund, field guards and common irrigators much like Kottapalle, but that it all finished because of constant conflicts within the council. Given these conflicts, it may be that the predominant families found it more convenient to restrict their concern to their own water supplies and crop protection, and could afford to provide these services for themselves. But Polur is on the margin of the poor water supply zone, and it is not surprising that it did have some corporate organization in the past. Indeed, in 1982 Polur re-constituted a council, field guards, and a village fund, with the intention of adding common irrigators at the appropriate time.[17]

The relationship between inequality and collective provision

The comparison between Kottapalle, Nayaka and Polur seems to suggest that a more equal wealth and power distribution, at the top-end of the scale, makes corporate organization easier. In Kottapalle there is no small group of households whose position of clear pre-eminence allows them adequate field guarding and irrigation service. On the other hand, there is a sizable group of surplus farmers, with enough leisure to

---

[17] Letter from a Kottapalle informant, with whom I had visited Polur. He suggested that my discussions in Polur about their village organization, or lack of it, prompted them to start discussing the idea of re-forming the organization.

spend time in the discussion of public matters and enough assets distributed over the village area for them to demand a voice in these matters.

Two cases among the TS Canal villages have to qualify this argument. They show that a position of clear predominance is sometimes a substitute for a village council. TSC–2 and TSC–3 both have common irrigators and field guards with no council or standing fund. Both villages are dominated by one family. TSC–3's dominant family has included a member of the national parliament, a long-standing MLA, and a *Samiti* president. One member of the family is permanently resident in the village, and is its president and magistrate. He arranges such matters as field guards and common irrigators for the whole village, and arranges the acreage levy with which the field guards are paid. (The family has also arranged a dramatically better water supply than might be expected from the village's tail-end location. Its land is fed by a special supply channel (running parallel and adjacent to the 'official' channel) which takes off from the official channel near the *head* of the distributary and runs 7 miles down to this village, serving no other village en route. The special channel was constructed by the Irrigation Department but does not appear on maps of the channel network.) In TSC–2, also in a tail-end location, the dominant farmer and his brother do not hold state political office, but they do own more than 500 acres of land, making them by far the biggest landlords in the area. The eldest brother, assisted by the village magistrate, organizes common irrigators and field guards and generally acts on behalf of the village in the world of government.

These two cases show the dominant family acting in place of a council to provide some public goods; but there is no 'public realm'. Here we have an imposed solution; but imposed by a local power, not by the state.

Another TSC case qualifies the argument further. TSC–7 is located close to the main canal, at the head of the distributary of which TSC–2 is at the tail-end. It is probably the most equal village in the whole sample; it is also a relatively poor, non-Reddy village; and it has no corporate organization. In this case, then, a high degree of overall *equality* is not associated with any corporate organization, while a village some 10 miles down the same distributary, with a high degree of elite *inequality*, does have two of the corporate institutions.

So the earlier argument about the advantages of elite equality needs qualification. Where the material benefit/cost ratio of field guards and common irrigators is high, it is likely that these services will be provided even in villages marked by a high degree of elite inequality – but perhaps without the arena of civic politics that we find in villages like Kottapalle or Padu, and with a more restricted range of public goods and services. On the other hand, where the benefit/cost ratio of field guards and common irrigators is low (as it tends to be in top-end villages) then whether the structure of power and wealth is relatively equal or unequal makes little difference: public goods are unlikely to be provided. One would expect that it is mainly in villages 'on the margin' of tail-end location, such as Polur, where this feature of the system of human relations would make a significant difference to whether such services are provided or not.

Factions

In practice, the distribution of wealth and power is closely connected to the existence and strength of factions. Where several households are very much wealthier than the rest and approximately equal to each other, factional conflict is likely. The clearest case among the villages considered so far is Polur (MNC–7). Polur is widely known as a village of 'parties' – its factions erupt into physical fights from time to time, a point which Kottapalle informants are not slow to highlight by way of contrast with their own village. We have already noted that while Polur had the full set of corporate organizations some 10 to 15 years ago they ceased because (informants say) of chronic conflicts within the council.

This suggests the entirely plausible idea that factions make corporate organization more difficult to sustain. However, it is certainly not the case that all or most of the relatively highly corporate villages have no factions or only feeble ones. On the contrary, Kottapalle had severe factional conflict in 1925–7 and 1952–4, during which time the corporate organization apparently continued. In Padu (MNC–16) a faction fight resulted in the burning of half the village's haystacks in 1980 – the arson was directed at one of the henchmen of the opposite faction but the fire spread, burning the hay of many in the arsonist's own faction (he fled the village for his life). Yet Padu has maintained a steady pattern of corporate organization. MNC–11, another relatively active village, is also known for the violence of its factional fights. Dry village 3 has a village council and field guards; and in 1981 its long-running factional conflict resulted in the murder of one of the faction leaders in Nowk, at the bus station in broad daylight. The converse also holds; there are villages without strong factions which do not show any sign of corporate organization (for instance MNC–8). In short, whether there are strong factions or not does not seem to be closely connected with the presence or absence of corporate organization; the pattern of organization can survive bouts of quite intense factional conflict.

In talking of a relatively stable pattern of collective control, then, one is not saying that the level of conflict is either steady or low. It is quite possible that the level of conflict moves in a cycle, connected with the emergence of new leaders and the creation of new links between local and regional networks (Attwood 1979). Variations in level and type of conflict between villages at *any one point in time* may be due simply to their being at different points of a more or less uniform 'conflict cycle'. However it seems quite unlikely that inter-village variations in patterns of corporate organization, such as we are talking of here, could be explained in terms of such a conflict cycle. The reason is, first, that it is difficult to see any *a priori* grounds for expecting the conflict cycle to vary systematically down a catchment, yet we find that corporate organization does vary in this way. Second, we have just noted that there seems to be no close connection between levels of conflict and the presence or absence of corporate organization: corporate organization of this sort can survive bouts of intense factionalism.

A similar point applies to the social structural variable which Beals uses to explain type and level of conflict in a sample of 30 villages in a district of Karnataka state (which adjoins Andhra Pradesh). He finds evidence to support the proposition that whether or not a village has 'parties' ('parties' in his usage simply indicate a recognition that the village is divided into two opposed, relatively stable groups) depends on the relative and absolute population size of what he calls the middle rank *jatis* (or castes) – those of the 'small landholders'. In his words, 'the ideal situation for party conflict would appear to be one in which [middle] jatis were numerically dominant... and could be divided easily into two groups of more than twenty-five households each' (1969: 39). It might be thought that the presence or absence of corporate organization would similarly be related to variables of this sort. Yet again, it is difficult to see any reasons why such variables differ systematically down a catchment, as do the components of corporate organization.

Kinship-based explanations are implausible for the same reason. It might be argued, especially by anthropologists, that a public realm of the Kottapalle type would appear only when kinship practices failed to produce suitably cooperative groups of field neighbours, among whom water could be shared and conflicts resolved without the need for common irrigators and a formal council. If so, *non*-active villages could be expected to show kinship practices that encourage close relationships among people who have contiguous irrigated fields: practices like bilateral inheritance (inheritance to all children regardless of sex) and endogamy (marriage amongst co-owners of the irrigated land). Active and highly active villages would show practices in the other direction. Again, the problem with this argument is the absence of any plausible reason why such practices should vary systematically down catchments of the size we are considering. We need an explanation founded on ecological rather than sociological variables.

9

Variation between villages (2): ecology and risk

Let us recall the results. Of the eight irrigated villages with all four corporate institutions, all are in tail-end locations (one of them, MNC–12, has land in both tail-end and top-end locations). Of the 11 irrigated villages in top-end locations none has all four corporate institutions and only 1 has two or more. Note in particular the tendency for field guards to be found only in tail-end locations: of 12 tail-end villages, *all* have field guards; of 11 top-end villages, only *one* has field guards. Why should the presence of field guards be correlated with head or tail location with respect to water supply? If all the top and tail-end villages were clustered close together, one might say that the reason for variation in corporate organization had to do with things only incidentally connected to water supply location. In fact, however, the tail-end villages are in five quite separate locations and the top-end villages in six separate locations; which enhances confidence that we are dealing with a genuine 'head to tail' difference.[1]

The argument of chapter 8 was that social structural variables are not able to explain this pattern. The present chapter outlines an explanation in terms of ecology and risk. It also suggests, more briefly, why institutionalization tends to take place with reference to the village as the unit, rather than either clusters of villages, sub-units of villages, or cross-village groups of field neighbours. For this second question sociological variables do matter.

Common irrigators

All the villages with common irrigators – 10 in the sample of 31 irrigated villages – institutionalize their employment in much the same way as Kottapalle does. But, depending partly on local hydrology and topography, the average density may be as high as one common irrigator for 50 acres in some villages, and in others as low as one for 200 acres. In

---

[1] Separate tail-end locations: (i) MNC–1 to -6, -18, -19; (ii) MNC–16; (iii) MNC–17; (iv) TSC–1, -3; (v) TSC–2. Separate top-end locations: (i) MNC–13 to -15; (ii) MNC–20; (iii) MNC–21, -22; (iv) MNC–23, -24; (v) TSC–5, -6; (vi) TSC–7.

all except 2 villages they are employed only for paddy irrigation; in the 2 exceptions, the common irrigators bring water only to the field boundary of the non-paddy crops, without undertaking application to the crop. In all cases they are employed only for first season, not second season, paddy (except in very unusual circumstances, like the unexpected shortage of canal water in Kottapalle after the second season crop had been planted in 1980–1). And they are employed only when the transplantation is complete, not at the start of the irrigation season. Before we go on to consider why some villages have common irrigators and others do not, we need to ask why these limits are placed on their employment.

Why are they employed only for paddy, with but two exceptions?[2] There are three main reasons. First, paddy needs more water than other crops, so concerted action to obtain more water from higher up the distributary is more necessary than for non-paddy. Second, the externalities of paddy irrigation are greater than for non-paddy irrigation, in the following sense. The crop–water response function for paddy is such that if soil moisture falls below the saturation point[3] water stress sets in after a shorter time (because the rice plant has more difficulty than other plants in extracting water from unsaturated soils); and the decline in yield as a result of that stress is greater (Levine 1977). In other words, the yields of paddy are more sensitive to *under*-watering than are the yields of other crops. So if a group of head-end farmers wish to keep all the water in a field channel flowing into their paddies until the depth builds up as high as the bunds will permit, they may cause lower-down paddies to experience a disastrous water stress. They may well want to take as much water as their paddy bunds can hold, because on the one hand *over*-watering causes little harm to paddy yields (paddy is the only crop which can grow in almost constantly saturated soils), and on the other, they can then irrigate less frequently and so save on irrigation labour, and possibly weed growth will be retarded so they save on weeding labour as well.

Thirdly, paddy irrigation is easier to assign to community agents than non-paddy irrigation is. Over-irrigation, as just noted, is not a problem for paddy, but can be damaging for non-paddy; so community agents can do less damage through carelessness. But also, it is much easier to

---

[2] One of the exceptions (MNC–16) occurred only recently, when chronic water scarcity in the first season became so severe that the council and assembly decided to prohibit paddy anywhere on the village's land. The existing common irrigator organization then simply switched to servicing the lightly irrigated crops that farmers planted in place of paddy (ch. 8, p. 140).

[3] More exactly, below field capacity, which is a little less than saturation point.

monitor whether a paddy field has been adequately irrigated than a non-paddy field. Three impartial people could look at a paddy field and agree that it had received an adequate irrigation simply by noting the depth of water in the field; whereas with a non-paddy crop like sorghum, these could be three quite different judgements, because the soil profile cannot be seen. So irrigating non-paddy crops is a more skilled operation than irrigating levelled, bunded paddies. Careful judgements have to be made about depth of water application and rates of flow, so as to match them to the infiltration rate of the soil and the varying water requirements of the different crops. In addition, the costs for some lightly irrigated crops like cotton and groundnut tend to be higher than for paddy, so the farmer has more investment at stake. All these reasons make it more difficult, sociologically, to take irrigation of lightly irrigated crops out of the hands of the cultivators themselves.

Why are common irrigators usually not employed for second season paddy? The second season paddy area is usually much smaller than the first season area in the villages which have common irrigators (in Kottapalle, a tenth). Within each village the area is concentrated in a few locations, rather than in scattered plots surrounded by non-paddy. And for most farmers the second paddy crop is less important than the first paddy crop; it is a supplement, destined for sale, whereas the first crop provides the subsistence of the household. For these reasons the village council usually does not become involved with the second season paddy crop.

The central question, then, is why common irrigators are found only in tail-end villages (those in the bottom third of longish distributaries)?[4]

---

[4] MNC–12 seems well placed for water close by the main canal, yet it does have common irrigators. Its water difficulties arise from the fact that water for one of its two blocks of irrigated land (with a zoned area of 1,650 acres) comes across the land of another village (15). (The block is not shown on map 2.2 – it is irrigated directly from the main canal, and lies on the far side of the canal from the village.) In the first season about 500 acres of paddy are raised in this block without authorization, the land not being zoned for any irrigated crop in the first season. To get enough water across 15's land requires constant vigilance; and the water must be allocated carefully within the block. Significantly, common irrigators are *not* employed for the village's other, and bigger, block of irrigated land, which is fed directly from the V Distributary and does not experience supply difficulties. MNC–19 is another village in a similar situation, with most of its land well fed from the main canal but with a second block, in this case much smaller than MNC–11's, in a tail-end location fed from a branch of the channel which passes through Kottapalle. In MNC–19 the social response is more localized: not village-appointed common irrigators, but common irrigators appointed by the farmers with land in that particular block, which reflects the small size of the block and the small number of farmers who hold land within it. Insofar as MNC–12 is the main exception to the generalization that common irrigators are found only in tail-end villages, it turns out on closer inspection not to be an exception at all: the issue is rather to do with the operational definition of 'tail-end'.

The basic argument is simply that the benefits of common irrigators are higher in tail-end villages, the costs are no higher, and therefore the net incentive to organize common irrigators is higher than in villages in better water supply locations. This incentive can be translated into collective action because free riding on the common irrigator service can be checked by selective punishment. An irrigator who refuses to pay the amount of grain stipulated by the council (in all villages this is the method of payment, not payment from a standing fund) might find that the following year's common irrigators would threaten to disrupt his water supply if he continues to fail to pay for the previous year; and he knows that such a threat is plausible. In addition, the payment is made in a lump sum straight after the harvest, when payment is easiest. Now let us consider why some of the benefits, as described earlier for Kottapalle, are greater in tail-end than in top-end villages.

(1) *Improved water supply to the village*: Villages towards the tail-end of an irrigation distributary tend to have a less adequate, more unreliable water supply than villages higher up. Of course, one of the functions of the Irrigation Department is to ration out water between top-end and tail-end villages, which means, above all, preventing top-end villages from taking too much. But the Irrigation Department, both in this village and in the rest of the state, is unable to do much rationing of the supply; it simply lacks the authority and its staff lack the inclination to do so, except under the threat of political outcry or the incentive of bribes. At the lower levels of the distribution network, canals are like man-made rivers. The workable authority of government in the countryside is generally weak, so in this respect the Irrigation Department is not peculiar. If anything, there are signs that the ability of the department to ration water during a drought is greater today than at any time over the past century (Wade 1980a; 1984c). Nevertheless tail-end villages like Kottapalle still cannot rely heavily on the Irrigation Department to assure them of an adequate supply, and consequently take action of their own.

(2) *Reduced drainage losses*: Coordinated management can reduce the amount of water lost to drainage from the tail-end of irrigation blocks. This is of more benefit the scarcer the water supply; the saving is of little consequence in top-end villages where supply is abundant, but is valuable in tail-end villages where it is not.

(3) *Improved water supply to more distant fields*: Tail-end villages are more likely to have to arrange rotational delivery of water to the fields, and to check the water flows in a channel so as to raise the level of the water in relation to the land.

In tail-end villages the water level in the distributary tends to be lower in relation to the surrounding land than is normal in upper-reach villages. This is partly because of deeper soils lower down the distributary (so the distributary tends to be dug deeper, to save building up the banks), and partly because siltation is less (the silt having settled higher up). The effect is that some degree of deliberate checking of the water flow at each outlet, in order to raise the water level at the outlet and so increase the discharge through it, is necessary if sufficient water is to flow through the outlet to reach the tail-end of the block. In principle, this checking ('cross-bunding') is meant to be done by Irrigation Department staff. In practice, for a variety of reasons, farmers of tail-end villages do it themselves. It may also be done in middle-reach villages, to increase the speed of flow within the blocks and reduce the need for night irrigation. In these middle-reach villages, however, the volume of flow in the distributary is normally sufficiently great so that even without cross-bunding enough water will still flow down to lower outlets within the village's land for farmers beneath those outlets to get water. In tail-end villages, on the other hand, the total flow in the distributary is commonly so low that if the checking of flows is left to the independent initiatives of the farmers under each outlet, outlets towards the end of the stretch of the distributary within the village land would get insufficient water. Hence there is an incentive to put this function of cross-checking the distributary's flows into the hands of common irrigators, who are responsible not to local groups of farmers but to a village-wide authority, in order to reduce competition for water *between outlets* within the village's land.

The same applies within blocks. In tail-end villages after the rains stop, if the water coming into the block from the outlet were not rotated to segments of the block in turn, the level of water reaching tail-end parts of the block would be insufficient to ensure efficient and quick delivery to the fields in the tail-end parts. Either the water would not flow onto the tail-end fields at all or it would flow so slowly that farmers of fields higher up the block would begin taking water for their lands again before the tail-enders had adequately ponded their fields, and so cut off the tail-enders' water. The tail-end fields of each block would suffer. In villages higher up the distributary water coming into the blocks normally has sufficient level at the tail-ends of the blocks even with continuous rather than rotational flow.

How much more area under paddy is made possible with common irrigators than without – in other words, by how much are the common irrigators able to stretch the water supply? Such a calculation is extremely difficult, and was not attempted in this study. As a crude indicator, however, one might look at the ratio of irrigated area to zoned area. Kottapalle has a far higher ratio – that is, a much higher proportion of its zoned land is actually irrigated – than the two villages down the other side of the fork in the distribution channel (villages 5 and 6), which lack common irrigators. These two villages, which like Kottapalle are in the bottom third of the distributary system, have an average area under first season paddy equal to only 39 per cent of their zoned paddy area; while Kottapalle plus the other two distributary villages in the bottom third of the distributary, which *do* have common irrigators, have a first season paddy area equal to 114 per cent of their zoned area. On the face of it this would suggest that common irrigators have powerful water stretching capabilities. However there are also topographical and land ownership reasons why the ratio is lower in the two villages down the other side of the fork: more of their zoned land appears to be physically uncommandable, and in one of them the land near the channel is owned by one dominant lineage, which is reluctant to allow field channels to be built across the land of its members to irrigate zoned land further away (see chapter 8).

Although it is difficult to know how much extra area is made possible by common irrigators in tail-end villages, we can be sure that each additional irrigated acre in tail-end villages is more valuable to the village economy and to the owner's household economy than an additional acre in upper-reach villages. There are two reasons for this. Tail-end villages tend to have a smaller area under irrigation per head of population (and more area under rainfed cultivation).[5] Since the returns to irrigated land are much higher than returns to rainfed land, there is greater incentive to protect those returns by organization even if the risks of water stress were the same in top and tail. Moreover, the extra irrigated area made possible by organization tends to be more fertile than land already irrigated. This is because in tail-end villages soils towards the tail-end of blocks tend to be more impermeable and more fertile than soils closer to the ridge. Upper-reach villages by contrast, show much less variation in soil type within the village land between

---

[5] The ratio of population to gross irrigated area is 2.7 persons per gross irrigated acre in III villages of the MNC; 1.4 in II villages; 1.3 in I villages. The overall average is 1.9, standard deviation is 1.2 (19 cases; village I is excluded because its figure is far above all the others, 17 excluded for lack of data, 12 and 19 excluded because they have both I and II location), so tail-end villages have a higher density of population in relation to irrigated area than top-end villages. Population density on total geographical area is, however, about the same in top and tail (with reference to the MNC villages): about 145 persons per sq. km. in top and tail (7 cases and 9 cases respectively), about 128 in II villages (excluding 11, 4 cases), and an overall average of 141 (excluding 11). This suggests that tail-end villages tend to have a higher density of population on rainfed cultivation. The 8 dry villages on the MNC side of the district have the same average population density as the irrigated villages, 146 persons per sq. km.

'ridge' and 'valley'. The village at the top of V Distributary System (MNC–14), for instance, has over 50 per cent of its area in inferior sandy loams, and only 8 per cent in relatively impermeable clays. Tail-end villages have 70–80 per cent of their area in clays (though close to the distributary the soils are similar to those which prevail in upper-reach villages if, as is usual, the distributary runs on the ridge rather than along a contour off the ridge). Consequently the productivity gains made possible by rotational irrigation on clay soils are not possible to any significant extent in top-end villages.

So the benefits of stretching the water supply to cover more distant fields are greater in tail-end than in top-end villages. There may also be stronger incentives to translate these benefits into collective action, because the degree of scattering of holdings may be greater in tail-end villages. The reason has to do with the greater variety of soil types in tail-end villages and the greater complexity of underground movement of seepage water from the distributary. Because of these factors, the desirability of a specific field's location is a more complex matter in tail-end villages than in top-end villages. It depends on (a) nearness to the channel; (b) soil moisture retentiveness; (c) soil fertility; (d) adequacy of drainage; (e) vulnerability to flash floods; (f) movement of the water table at that specific location. It also depends on (g) nearness to the village and field access roads. A field far from the channel may yet be well supplied with water if the water table rises near the surface at this point – better supplied than some fields closer to the channel even though the over-ground water supply is worse; and fields far from the channel, in the 'valley', tend to be both more fertile and to retain moisture better. These considerations indicate the desirability from the farmer's point of view of reducing risk by having his land in several locations. Variations in micro-climate indicate the same conclusion. In top-end villages, by contrast, it would seem to be less important for a big farmer to have his land spread about, for the criteria of locational desirability are less conflicting than in the tails.[6]

To be able to obtain the benefits of rushed supplies and higher head which rotational deliveries permit there must evidently be a reasonably dense field channel network in place. We noted earlier that in two parts of Kottapalle's paddy land (one close to the channel and the other far from it) the density was about 80 metres per hectare, which is high by average South and Southeast Asian standards, and much higher than in head-reach villages in the sample. Field channels are a technical

---

[6] I have no data on degree of scattering for any village other than Kottapalle.

response to water scarcity,[7] a complement to common irrigators as a social response. To obtain the potential advantage of rotational irrigation, the field channel network must also be well maintained; if the channels are full of weeds, stones, and holes, the benefits will be reduced. Indeed, maintenance of field channels in tail-end villages tends to be done not at the start of the irrigation season but later, at about the time the common irrigators are appointed and deliveries begin to be rotated.

(4) *Other benefits*: We noted several other benefits of common irrigators in Kottapalle, including saving of labour time, repair of field access roads, and added crop protection at harvest. There is no reason to suppose that the first two are higher in tail-end villages than elsewhere; the third probably is, given that crop theft and animal damage is more likely with a mixed cropping pattern than with a rice monoculture. In any case, these are secondary, not primary benefits of common irrigators. The timing of appointment makes this clear. In all villages which have them, common irrigators are appointed in late September or October. If they were primarily about saving labour time they would presumably be appointed earlier; likewise if they were about repairing the environmental damage of heavy rainfall. Instead, the months of their employment are months when the deficit of long-run rainfall in relation to potential evapotranspiration is greatest, when, in other words, the dependence on canal supplies is heavy, the risk of water stress high (Table 3.1). In July and August, by contrast, rainfall is usually greater than potential evapotranspiration.

Given the erratic rainfall and the problems of canal supply, why do farmers in tail-end villages compound the problems by growing paddy rather than less water-consumptive crops? Paddy is the main subsistence crop; even landless labourers eat more paddy than one would expect from the price and calorie differential in favour of, say, sorghum, and farmers have a strong preference for growing their own paddy rather than buying it with the proceeds of sale of non-paddy crops. Moreover, paddy is in many ways a very convenient crop, *once water supply is assured*. It is reliable, giving a moderate yield year after year even without fertilizer and manure – for the reason that paddy, unlike other cereals, is able to obtain much of its nourishment from the water rather than from the soil in which it is rooted (Grist 1975). As Masefield observes, 'There are rice fields in Asia which have probably been

---

[7] But field channel density is in general not related only to water scarcity. Svendsen (1983) found a correlation between density and unevenness of topography in some Philippines' systems, and one can readily imagine other influences on density. It is implausible that water scarcity is a sufficient condition of high density.

continuously under the crop for centuries without any conscious input of plant nutrients by the cultivators, but which can still be relied upon, provided that water is available, to produce a steady half ton of paddy per acre. No other cereal can emulate this feat' (1977:21–2).

Another advantage is that paddy is the only cereal which can grow in almost continuously saturated soils.[8] In a drought-prone area, with average rainfall less than 750 millimetres a year, it is ironic that water logging is often a problem in lands close to the main water distribution network. The distribution network is unlined, and where the distributaries are on ridges the surrounding soils are highly porous. In many places, whenever the water is flowing in the channels the immediately surrounding land becomes more or less saturated. Crops susceptible to water logging would be destroyed on this 'seepage-affected' land. Hence the owners of this land tend to plant paddy. But if *they* plant paddy, everyone else in the same mini-catchment must also grow paddy, because drainage water from the paddies up near the channel would tend to prevent non-paddy crops from growing. Hence in upper-reach villages one sees vast extensions of paddy, often out-of-zone: with the bedrock close to the surface seepage from the distributary keeps the soil continuously saturated even at considerable distances from the source. In a sense, upper-reach villages solve the drainage problem by growing mostly paddy on their irrigated land, two crops a year, year after year, regardless of government's attempts to give legislative protection to lower-down villages by entitling only a very small area to two paddy crops.

In tail-end villages, on the other hand, there is more of a conflict of interests between farmers with land close to the channel and those with land far away. While the former may have to grow paddy because seepage from the distributary makes their land unfit for anything else, the latter would not have to grow it for reasons of underground seepage, but only because of surface drainage from those higher up. If those higher up could be prevented from growing it, those lower down could grow a more profitable crop, like groundnut or cotton. In 1981, for example, the Irrigation Department announced that water was unusually short in the reservoir, and warned farmers in tail-end villages not to grow paddy. Some Kottapalle farmers with land in a certain block succeeded in getting an agreement at the general assembly meeting at the start of the season that no paddy would be grown in their block. In past

---

[8] But some lands in Kottapalle, mostly very close to the distributary and the outlet, are saturated all the time water flows in the distributary, year after year (such lands are called *kapu*). Here even rice does not flourish – some drying of the roots is desirable even for rice.

years this block normally grew paddy even though not zoned for paddy, because of seepage-affected land near the channel. The farmers who took the initiative in securing the agreement against paddy in the first season of 1981 had land towards the middle and end of the block, and their lands were not affected by underground seepage – only by surface drainage from irrigators of paddy higher up the block. They wanted to grow lightly irrigated crops and seized the chance of a likely water shortage in 1981 to get a collective agreement. But as the time for planting paddy seedbeds came, a few seedbeds appeared in the block up near the channel as farmers of those lands went against the collective decision and planted paddy as usual despite the risk of water shortage. At which the lower-down farmers also began to plant seedbeds as a protective measure, so that if the upper farmers went ahead and transplanted paddy they would not then be faced with the prospect of having no crop on the land – they also would be ready to plant paddy, the only crop which would grow if the upper farmers planted it.

In Padu (MNC–16), as we saw, the problems of getting enough water down the distributary for paddy were so great that a few years ago the council itself ruled that *no one* should grow paddy in either season. Without such a superordinate political authority to decide it is likely that some individuals with land in good water supply locations within the village's land would try to grow paddy, and their decision might then put surrounding land out of production for any other crops. Kottapalle's water supply position is a degree less serious than Padu's, and paddy continues to be grown over a large area. This forces the council to try to provide the large paddy area with enough water, partly by appointing and supervising common irrigators.

Field guards

Why are field guards more likely to be found in tail-end than in top-end villages?

Sheep-shit economics

Villages high up and villages low down a catchment show a characteristic variation in soil types, which is typical of the wet and dry tropics generally. Tail-end villages tend to have a higher proportion of fine, deep soils than top-end villages, which are much more retentive of moisture than the soils typical of top-end villages (map 2.3). Therefore the supply of fodder is greater in tail-end villages for a longer period after the rains stop; in villages higher up the catchment, areas of rainfed agriculture dry

Table 9.1 *Cropping pattern in head-reach and tail-reach villages of V Distributary System, 1901–05 (% of rainfed area)*

| | Head-reach | | Tail-reach | |
| | | | | |
Crop	MNC–14	MNC–12	MNC–2 (Kottapalle)	MNC–3
Millet	39	26	7	8
Sorghum	27	35	44	47
Cotton	1	5	26	28

Source: Settlement Registers

out and lose their fodder much earlier after the rains than in lower villages. Moreover, much of the rainfed area of lower villages is under sorghum. After the harvest, sorghum produces new growth ('ratoons'). The new growth is rich in protein, which is scarce in the diet of sheep and goats after the rains stop. The sorghum goes on ratooning until May, whereas the last significant rains are normally towards the end of October. (For this reason farmers do not clear the sorghum fields until shortly before the new planting season.) Cotton is another popular crop for heavy soils. The left-overs from the cotton pickings provide a nutritious feed for grazing animals, and the grasses between the cotton plants, growing abundantly on fertilizer provided for the cotton and not weeded out once the cotton plants have become established, are yet another good source of fodder. In contrast, the more common light soil crops, such as millet, do not continue to provide fodder for as long after the harvest.

Thus, the difference in soil type between top-end and tail-end villages gives rise to a characteristic difference in the rainfed cropping pattern, and so to a characteristic difference in fodder supply. To illustrate the contrast in cropping patterns we take data from the Settlement Registers of 1907, which refer to the average proportion of villages' rainfed area under different crops between 1901 and 1905. Table 9.1 shows that the two head-reach villages had a much higher proportion of their rainfed area under millet than did the two tail-end villages, while the two tail-end villages had much more under cotton. This reflects the fact that cotton cannot be profitably grown on the sandy loam red soils of the head-reach villages, whose cultivators had no option but to grow less profitable millet. Sorghum on the other hand was grown over large areas in both top-end and tail-end villages, being adapted to a wide range of soils.

In addition to the top and tail contrast in cropping patterns (still seen today), there is a difference in the area under rainfed cultivation – in the area on which stock might graze after the harvest. As a proportion of total cultivated area, the area under rainfed crops is greater in tail-end villages than in higher villages.[9] Since canal irrigation came, villages at the top of the V Distributary tend to have a much larger proportion of cultivated area under irrigated crops, in the second season as well as the first. So in terms of the cropping calendar shown in figure 3.1 (p. 41) for Kottapalle, head-end villages have a much smaller blank space between March and June, indicating a smaller potential area for stock grazing.

Therefore, for reasons to do with soils, cropping pattern and area, the supply of fodder after the rains stop tends to be greater in villages lower down a distributary than in villages higher up.

During the rainy season a high proportion of the geographic area of tail-end villages is usually under crops, and the area on which animals can graze or from which fodder can be cut is relatively small. The number of animals which can be carried *for the whole year* is thus low in relation to the number which can be carried later on the stubble of the rainfed crops. The number of locally owned animals is thus relatively small – and consists mostly of buffalo and oxen, not sheep and goats, because the former, being needed for working the land and for milk, have first claim on the year-round supply of fodder.

With tail-end villages having an *excess supply of fodder* in relation to local demand (compared to light-soil villages higher up the catchment), there is greater demand from outside herders to bring sheep and goats to graze their fields. Herders are more concerned with getting good fodder and water for their animals than with the price they receive for folding.

There also tends to be a *stronger demand for sheep and goat manure* in tail-end villages than in top-end villages. Sheep and goat manure is used for rainfed and lightly irrigated crops, not for paddy.[10] Tail-end villages have proportionately more of their land under rainfed and lightly irrigated crops, proportionately less under paddy. It will be recalled that

[9] This is inferred because official statistics on rainfed areas are wildly inaccurate. One indication is that population per irrigated acre is greater in the tails, but population per acre of geographic area is about the same, which suggests that the ratio of rainfed to irrigated area is higher in the tails. A second indication is that the ratio of total geographic area to gross irrigated area is much higher in III and I villages (5.5 compared to 2.3, using MNC villages), suggesting a higher proportion of rainfed to geographic area in the tails. Of course, fodder is not only a function of the stubble area, but also of fallow and waste. Villages near the head of V Distributary tend to have a large area of very poor wasteland included within their boundaries, while this is not so in general of tail-end villages (MNC–5 is an exception).

[10] Of the manures, pig manure, brought in from outside the area, is preferred for paddy (also for rainfed lands where soils are very saline).

around 10,000 head of sheep and goats are brought into Kottapalle in March and April, mostly from the hilly tracts of one-bite grasses on either side of the Nowk valley.

If several thousand sheep and goats come into a village when the second season irrigated crops are still standing the danger of stock damage to the standing crops is acute, and the standing crops in tail-end villages generally include high cost, high profit crops like irrigated cotton, groundnut and turmeric. If the flocks are not carefully guarded the crops might be decimated. We have noted the elaborate rules laid down by Kottapalle's village council to prevent stock damage to crops. And we noted that in 1981 the farmers of second season irrigated crops pressed to have the outside herders allowed in only after all their crops were harvested, even though this would result in a substantial fall in income from the sheep-folding auction. The provision of field guards is part of the social response to the risks to standing crops posed by allowing in large numbers of sheep and goats, in conditions in which fencing is not feasible other than for small, precious areas like citrus groves or threshing floors. Field guards also help reduce the risk of stock theft, which otherwise would be higher with so many animals in the villages. A secure environment for their stock makes a village with field guards more attractive to outside herders than one without, and may induce them to accept a lower return per animal than they could get in non-field guard villages.

Features of the supply and demand for sheep and goats help to explain why village field guards are provided at the time when large numbers of animals come into the village land. Once organized for that period, it is then not difficult to organize their employment for a much longer period. And – a third part of the explanation – the higher demand from outside herders to bring their flocks into tail-end villages means there is more potential for 'the village' to raise money by levying an entrance tax on the herders. The entrance tax, or franchise fee, can then be used to cover field guard salaries for most of the year.

Free riding

This last point is important, because the establishment of field guards by *annual levies* on land-owning households is vulnerable to free riding: to the attempt by some households to avoid paying in the expectation that others will continue paying and they will receive the service free. So there are strong advantages in having field guards paid from a fund which is independent of specific household contributions. (On the other hand, 2 out of 17 irrigated villages with field guards, both under the TS Canal, do use annual levies to pay field guards' salaries – TSC–2 and TSC–3 – both dominated by one family. And 2 out of 8 dry villages with field guards also use annual levies, D–3 and D–9. But D–7 recently switched from annual levies to the leasing method precisely to avoid the free-rider problem.) If field guards are more likely to be sustained where they can be paid independently of direct levies on landowners, then tail-end villages are more likely to be able to sustain field guards because of the greater opportunities there to raise large amounts of revenue by the leasing or auction methods. In virtually all villages with a standing fund sheep folding is the major source of income.

It is not clear, however, who bears the incidence of the payment to the village fund. Herders and their flocks are mobile, and *if* the objective is to maximize the return on sale of manure one would expect them to distribute themselves between villages so as to equalize the return per head of stock. If so, the difference between villages with 'leasing' or 'auction' methods of raising revenue and those without (where herders come at will and negotiate farmer by farmer) is that in the former, farmers who pay for the sheep to be folded on their land are paying *more* per head of stock than are farmers in villages without such arrangements, with the extra going to the village fund. In effect, there is an intra-village transfer payment from those who get the manure on their fields to the collectivity of owners of standing crops, which is used to provide the latter with protection. But since the amount raised is generally sufficient to meet all or most of the cost of field guards for most of the year, it is a transfer from those who get the manure to *all* landowners. This is the element highlighted by the 'auction' method, in which half of the winning bid goes to the village fund.

On the other hand, to the extent that the herders accept less per head in tail-end villages because the fodder is more abundant than higher up they make a net contribution to the village fund. Their contribution is a way of socializing rents. In theory, it would be possible for each herder to negotiate a deal with each landowner whereby the former pays the latter to graze his flock during the day (the amount depending on how good the fodder supply is), and the landowner pays the herder to keep his sheep on his land during the night (the amount also depending on how good the fodder is). But the scattering of village landholdings makes the transaction cost of such an arrangement very high, even among big landowners. So if the rents were not socialized by being levied (directly or indirectly) for entry to the village land as a single unit, they would not be collected by anyone – as they are not collected in villages without field guards and a fund. 'Leasing' and 'auction' ensure that the rents are socialized and made to benefit *all* landowners via the employment of field guards plus the other services financed by the village fund.[11]

Risk of crop theft and animal trespass

One other advantage of field guards is also greater in tail-end villages. Thefts are more likely of rainfed and lightly irrigated crops than of paddy – partly because more of the former can be eaten raw, and partly because once planted most of them required less frequent attention than paddy. Moreover, paddy is normally grown in large, flat extensions on which uninvited people or animals can be spotted from a distance; whereas the irregular and often tall stands of rainfed and lightly irrigated crops better conceal. Tail-end villages, having more of their

[11] It is not clear what determines which method, 'leasing' or 'auction', a village will adopt. Three points might be made. There seems to be some correlation between sub-region and one or other of the methods: in the sub-region of the Nowk valley south of Nowk villages are more likely to use 'leasing', while to the north of Nowk 'auctioning' is more common. Second, there is probably not much difference between the two methods in cost of folding to the farmer or in return to the herder. In Kottapalle's auctions of 1980 the average price paid by farmers per head of stock per night was Rs. 0.038, of which half, or Rs. 0.019 went to the herder; since the herders did not pay to come into the land this represents their net profit. In D–7 in 1980 (see chapter 8) the herders paid Rs. 600 to buy the rights to their own village plus Rs. 2,400 for the next village, a total of Rs. 3,000 for rights to about 3,600 acres. They charged 32 *pallu* of sorghum (at 1 *paddi* of sorghum = 1.5 kg.) per night, for folding their 1,200–1,500 sheep. The price of 32 *pallu* of sorghum was about Rs. 48. At Rs. 48 per night they get Rs. 0.032 – Rs. 0.04 per head of stock. But they have to pay for the grazing rights at about Rs. 2.0 – Rs. 2.5 per head. If they take about 100 days' grazing the cost of the grazing is Rs. 0.2 – Rs. 0.25 per head per day. This leaves the herder with a net profit per head of stock of about Rs. 0.012 – Rs. 0.015 per day, a little less than in Kottapalle (but the margins of error are too large to attribute significance to the lower return in the 'leasing' case).

As for cost to the farmer, Kottapalle and D–2 are both in the same general area (about 12 kilometres apart) and both use the 'auction'; cost to the farmer is about Rs. 0.038 per head per night in Kottapalle, and Rs. 0.03 – Rs. 0.037 in D–4. D–1 is also in the same general area but uses 'leasing'; cost to the farmer is about Rs. 0.04 per head. D–7 also uses 'leasing', and cost to the farmer is about Rs. 0.032 – Rs. 0.04. Harriss' figures for Randam village in northern Tamil Nadu suggest a cost to the farmer of about Rs. 0.032 (taking the cost of four meals as Rs. 3: 1982:90). If costs to the farmers are not systematically greater with one than the other, the important factors in which is chosen may be (i) that 'leasing' is easier to administer (it involves a one-off negotiation, rather than recurrent auctions and collections of bid money), and (ii) 'auctioning' gives both shepherds and farmers greater flexibility. With 'auctions' the herders do not forfeit any money if they leave early (which they might want to do if the fodder supply is less good than expected), and farmers have more influence over how long they stay and how many sheep come. With 'leasing' the herders buy exclusive rights and can stay as long as *they* wish (until the new planting); while with 'auctioning' the herders have exclusive rights only for a fixed period (16 days in Kottapalle).

area under rainfed and lightly irrigated crops, derive correspondingly more benefit from village-provided field guards.

We have now explained the head to tail variation in common irrigators and field guards. The same explanation covers the variation in council and standing fund, because the sample results show not a single case where council and fund are present without either field guards or common irrigators, though there are a few cases where the latter are present without the former.

Amply irrigated, poorly irrigated, and dry villages

Whereas only 1 out of 11 amply irrigated villages has field guards, 8 out of the 10 *dry* villages have field guards, and 5 of these 8 also have a council and standing fund. So most of the dry villages are more 'active' than the amply irrigated villages. The reasons are much the same as explain why poorly irrigated villages are more likely to have field guards than amply irrigated villages. Non-paddy crops are more vulnerable to theft and animal damage. And many dry villages in the sample have substantial flocks of sheep and goats resident within the village, so the year-round risk of animal damage to standing crops is greater. Moreover, in dry villages with black soils (similar to those of tail-end irrigated villages) the village's own animals are generally added to by outside herders bringing their flocks to graze the relatively abundant fodder. Whether the flocks belong within the village or outside, it is possible for the village to charge a rent for the stubble grazing, and so raise income to pay for year-round protection. Half of the 10 dry villages are, in fact, 'tail-end' villages – in the specific sense that they are located further down the same catchments as Kottapalle and Nayaka, and indeed have land zoned for distributary irrigation from V Distributary – but receive no water. The one dry village which is unambiguously 'top-end' in soil type (D–8) has no field guards or council or fund. Another village (D–6 – soil type not known) suffers from a problem which independently of soil type can prompt field guard organization: risk of large-scale thefts by outsiders, in this case 'tribals' who live not far away. Indeed, this village employs some 16 'tribals' as its field guards at harvest time, on high salaries, the logic being that tribal field guards will be the best protectors against stealing by their fellow tribals as long as they do not wish to lose their jobs.[12] One of the TSC villages (D–9) reported a serious problem of thefts by 'tribals' and had also instituted field guards as a response. On the other

---

[12] I heard of no other cases where field guards were non-residents.

hand, none of the irrigated villages reported a *big* problem of thefts by 'tribals'.

One can thus think of two distinct sets of causal connections. The 'water security' nexus links difficulties of water supply to a superordinate council which appoints and supervises common irrigators and sanctions those who interfere with their work. The 'crop protection' nexus links risks of crop loss due to animals and thieves to a superordinate council which similarly appoints, supervises and sanctions the work of field guards, and also raises money to pay the field guards' salaries. The crop protection nexus operates in dry villages as in poorly irrigated villages. But in every dry village case the village fund is too small to do much more than pay the field guards' salaries. It is where *both* sets of causal connections intertwine that one finds the Kottapalle type of corporate organization: in poorly irrigated villages. Here one is likely to find a council which is authoritative enough to raise money from sources in addition to the rent of village grazing, and so is able to finance intervention across a wide range of village contexts. Here one is likely to find a clearly demarcated 'public realm' and the processes of civic politics.[13]

On the other hand, the implication is that a majority of the total villages irrigated from the MNC and TSC would *not* be expected to show a high level of public activeness, because a majority of villages are not in the bottom third of distributaries – or more exactly, a majority do not have canal supplies which are sufficient to irrigate a large area but problematic in adequacy and reliability; and so a majority probably do not have common irrigators.

Institutionalization of the village

With just a few exceptions field guards and common irrigators are appointed by a village-wide authority for the whole of the relevant area of the village, rather than either by sub-units within the village or by units which cross-cut villages. The reasons for this are contained in

---

[13] But not every village with field guards and common irrigators has a council and fund; the statement is about probability. Notice, too, the ecological influences on possible revenue raising sources. To raise money for the fund by auctioning the franchise to collect dung at the village watering place the village should have a largish area where the animals are left to roam, such as the flat bed of a river. In Kottapalle, crops surround the village, and animals are either brought water in the yard or stable or are closely supervised as they drink – and their dung is then picked up by their owners. The determinants of other methods are not clear; for example it is not obvious why some villages auction the franchise to collect a levy on the sale of grains while others do not, but the practice seems more common south of Nowk and less common north of Nowk.

arguments already presented, and can be given here in summary form.

There is no organization which links villages. Villages have mutually exclusive boundaries, and virtually all the land within the village boundaries is owned by village residents. Cases where a resident of one village owns land within the boundary of an adjacent village are uncommon (which correlates with the unimportance of tenancy). Irrigation blocks are designed so that in most cases each block is wholly contained within the boundaries of one village; so in few cases does more than one village depend on the same outlet. And in the framework of governmental political institutions, the single village has for centuries been taken as the basic unit, each village linked to higher levels of government authority but not horizontally to each other. The government has not, for example, attempted to form associations of water users for whole distributaries (nor indeed for single villages).

Field guards and common irrigators are established for the whole village rather than for sub-village segments for reasons to do with economies of scale. Take field guards first: from the point of view of a big farmer with scattered fields, it would clearly be cheaper in terms of transaction costs to have only one authority responsible for all field guards, rather than have independent arrangements in each or some of the various sectors in which his land happens to be located. These are *managerial* economies of scale. There are also two sorts of financial economies of scale. Where field guards are recruited by private groups of landowners they tend to be more expensive per acre. The reason is that the size of the cooperating group for this one task would be relatively small – it would be difficult and time-consuming to secure agreement from all owners in blocks of more than, say, 100 acres, whereas each village-wide field guard usually looks after well over 600 acres on average. The second sort of financial economy has to do with the relative ease of selling franchises for the village as a unit rather than for sub-sectors of it. This is obvious in the case of the liquor franchise. As for the grazing franchise, it *might* be possible to identify well-bounded segments of the village's stubble land so as to raise a franchise fee on herders for entry to each segment; but it is entirely possible that the group of landowners within each segment may not agree to cooperate in employing field guards, that the feasible unit for revenue-raising may not coincide with a potentially cooperative social group. This then points to the advantages of institutionalizing revenue-raising at the village level.

With reference to common irrigators, the same point about *managerial* economies of scale also applies. Big farmers, having scattered holdings, cannot limit their attention to ensuring adequate water supplies to the one place where their own holdings are located, but rather have an interest in seeing that water is spread about the whole area; and it is cheaper in terms of transaction costs to have only one authority for all common irrigators than to negotiate independent arrangements in several sectors. Village-wide common irrigators also reduce competition between common irrigator outlet groups for water – if all common irrigators were not responsible to a superordinate authority competition between outlets would be fierce, especially in a drought, and the even distribution of water over the village area would be jeopardized. Likewise, village-wide common irrigators will be more energetic in attempting to bring down more water for the whole village; sub-village common irrigators would presumably be concerned to bring down extra water only insofar as they could appropriate the extra water for their own jurisdictions. So sub-village common irrigators might generate 'external' costs to irrigators outside their own jurisdictions by competing for water and by restricting their efforts to bring more water to what they can appropriate; village-wide common irrigators eliminate *externalities*.

Village-level institutionalization has clear advantages in the case of both field guards and common irrigators. And the same point made about the absence of institutionalization for clusters of villages also applies here: in the structure of wider political institutions the village is taken as the basic unit, equipped with its own state-backed structure of authority (in the form of the village officers, like accountant and magistrate); whereas there are no pre-existing authority structures based on sets of contiguous landowners.

10

Conclusions (1): the conditions for collective action

The tendency in peasant studies today is to identify the relations of power between the peasantry and external groups as *the* salient characteristic of the peasantry. Useful as this perspective is for many problems, it does tend to occlude the extent to which peasants manage their own affairs without external intervention – even today, when the technology is available to close great distances. It tends to direct attention away from the ways peasants handle problems arising from joint dependence on a particular tract of land. To improve upon the sweeping characterizations of 'peasant society' offered by Scott, Popkin, Foster and others, these problems need to be more centrally placed.

Homo hierarchicus has to eat

Dumont is an extreme case in point. He goes to some effort to deny that the village is a significant unit of social action in India, arguing specifically that what is generally called a 'village *panchayat*' in the literature is actually a 'caste *panchayat*', because it is *'first and foremost* a matter for the dominant caste' (1972:216–7). By this he means that the village *panchayat* is (was) composed of members of the dominant caste, that it is not representative of all (caste) groups in the village. But to say that its representativeness determines whether it is to be understood as a village or caste-based organization is a very partial logic. The equally important criterion is what the *panchayat* does.

By his own account, it is a body of persons having general authority to take decisions affecting all the village, 'to settle the common business of the "village", whether...a question of collecting taxes or of the administration of the village in general' (1972:216). Just what the 'administration of the village in general' might consist of is not a matter which interests him, but apparently he has in mind the administration of justice, the settlement of disputes. This is one major activity which councils of the Kottapalle type do *not* undertake; for the good reason that it would involve them in making judgements about the allocation of privatizable benefits, and would therefore be threatened by the politici-zation of the case as the loser attempted to enlist factional support to get a more favourable judgement. Its ability to continue to provide goods and services of vital common interest would be jeopardized. Dumont's sociology of Indian society is remarkably insensitive to the point that *homo hierarchicus* has to eat. So he has little to say about how people handle those common problems of resource use to which this study is devoted. Hence he is able to preserve the original Cartesian axiom, that caste ideology is primary.

But it is also true that Dumont and other theorists of Indian society have been poorly served by the existing village studies. The capacity of villagers to organize their public life (apart from the settlement of disputes) has not been thought to need explanation. An examination of fifteen village studies, mostly of South Indian villages, failed to give more than occasional hints of patterns of organization similar to those reported here.[1] Dube's study of a village a few hundred kilometres north of Kottapalle provides, relatively speaking, an unusually full account. Here is his description of irrigation organization for the village's tank:

At present there are three Neerudis in the village, two of whom are Malas and one a Madiga. It is their duty to look after the tank bund, particularly to keep a watch on the flood-gates ... They should also periodically check the water-level in the tank and keep the superior village officers informed. The three Neerudis hold together seven acres of rent-free wet land granted to them *by the government* (1955:52, emphasis added).

As for sheep folding,

After the harvest ... the agriculturalists ask the Gollas [Shepherds] to graze their herds on their fields and keep them penned in during the night ... this service is much in demand by the agriculturalists. The shepherds often fix days with the agriculturalists, and each one has his turn only on a limited number of days. According to the nature of the agreement between the cultivators and the shepherds, the payment is either in cash or the latter collect their dues from the fields at the time of harvesting (1955:64).

Beals' study of Gopalpur, a few hundred kilometres west of Kot-

---

[1] South Indian studies: Beals 1963; Beals 1974; Dube 1955; Epstein 1962; Gough 1961; Harriss 1982; Hiebert 1971; Ishwaran 1966; Ishwaran 1968; Srinivas 1976. Others: Bailey 1957; Berreman 1963; Orenstein 1965; Sharma 1978; Wiser and Wiser 1971. Over a thousand reports and monographs on Indian villages were examined as part of the Village Studies Project at the Institute of Development Studies, University of Sussex (Moore *et al.* 1976). The coding used in this exercise would not have picked up the Kottapalle of organization in any case; but it is the assessment of Mick Moore, who himself coded hundreds, that no more than hints appeared of such organization (personal communication). The continuing research by Priti Ramamurthy is an important exception. In a district adjacent to Kurnool district she found a pattern of organization similar in many ways to that described here. See also Farmer (ed.) 1977; Wade 1982e.

tapalle, mentions a problem of crop theft: 'When the watchmen are not looking, passers-by stop to cut the ripening [sorghum] canes and then move on, chewing the sweet pith and spitting it out along the pathway' (1963:4). The watchmen are not provided by the village, however:

After thinning and weeding has been completed, one member of the family must remain in the field at all times, day and night, to guard against theft by men, cattle, birds and antelope. This watch must be maintained for two and a half to three months, until the crop is harvested (1963:7).

This is a relatively full account of the response to crop theft and animal damage. Beals mentions nothing about village-wide organization, village work groups, etc. Some of the studies mention a village-wide *panchayat* for dispute settlement, but none mention a village committee or council with functions similar to Kottapalle's.

It may be, of course, that our area is somehow quite exceptional, that such organization really does not exist elsewhere on the South Indian uplands. There is one major argument against this conclusion, however. None of the fifteen village studies emphasizes the problem of 'externalities' inherent in a mixed livestock and arable husbandry when holdings are scattered and fields unfenced, and when fodder is short. Yet almost certainly these conditions apply in most of the 15 villages. Even just the fact of scattering is barely noticed. Moreover several of the villages are irrigated by surface-flow schemes, so one would expect externalities or neighbourhood effects to be important sources of conflict when water is scarce. Yet none describes how water distribution is organized in anything more than passing detail. Epstein's celebrated study of two villages, one irrigated from a large canal, reports that 'competing interests for a limited supply of water to the fields is *the most frequent cause of quarrels* in Wangala' (1962:26, emphasis added), but says virtually nothing more about water distribution. The Hunts, after a thorough search of the world-wide literature on irrigation and local social structure, comment that 'South Asia still presents a serious problem. India is the country with the second highest total of irrigated hectares in the world and the country for which good community-level data are hardest to find' (1976:406, cf. Farmer (ed.) 1977).

In short, studies of Indian village are remarkably thin on what I have identified as the two main impetuses to central (village) control. Questions of irrigation organization, of scattered holdings, of competition between livestock and humans for food, of the social response to risk, have simply not been of much interest. So the absence of the Kottapalle type of organization from the literature does not mean its absence in the Indian countryside.

The medieval European parallel

This argument is strengthened by the point that in the circumstances of scattered fields and population pressure in medieval and early modern northern Europe, cultivators often responded in ways somewhat similar to the cultivators of Kottapalle. Kerridge writes about England in the early modern period:

> The man with only a few score sheep could not fold his arable with these alone, and it would not be worth his while to keep his own shepherd ... most farmers had too few sheep for the fold. Therefore, in order to be able to fold their arable and to be able to grow corn, the small farmers of most townships put their sheep into a common flock ... for the sustenance and employment of this common flock it was necessary for the tenantry to treat the whole of their open land meadow and pasture as one single unit for all purposes of flock and fold. They had *to consult together, to abide by mutually agreed regulations and form and administer a common purse* ... The common shepherd managed the flock according to the decisions of the tenantry themselves
> (1953–4:282–4, emphasis added).

Stock damage to arable crops was a matter of intense concern in open-field by-laws; and a second focus was the regulation of the harvest, especially so as to reduce the danger of crop theft. Elected wardens were often appointed to police the regulations and collect the fines. In contrast to the Kottapalle field guards the wardens were not paid (in England): and tended to be 'among the more substantial and responsible members of the community' (Ault 1972:61). The fines were usually paid to the lord of the manor, but sometimes half went to the church, and sometimes the wardens kept one third of the fine, the balance going to the lord (rather than, as in Kottapalle, to a common fund).

I do not want to push the parallels with the Kottapalle type of organization too far; it is clear that English open-field villages did not have a standing fund financed by franchises, nor a body of village employees such as Kottapalle's field guards and common irrigators. Farmers in English open-field villages had to maintain the field access roads and ditches themselves – if they failed to do so village by-laws often prescribed fines (Ault 1972:56–7, 126, 139). There seems to have been no notion of a council responsible to the larger village assembly; the assembly itself was the decisionmaking body.

Yet one can see that the problems to which the by-laws were a response are in many ways similar to those which have prompted Kottapalle's organization. This underlines the point that 'sheep-and-corn' farming on scattered open parcels creates certain problems to which a corporate response, a unified system of rule, is a distinct possibility; which makes it all the more surprising that other monographs on Indian villages have little to say about them.

The social response to scarcity and risk

However, any explanation of why Kottapalle and several other villages in our sample are relatively corporate must be related logically to the explanation of why many other villages in the sample are not. I have attempted to provide a consistent body of reasoning that rationalizes both the presence of Kottapalle-type organization and its absence; that shows how changes in the same variables can give rise to different village forms (Barth 1965). The central variable is the risk of crop loss and social conflict faced by many or all cultivators as a result of the actions of other people or animals. The magnitude of this risk sets the premium on the village's ability to tighten its internal ordering, to create institutions of unitary rule which are continuous, calculable and effective.

Let us restate the argument in more general terms. It concerns two resources, water and grazing. These we earlier called common property resources, but they might better be called 'common-pool resources' so as to make a clearer distinction between the nature of the resource and the institutional arrangements by which it is exploited. Common-pool resources are a sub-set of public goods. All public goods have the property that many can use them at the same time, because exclusion is difficult. But some public goods yield infinite benefits, in the sense that if A uses more there is no reduction in the amount available for others (lighthouses and weather forecasts, for example). Common-pool resources, by contrast, are public goods with finite, or subtractive, benefits; if A uses more, less remains for others. Common-pool resources are therefore potentially subject to congestion, depletion or degradation: use which is pushed beyond the limits of sustainable yield (Ostrom 1985b, Randall 1983).

Canal water is a common-pool resource: it can be used jointly, because of the high cost of excluding a landowner with irrigable land; and its consumption is subtractive in the sense that water applied to A's land is not available at the same time to be applied to B's land. So when water is scarce congestion is likely, manifested in conflict and yield reductions where water arrives too late.

Grazing is also subject to joint use and subtractive consumption. However with grazing it is not so much the limits to the sustainable yield of common grazing that drive the attempt to regulate in these villages. It is rather the fact that joint use imposes costs on the owners of nearby crops; and the larger the number of animals, the greater the risks of such costs will be. So grazing is common-pool resource where the problem is not so much congestion of the resource itself as the externalities inflicted on non-users.

In these terms we can distinguish commons situations and commons dilemmas (Blomquist and Ostrom 1985). The exploitation of a common-pool resource is always a commons situation, in the sense that any resource characterized by joint use and subtractive benefits is *potentially* subject to crowding, depletion and degradation. But only some commons situations become commons dilemmas: those where joint use and subtractive benefits are coupled with scarcity, and where in consequence joint users start to interfere with each other's use. Here the private costs resulting from private behaviour, without collective organization, are relatively high, and may exceed the costs of organization. The short answer, then, to the question of variation between the villages in this study is that corporate organization is found only in villages where commons situations have become commons dilemmas.

So it is not the fact of gravity-flow irrigation which matters for central control at village level, many anthropological generalizations notwithstanding. Most of the irrigated villages in our sample have *no* community organization or formal rules. Rather, the relevant variable is the *reliability and adequacy of water supply*, and this varies systematically between top-end and tail-end irrigated villages. Water supply is more unreliable and less adequate in tail-end villages and so the risks of crop loss and water conflict are greater in tail-end villages.

Nor is the morphological layout of scattered, unfenced holding itself a strong condition prompting collective arrangements; nor even common stubble pasturage *per se*. All villages in our sample meet these two conditions, yet many do not have any village-based organization. What matters is the *density of grazing livestock*, for the greater the density the greater the risk of crop loss and conflict. The density is related in turn to cropping pattern and soil type, which are themselves related to position of the village on a catchment. Top-end villages tend to have lighter, less water-retentive soils, therefore have less fodder supply available for common stubble pasturage; and so receive after the harvest a much smaller influx of livestock. Further, irrigated top-end villages tend for reasons relating to water supply and drainage to plant most of their irrigated area with two crops of paddy a year, leaving little of the first season irrigated area available for common stubble pasturage after the harvest. In any case, sheep and goat manure is not wanted for paddy fields. So for both supply and demand reasons, the density of potentially wayward animals in top-end irrigated villages is relatively low. Tail-end villages tend to have more water-retentive soils, therefore have a bigger supply of fodder available after the harvest. Irrigated tail-end villages tend to grow more of their irrigated area under non-paddy crops, which benefit more than paddy from sheep and goat manure. So the density of livestock in irrigated tail-end villages is relatively high.

Moreover, I have suggested that the degree of scattering of holdings may also vary systematically down a catchment, reflecting the differential need to hold a diversified portfolio of land locations: less at the top-end, more at the bottom-end. The greater the degree of scattering, the stronger are likely to be the externalities of both grazing and irrigation.

With irrigation there is a further point. If holdings are *not* scattered, the externalities of water use are 'uni-directional': the actions of irrigators with land at the head of the block impose costs on those towards the tail, but not vice-versa. In this case there is a clear difference of interest between top-enders and tail-enders, the latter having a stronger incentive than the former to agree to strong community organization and formal rules. If holdings are scattered, on the other hand, an irrigator with land near the top end of one block may have another plot near the bottom end of another block, which diffuses the direction of the externality and helps to create a common interest in rules and organization.

It is where the risks of *both* grazing and irrigation are high that one tends to find a corporate response as strong as Kottapalle's: in villages fed from near the tail-end of a more-than-several-miles-long irrigation channel, with fine, water retentive soils.[2] In dry villages with fine, water retentive soils there are high grazing risks, which tend to generate only an intermediate level of corporate organization. On the other hand, in top-end irrigated villages, the risks of both irrigation and grazing are relatively low, and the level of corporate organization tends to be *less* than that of many dry villages.

This statement of the connection between risk and corporate organization runs in terms of more or less risk and more or less corporate organization, and it would of course be desirable to be more precise. My data do not permit a more exact specification, however. With reference to irrigation, the fact that common irrigators are only found in villages in the bottom third of distributaries is consistent with the proposition that risk of crop water stress and water conflict increases steadily down the length of distributary, *or* with the proposition that risk increases sharply in the bottom third. The decision to have common

---

[2] Above an upper limit or risk the response is more individualistic – a switch in cropping pattern out of water-consumptive paddy. MNC–1, the village below Kottapalle, and MNC–16, exemplify this response.

irrigators is a yes–no decision, and either proposition is consistent with the balance of advantage flipping from no to yes in the bottom third. Much the same point applies to field guards.

So while risk may change continuously or discontinuously, changes in corporate organization are discontinuous. All the more so because there is little corporate organization in our villages which is *not* village-wide: that is, there are few cases where 'common irrigators' are provided for a segment of a village's land by the farmers who have land in that segment; and similarly for field guards. Institutionalization tends to take place, if at all, village-wide, for reasons to do with economies of scale and the prior existence of a formal local government establishment with village-wide jurisdiction (or conversely, the absence of any other experience of formal organization by sub-village groups of field neighbours). Hence the distinction I have drawn between an intermediate and a high level of corporateness or activeness relates not to the size of unit (whether sub-village or village) but to the range of public goods and services supplied and the amount of resources mobilized in excess of the field guards' salaries.

The evidence from my sample of irrigated and dry villages, then, supports the following two propositions: (1) that deliberately concerted action of the kind considered here arises only when the net material benefits to be provided to all or most cultivators are high – when without it all or most cultivators would face continual collision and substantial risk of crop loss; and (2) that such unified action is very likely when these risks are high. Notice that this is no tautology. Whether benefits are high or not is not inferred from the fact of collaboration, but independently established on the basis of ecological factors translated into household preferences. The critical evidence is the tendency for village organization to vary systematically down a catchment with variations in water supply and soil type.

This argument can be seen as a special case of Boserup's more general theory of agricultural intensification, that people will pay the social costs that come with intensification only when it is absolutely necessary (1965, 1981). And it is in line with recent research findings on the topic whose parallels with South Indian village organization have been stressed at several points – the open-field system of husbandry in medieval Europe. According to Hoffman (1975) and Thirsk (1967), the tight communal regulation of the open-field system evolved from a previous more individualistic agriculture of scattered farms and few communal regulations, in response to the growing scarcity of grazing land as population pressure increased. The more familiar response to growing scarcity is the shift from loosely defined communal rights to more tightly defined private rights, and the basic reason why the response in medieval Europe was to tighten control on communal property was, they argue, the high cost of policing private grazing rights where fields were scattered.[3] McCloskey (1975) links variations in the timing and extent of enclosures (which reduced scattering) to variations in risk. Specifically, he argues that the main reason the English Midlands were enclosed more slowly and later than eastern England was not that the Midlands peasants had a greater love of the egalitarian community than those further east, but that the clay soils of the Midlands were more sensitive to weather than the free-draining sands of eastern England, and so greater risk-averting advantages were to be had from persisting with scattered fields.

I shall argue later, however, that McCloskey's explanation is too simple by half. Any comprehensive explanation must treat not only variations in the demand for enclosures, but also variations in the power of those who wanted enclosures compared to the power of those who did not.

In the present case, however, enclosure or privatization of the water and grazing is not an option. The options, rather, are to organize in something like the Kottapalle way, or not organize at all except in casual small group arrangements. It turns out that to explain which villages organize a public domain and which do not, we need give no more than a little weight to sociological variables such as power structure, factions, inheritance and marriage rules, or general norms of solidarity and cooperation; or to the kinds of variables that are prominent in some theories of collective action, such as selective incentives or the size of the group. The reason is that variance in these factors is small within the study area, and there are no grounds for supposing that it could account for the pattern of geographic variation in village organization found on the ground. On the other hand, if one were to take an all-India or world sample of villages, the sociological variables would certainly explain much more.

From collective incentives to unified action

As it stands, my argument seems to make a starkly deterministic connection between ecological conditions, risk, and social organization.

---

[3] Similarly, Thirsk shows how variations in communal organization and rules in east Midlands villages correlated with variations in fodder supply (1973). Broadly speaking, stricter rules of grazing were found where grazing was less abundant (though type of grazing also had an independent influence). However, the general argument about open-field systems being generated by high and rising population density has recently come under strong challenge in the English context (Campbell 1981).

It seems to say that where risks associated with irrigation and common grazing are high cultivators will straightforwardly come together to follow corporate arrangements designed to reduce those risks. In the same way, Hoffman and McCloskey portray the social response to the risks of mixed arable and animal husbandry as unproblematic; the problem is to identify the sources and nature of the risks which generated the observed response. Orthodox group theorists in political science, such as David Truman (1951), likewise assume that the formation of pressure groups is unproblematic once it can be shown to be in the interests of rational individuals. And some orthodox Marxists assume that when a certain type of state intervention can be shown to be in line with the 'needs of capital', the appearance of interventions of that type is sufficiently explained (Althusser 1971).

As the collective action theorists have shown, explanations of this sort are insufficient. The concerting of action is itself something in need of explanation even once the incentives or 'needs of capital' have been identified. In the peasant context, even where all or most cultivators in a village could benefit from joint action that action will by no means be automatically forthcoming. As Popkin says, 'it is frequently the case that the actions of individually rational peasants in both market and non-market situations do not aggregate to a "rational" village' (1979:31).

Let us then consider the question of why a substantial level of provision of public goods is achieved in the tail-end villages of this study. How do the strong incentives for unified action in tail-end villages get transformed into a supply of public goods and services? It is convenient, following Elinor Ostrom's framework (1985b), to distinguish between the conditions that aid the emergence of corporate organization of the Kottapalle kind, and those that subsequently help to sustain it. Both types of conditions affect organization by means of their influence on rational choice. The essential argument is that in the conditions to be described, cooperation to establish and maintain a locally-based enforcer of agreements is a rational strategy for self-interested individuals.

The origin of corporate organization

The conditions of origin can be divided into those relating to the character of the resources which the corporate organization manages, those relating to the group of users, and those concerning relations between the group and the state (Ostrom 1985b, Oakerson 1985).

Resources

The grazing land, it will be recalled, is not a single contiguous area permanently or annually available for common grazing. It is the cropland after the harvest, plus the field margins and roadside verges all through the year. Given scattered holdings, the option of privatization through fencing is too expensive for all but the most valuable of crops (generally only citrus groves). The external boundaries of the grazing land are well-defined, being the legal boundaries of the village land area itself; and by the same token the boundaries are relatively small. Accurate knowledge of the state of the resource is easy to get, and the incidence of disputes over crop damage provides a clear indicator of congestion. Undiscovered cheating on the grazing rules is difficult, for violations can be seen from a distance (especially if the crop is low-growing paddy); anyone who sees an animal grazing a standing crop knows that it should not be there. These factors make collective management easier.

With respect to water, the option of privatization by means of wells sunk into the command area to capture the underground flow of canal water is not used, presumably for reasons of expense and scattered holdings. The external boundaries are in this case (unlike grazing) poorly defined. The amount of the resource available to any village depends on the water supply higher up the canal network and in the reservoir, about which farmers have little knowledge. On the other hand, the conditions of supply mean that the amount obtained by any village is open to influence by concerted action (to bribe officials, intimidate upstream water-stealers, and so on). And once the water reaches a point a few miles upstream it is then readily monitored and controlled.

Social group

The social group of users has clear spatial boundaries; it is relatively small in size; and resides in the middle of the resources it exploits. It is homogeneous in the sense that most members of the village share a common dependence on the same tract of land, which they all wish to use in basically the same way, and share the same perception of risk of congestion.

Land holdings are scattered. So as a household acquires more land it will generally acquire an interest in what happens over an increasing proportion of the village area. This greatly strengthens the sense of common interest with respect to the village land as, a single unit.

Asset ownership is not homogeneous. Kottapalle has a 'power elite' of perhaps 60 to 90 households out of 575, from which come the active participants in decisionmaking. They are all in solid agricultural surplus, and virtually all from the Reddy caste. Since benefits of corporate organization are positively related to land area, the claims that these households can make are sufficiently large for some of them to be motivated to pay a major share of the organizational costs. Debate and compromise are easier in a sub-group of this kind than in a larger and more heterogeneous group with more diverse preferences; so consensus about levels of provision is more readily reached. On the other hand, beyond a certain point of asset inequality there may be no village council or popular involvement, even if some public goods and services are provided. Where one or two families are overwhelmingly dominant and where the village is in a tail-end location, there may be field guards and common irrigators but no council, no standing fund, no general meeting. TSC–2 and TSC–3 fit this pattern. In these two villages the dominant family arranges an acreage levy and appoints the work groups.

The nature of class relations also matters. The reality which the village councils face is not one of social classes or castes in confrontation, for the reason that the subordinate groups have not coalesced to give expression to their interests. Whereas in some other parts of South India village festivals have been cancelled by the dominant caste because the festivals came to be an occasion for the subordinate castes to claim higher rank (chapter 3), such conflict is not seen in this area. Nor is the violence directed towards 'untouchables' by members of the dominant castes, a regular feature of life in some parts of India, common here.

The state

The arm of the state does not exercise enough force at the village level to be able to prevent the users from making their own arrangements. Indeed, state officials outside the village barely know of the organization's existence. At the same time, the state's models of local government forms have provided ideas for independent arrangements.

State officials often respond to pressure or bribes, as we have seen for irrigation, and the same applies to agricultural extension, veterinary service, electricity supply, or village access roads (Wade 1982a, 1985b). The implication of market-like relations in the allocation of state benefits is that villages which can organize to collect quickly the required amounts of money or contacts have advantages over those less well organized. Which raises the premium for the village to strengthen its internal ordering and act as a benefit-maximizing group.

These various conditions relating to the resources, the social group, and the state have the effect of lowering the costs of organization or raising the benefits. In so doing they help organization to emerge.

Sustaining corporate organization

The conditions for sustaining corporate organization relate primarily to features of the organizational design itself.

The structure of authority

The structure of authority includes three levels – the level of the work groups of field guards and common irrigators, that of the council, and that of the general assembly. At the first level, a single person or small group makes decisions about immediate problems in a specified jurisdiction; at the second, the council discusses major problems, formulates general rules, and assesses penalties in particular cases. At the third level decisions are made or ratified which require considerable sacrifice on the part of individuals or which affect the basic scope of the organization. The distinction between the second and third levels is not, of course, clear cut. But some such complex and tripartite arrangement seems to be necessary to allow the organization to take quick decisions both in response to rapidly changing exogenous conditions and to ensure that the organization continues to elicit feelings of acceptance on the part of the villagers at large (Ostrom 1985b).

Types of benefits

The organization limits itself to supplying non-privatizable goods. This avoids the quarrels which would result from attempts to allocate privatizable benefits (and did result in the one major exception, the distribution of subsidized sugar). Such quarrels among the landed would jeopardize the council's ability to continue to provide for common interests. Hence the Kottapalle council is not involved in input supply other than water, or in settling disputes unrelated to water or husbandry, or in compensating the owner of animal-damaged crops with the fine levied upon the animal owner. These things would cause disputes over the amount that individuals could appropriate. It is also not involved in fixing wages, or disciplining labourers on behalf of land owners, which would place it in the middle of conflicting class interests. Finally, it stays out of households' investment decisions, such as how many livestock to own or how much paddy area to plant; rather, it limits itself to trying to offset some of the externalities which those decisions cause.

On the whole, the organization's benefits are of a prophylactic kind, to do with defence of what people already have rather than with net additions. This makes collective action easier, for people organize more easily and stay organized when they feel their existing interests threatened than when they wish to further interests they do not already have (R. Hardin 1982; Kimber and Richardson 1974). The benefits also arise not from the investment of tangible resources, but from people behaving one way when a narrower view of self-interest would indicate another way. This too makes collective action easier, for when there must be a commitment to provide a future flow of investment resources from each individual, any one person is more likely to be tempted to free ride on the assumption that others, having sacrificed some of their resources already, will continue to take up the shortfall caused by their withdrawal so as to be sure of getting something back (Laver 1981:158). Finally, withdrawal of one of the two central services, common irrigating, would cause an emergency or crisis for the group, which again makes collective action easier to sustain than where withdrawal of the service would not have such a dire effect; for free riding is less likely in the former situation (Kimber 1981).

Rules

The rules of behaviour which the council lays down – rules of access to canal water once the common irrigators are appointed, rules about where animals can graze, rules of harvesting, and so on – are simple in terms of the amount of information they require; which makes them easy to remember and enforce.

Enforcement

Whereas consensus is sufficient to explain the origin of collective organization some degree of coercion is a necessary condition for sustaining it. The council has clear and powerful enforcement mechanisms in place to check the temptation to cheat on the rules of restrained access, and has found ways to bypass the temptation to cheat on the financing of those mechanisms.

The ease of enforcement is related to (a) the possibility of undetected cheating; (b) the bite of available sanctions; (c) the costs of conforming; and (d) habit. Habit matters because when rules are well-established as in the present case, people rarely stop to calculate the costs and benefits of not obeying. As for the other elements, the more possibilities for undetected cheating (or free riding), the more difficult is the enforcement. In our villages these possibilities are limited for both irrigation and grazing; the problem is less detection than resolving the conflicts between those seen to be cheating and those who see themselves as harmed by their cheating. However detection is more difficult for irrigation than for grazing, because violations of the grazing rules can be more easily seen from a distance. Partly for this reason there are many more common irrigators than field guards.

The available sanctions include fines of non-trivial amounts – a day's field wages for an animal caught at night, and much more for water infringements. The field guards' salaries are set at less than the daily wage of an agricultural labourer so as to give them a strong incentive to collect the fines, for they keep all of the small fines and a fixed percentage of the larger ones. The deterrence effect of fines is reinforced by considerations of reputation (Akerloff 1980, Runge 1986). Whether because the desire for social acceptance by a group is a fundamental principle of social behavior or because reputation loss has material consequences for an individual in terms of contracts foregone, reputation in a small agricultural community is not lightly exposed to attack. We have seen the council deliberately seeking to activate reputation sanctions, as in its strategy of bringing the maximum number of 'influentials' to council meetings at times of crises to signify by their presence and non-disagreement their acceptance of the decision. By demonstrating that a high proportion of the influential population subscribe to the decisions, the council increases the cost to an individual's reputation of disobeying. Also, in cases of serious water or grazing infringement the defendant must argue his case before the council and its public, and can here be exposed to serious criticism.

The effects of fines and reputation loss are reinforced by stratification. Many who might be tempted to free ride are socially subordinate to others in the user group, and are checked from doing so by sanctions which derive from the wider order of caste and property without the council having to use its own authority. On the other hand, where stratification breeds class antagonism, as in some other parts of India, the bite of reputation loss may be reduced, because the reference group is confined to the subordinate class and collective free riding by members of the subordinate group might be encouraged.

The costs of conforming can refer to both the material costs (water foregone, for example) and the financial costs that have to be met to ensure enforcement of the rules. Let us concentrate on the financial costs. From the council's point of view it would be administratively easier to finance its operation through acreage levies than through mechanisms it in fact uses. But it is very difficult to enforce household collections except at times of crisis (when money has to be found to bribe water from the Irrigation Department during a drought, for example). People complain that they don't have the money available, say they will pay next week; they are very aware of the clash between private and public interest on the expenditure side.[4] The sale of franchises allows the free rider problem to be by-passed – or more exactly, displaced to where it is easier to deal with. The council still has to use its authority to sanction the auctioned franchises, as when it announced a boycott of the liquor agent who had refused to pay the fund and threatened severe fines on anyone who failed to observe it. But free riding behaviour with respect to the franchises is more easily checked than free riding with respect to direct contributions to, say, the field guards' salary. Broadly speaking, what the council does is to pay for the non-excludable service of field guarding by the sale of excludable franchises, much as non-excludable lighthouse services can be financed by excludable port charges. The money raised by these methods is often sufficient, in tail-end villages to provide many other public goods in the same free-rider-invulnerable way.

Common irrigators, on the other hand, are paid from acreage levies. Free riding on common irrigator services is held in check by knowledge that termination of common irrigator services, when water is scarce, would produce an immediate crisis for everyone with land in a tail-end location within the village. Also, people know that non-payment one year can be penalized the following year by the common irrigators themselves; it will cost the common irrigators some extra effort, but it is possible for them to interrupt a non-payer's water supply until his crops suffer yield-reducing stress. So the common irrigator service is not a 'pure' public good, because non-contributors can, with difficulty, be excluded. Finally, the levy is made at the one time of year when all cultivators can pay – straight after the first harvest, in kind rather than cash. Payment of the field guards at the same time would imply payment *in advance* for their work to the end of the second season, and this requires a level of trust which is not forthcoming.

---

[4] Collection difficulties may arise not only for fines, but also for any payment which goes to the fund. For example, the male progeny of the temple's cow are sold by auction under the council's supervision in Kottapalle, and the proceeds go to the village fund. The auction is covered by a written set of regulations which specify, amongst other things, that buyers must pay the due amount within two months of the sale, or face a fine of Rs. 400 per day (sic).

Conditions for collective action

Accountability

There is an inherent tension between enforcement and accountability; those who have the power to enforce may use that power to resist being held accountable for their actions. All the more so, given the lack of practice which people in small rural communities get of separating institutionalized role relationships from the totality of interpersonal relations. In these circumstances, personal or factional antagonisms and suspicions might easily burst the organization asunder. The Kottapalle organization meets this problem by giving these antagonisms and suspicions an institutionalized expression. Care is taken, for example, to balance the composition of the council between the two factions. One low caste member is nearly always included on the council. Decisions are taken by consensus, not majority vote. When tensions are high, two treasurers, one from each faction, are appointed, each providing a check on the other. Written accounts of fund income and expenditure are kept, and are read out at the annual general meeting. Council meetings are in a public place, so that anyone with the confidence to do so can monitor the proceedings from the sidelines and even take part in the discussions. While there is normally only one advertised general assembly meeting a year, council meetings on contentious issues often turn into *de facto* general meetings, and as noted, the council actually encourages this so as to enlist the consent of as many people of influence as possible. In these various ways the exercise of power is kept relatively depersonalized, and accountability maintained. One indication is the fines levied by the council on councillors who took water out of turn in the 1980 drought. The lawmaker is bound by its own laws.

These procedures are sufficient to keep factional conflict in check. Only in a small number of villages is factional conflict an influence on which way the yes–no decision flips; and these are *on the margin* between tail-end and middle-reach location. The next village upstream from Kottapalle, MNC-7, for example, had a Kottapalle-type of organization until about fifteen years ago, at which time it ceased because of factional stalemate on the council (though it is also possible that water supply down to that point in the distributary may have improved at about the same time, reducing the benefits to be gained by organization).

The moral basis

To what extent do people comply with the rules, even if by breaking them they could get immediate material gain, because they believe the rules to be right? It is striking how little people in these villages are steered by a sense of devotion or obligation to a non-self-regarding 'cause', such as 'the welfare of the village' or 'cooperative ways of doing things'. This is the sense of devotion that induces many to contribute to the Council for the Preservation of Rural England without expectation of any special benefit in return and many others to contribute to trade unions. I find little of it in these villages. Village-based organization, even after several decades or more, has only a weak claim to morally motivated obedience. If the village council were seen as the village personified or as the embodiment of the ideal of cooperative ways of doing things, one would expect to see some symbolism by which this representation is achieved; but there is none. The village public realm is about getting things done rather than about ceremony and symbolism – what Bagehot called 'efficiency' rather than 'dignity'. The farmers' involvement remains calculative rather than moral. After the general assembly meeting of 1981 had sharply curtailed the council's role in the village there was virtually no regret. This is not the response expected if there were any trace of a cooperative ideology, if the council had appealed to deeper and more demanding feelings and affections, if it had linked itself to the idea of the totality of its member's interests, to an idea of the village as moral entity. Rather, the response showed that the council and its work groups are seen as a functionally-specific machine, to be judged according to its ability to control and support the individual's search for his own advantage by rendering the interplay of 'antagonistic cooperators' more transparent, calculable and noncoercive. This, in a word, is why there is a fairly steady pattern of corporate organization, even though it lacks a strong underpinning of normative understanding that people *ought* to behave in a corporate kind of way.

However, to leave the matter at this point is too simple. There is another sense of 'ought' which springs from self-interest coupled with the moral capacity to recognize the related claims of others. This coupling produces the principle that I cannot expect others to pay their share unless I pay mine. It is a fine point, of course, to decide how much of this proceeds from a strictly self-interested calculation of the consequences for my own gains if others do not pay their share (or follow the rule), and how much proceeds from a general sense of reciprocity, of doing to others as you would have them do to you (or not doing what you would not have done to you). But in any case, the second and more moral component is present to some degree. It is reinforced by experience of past behaviour showing that (most) others *can* be trusted to do their share, to abide by the rules. Conversely, the 'ought' rapidly loses force if that trust is lost.

Then there is another sense of 'ought' which springs from identification with a collectivity contesting with other collectivities. The official who has to be bribed or entreated, the upstream village that has to be stopped from taking too much water, becomes an antagonistic 'them', and being reified, can enhance perception of a reified collective 'us'. The conception of the village (the power elite especially) as a benefit-maximizing group strengthens the individual's sense of obligation to follow the rules of the group; and so helps to increase the confidence of any one member of the power elite that others can be counted on to follow the council's decisions, making that individual more willing to do the same.

It is therefore too simple to say that the farmers' involvement in corporate institutions remains wholly calculative, as though one could explain the institutions in terms purely of the interests of rational individuals interested only in gains for themselves. The sense of obligation stemming from these two sources helps to weaken the temptation to free ride. But it should be remembered that for many in the population whatever sense of obligation they feel is probably secondary to the sanctions they would face as a result of their general social subordination.

Actual and optimal

I have explained why a 'substantial' level of provision of public goods is achieved. Whether it is in some sense optimal, given transaction and enforcement costs, is a question my data cannot answer. There is a presumption that the supply of public goods is fairly elastic, if one thinks of such events as how the council changed the field guards in 1981 after their unsatisfactory performance the preceding year, or how it increased the strength of the common irrigators as the 1981 drought worsened. There is a presumption, in other words, that the equilibrating mechanisms for adjusting supply to demand are good enough to keep the supply at something close to optimal levels. But harder evidence requires one to quantify the economic effects of the rules of restrained access. The best way would be through matching pairs of villages, alike in ecological conditions, one with corporate organization and one without. I could not find such pairs, however, and would not expect to find them if the underlying argument is valid. All one can say with confidence is that production and equity are higher in the villages with these rules than they would have been in the same villages in their absence.

The political effects are easier to be sure about. The Kottapalle type of organization represents a higher level of political development than less corporate villages, if by political development we mean the growth of a differentiated political domain (Eckstein 1982). Perhaps the best single indicator is that punishment for crop damage and water stealing is meted out according to well-established procedures, rather than being the responsibility of the offended party or his kin. More generally, the political realm of the corporate villages is clearly defined, open to many individuals and responsive to their views – especially if they are landed Reddys. The exercise of power is relatively civil, with aggression, usurpation and repression held in check. But as for whether these political benefits are provided at an optimal level, that again is a question my data cannot answer. The very concept of a political optimum is unclear.

A final point. I use a slightly qualified assumption of methodological individualism to explain why certain resource-management rules have emerged in some villages but not in others. This is to say, I do not think a sense of obligated group membership or a belief in cooperation as a desirable way to live are important factors, there being no grounds for supposing that general social norms vary between these villages. On the other hand, the rules and institutions I am concerned to explain are distinctly 'second-order'; they presuppose a more fundamental set of rules making for a general pattern of 'social order'. I do not believe that these 'first-order' rules and institutions can be explained in the same sort of terms, as the result of prior rounds of individual maximizing.

11

Conclusions (2): theories of collective action

As we have seen, many theories of collective action are pessimistic about the chances that people who would benefit from the provision of a public good if they organize themselves to supply it, will actually do so. Far-reaching proposals for institutional change in the management of common-pool resources have been justified by this conclusion, in the direction of either full private property rights or state control.

Yet a sweeping pessimism is ill-founded, both empirically and analytically. Empirically, we have well-documented examples of peasant communities managing forest and grazing commons over long periods of time without degradation of the commons – in Japan and Switzerland, for example. The open-field systems of medieval Europe, and of the present-day Andes, show peasant communities undertaking still more complex tasks of common property resource management. These cases are sufficient to negate the *necessity* of full private property rights or for control by a central authority in order to protect common-pool resources (Ostrom 1986).[1]

We also observe, in contexts beyond natural resource management, a good deal of voluntary contribution to public goods which is difficult to explain in terms of selective inducements. Many worthy citizens join the Council for the Preservation of Rural England for reasons which it would be whimsical to suggest are limited to the wine and cheese parties (Olson's selective inducements) it provides for its members (Kimber 1981). Experiments on free rider behaviour in North America have shown that even when the experiments are designed to maximize the attractiveness of free riding, much less free riding occurs than current collective action theory can explain. (One experiment found, however, that economists and students of economics are more likely to free ride than adherents of other disciplines: Marwell and Ames 1981.) Ford Runge concludes from this body of experimental evidence that expectations of others' behaviour and a desire to contribute a 'fair' share are important factors even when free riding is made very attractive (1984).

[1] See Netting 1972 for the Swiss case, and McKean 1984 for the Japanese case. For a comparison of open-field systems in the present-day Andes and medieval England, see Campbell and Godoy 1985. Runge 1986 cites several other studies of 'successful' cases.

So there is much empirical evidence against a sweeping pessimism about collective action in general or some kinds of common-pool resource management in particular. The analytical basis of the pessimism also turns out to be weak, in large part because the theories have been applied to village situations for which they are inappropriate.[2] A frequent failing is that situations of no property (*res nullius*) are not distinguished from situations of common property (*res communis*) (Randall 1983; Runge 1986). No property means completely unrestricted access (as in ocean fisheries or the atmosphere), and this is the situation which Garrett Hardin assumes in his analysis of the tragedy of the commons. Imagine, he begins, 'a pasture open to all'. The case is quite different where a joint ownership unit exists, and access is open only within the bounds of this unit (those outside the unit can be excluded). Here the chances of getting compliance with rules of restrained access are much better. Yet Hardin and others, by failing to make the distinction, inappropriately generalize their results for no property, or open access situations to cover common property as well. The above-mentioned peasant cases of successful common-pool resource management all involve common property rather than no property.

Frequently, too, the argument implicitly or explicitly uses Prisoners' Dilemma as the underlying model for situations whose structure makes it inappropriate. Both Hardin's 'tragedy of the commons' and Olson's 'logic of collective action' can be understood as variants of Prisoners' Dilemma.

Prisoners' Dilemma

The parable of Prisoners' Dilemma is well-known, and need only be summarized briefly here.[3] Two suspects are being separately interrogated about a crime they jointly committed. They know that if they both stay silent they will receive a light prison sentence. If one stays silent while the other confesses the first will receive a long prison sentence while the other goes free. If both confess they both receive a medium prison sentence. Each person can choose only once – which means that if one chooses to stay silent while the second confesses the first cannot then confess upon learning of his sentence. This is what creates the

---

[2] In making the following argument I have drawn on discussions with Keith Dowding, David Feeney, Richard Kimber, Ford Runge, and especially Elinor Ostrom.

[3] The literature on Prisoners' Dilemma is vast. Rapoport and Chammah 1965 is a standard source. Runge 1984, 1986, Wagner 1983, Lipton 1985, Snidal 1985, are amongst many useful critical discussions.

dilemma. Their joint interest is for both not to confess (that is, for them to 'cooperate' with each other). But the outcome is that both confess (both 'defect'). From the point of view of either one of them, staying silent while the other confesses would give the worst outcome, and confessing at least ensures that this outcome is avoided while it also opens the possibility that the confessor will go free if the other stays silent. In this single-period game the choice of best strategy is made regardless of the expected choice of the other player, and that is the important point for our purpose. Confessing is, in other words, the 'dominant' strategy.

This parable extends to common-pool resource use by regarding the choice as being either to cooperate with others in a rule of restrained access or to not cooperate. The argument is that each individual has a clear preference order of options:

(i) everyone else abides by the rule while the individual enjoys unrestrained access (he 'free rides' or 'shirks');
(ii) everyone, including himself, follows the rule ('cooperates');
(iii) no one follows the rule;
(iv) he follows the rule while no one else does (he is 'suckered').

Given this order of preferences, the stable group outcome is the third-ranked alternative: unrestrained access to all in the group. From the more desirable second-ranked alternative, each individual has an incentive to cheat and go for his first ranked alternative (restrained access by all except him). Even if it then turns out that no one else follows the rule, his cheating at least ensures that he avoids his own worst alternative – following the rule while no one else does (being the sucker). In other words, mutual rule-bound restraint is not a stable equilibrium, because each individual will try to cheat regardless of what he expects others to do.

In this situation the only solutions are either coercion from outside the group to force people to reach and maintain the social optimum (second preference), or a change in the rules from outside the group to a private property regime.

Prisoners' Dilemma has exercised a continuing fascination on social theorists because it appears to provide a solid basis for a profoundly disturbing conclusion – that rational people cannot achieve rational collective outcomes. It seems to be applicable to all situations in which it is possible for some to refuse to cooperate while others are willing to cooperate.[4]

---

[4] Several theorists have used this argument to provide the essentials of a theory of the state. The state is shown to be needed above all to enforce contracts and punish deviants,

(Cont. on next page)

However, two key assumptions must hold if a situation is to be plausibly modelled as a Prisoners' Dilemma and if, therefore, the pessimistic conclusions of Prisoners' Dilemma are to be applied to it. The first is that the players choose in ignorance of each other's choices. The second is that each player chooses only once before the payoffs are received, and so cannot change his mind upon finding out what the other has done (Wagner 1983). The first assumption has the important implication that the players cannot negotiate among themselves to change the rules of the game, so as to secure more desirable collective outcomes. The changes in rules must come, if at all, from outside the group.

These assumptions clearly fit the core parable, where the two suspects have no communication, no pre-existing ties, no Mafia-like code of honour, no expectations of future interaction, and each knows that if he remains silent (cooperates) while the other confesses (defects) he will not have another opportunity to confess. The same assumptions may also make a useful first approximation to situations of industrial pollution, depletion of ocean fisheries, or some cases of deforestation, for example. In such situations, monitoring the compliance with a rule of restrained access is difficult; so any one would-be polluter or ocean fisherman or tree user can calculate that his own cheating will not be noticed, and equally that were he to comply with the rule others would make the same calculation and therefore cheat, leaving him as the sucker.

Where, however, the situation is an enduring or recurrent one, the logic changes. If the players in a Prisoners' Dilemma know that the game will be played repeatedly into the future, the chances that they will cooperate today in the hope that others will then do so are much higher than where the game is played only once (Axelrod 1981). This is true even if the rules of each round of the game are consistent with the two key assumptions stated earlier; so that each player continues to make his choice in ignorance of what the other players have chosen in that round, and finds out what they did only when the payoffs are received.

If, in addition, we assume that the players learn quickly what the others have chosen and can alter their own choice before the payoffs of each round are received, then the rational strategy is – in sharp contrast to the simple Prisoners' Dilemma – one of *conditional cooperation*, or

(Contd. from page 201)

so that social order can be maintained. But the state may not simply be imposed. As long as individuals' costs in the form of taxes are less than the gains to them from social order, they will accept a state, with its coercive powers, voluntarily. State formation is thus based on a conjunction of contract and coercion (Buchanan and Tullock 1962; Nozick 1974). As a theory of the state, this argument has the fatal weakness that it ignores social groups and the way that the relative influence of groups affects the type of state that emerges (Moore 1967).

'cooperate first, defect if the other defects' – or more simply put, 'no first cheat'.

If, further, we assume that the players are able to negotiate *changes* in the rules of the game among themselves, then one likely rule change is the introduction of penalties for violating agreements. The effect of such penalties is to reinforce the tendency towards cooperation.

So with these new and by no means unrealistic assumptions it begins to seem that rational individuals can, after all, achieve rational collective outcomes. But what constitutes rational choice-making is now much more complex than in Prisoners' Dilemma. Here the rational individual must calculate the consequences of his own attempt to free ride (cheat or defect) on the extent of free riding by others in the group. If his own free riding is noticed and if others retaliate by themselves attempting to free ride, there may be no public good to free ride upon, in which case free riding is not a rational strategy even for a strictly self-interested individual. 'Cooperate first and defect if the other defects' is the more rational strategy. But if there are many players even this may not be rational, for the consequence of mass retaliatory defection may again be to stop provision of the public good. Here the players have an incentive to respond to signs of noncooperation by cooperating to increase each other's incentive to cooperate, through exhortation and stiffer penalties for noncooperation. In this more complex situation considerations of morality, power, and loyalty also intrude as checks on free riding, as when people choose not to free ride even when they know that others are cooperating, because to do so would run against moral standards of 'do not take advantage of others in the group', or expose them to reprisals from outside the game (reprisals based on property or caste relations, for example). Rawls (1971) has shown analytically how the compliance of one individual to a code of conduct can reinforce others in behaving likewise.

Free riding, in this view, remains a possibility, but not, as in Prisoners' Dilemma, an imperative (Runge 1984, Kimber 1981, Sugden 1984, Snidal 1985). Institutions which give people the assurance that if they do comply with the rules they will not be the sucker – that those others who do not comply will be punished – greatly increase the chances of voluntary compliance. This is important, because the law as a mechanical barrier – whether local law or national law – can be effective when only a tiny minority of the population is likely to break it. Most of the observance of rules has to be more voluntary, because the cost of enforcement when large numbers of people comply involuntarily (through a calculus of evasion and punishment) is likely to be prohibitively high.

How does all this relate to village resource use? In the typical village, the context of common-pool resource use resembles more closely the assumptions which lead rational choice-makers to cooperate than it resembles the assumptions of Prisoners' Dilemma. That is, village common-pool resource use should usually be modelled as a recurring game, in which the possibility of undetected free riding is fairly low, and in which the villagers generally do have some control over the structure of the situation in which they find themselves. Insofar as this is true, rational choice-making is different in village resource use from what is rational in anomic situations like the Prisoners' Dilemma parable. In villages rational individuals can (subject to other conditions to be discussed) voluntarily comply with rules of restrained access.

The main exception to this argument occurs when some people in the community become desperate. They may then contemplate short-run strategies which they would not contemplate in normal times. They may be tempted to be the first cheater. This is what happened in Kottapalle during the water crisis of 1980–1 (chapters 5 and 7). At that time there was a real danger that many people would start to calculate that those who did not break the water rules first would not get any water (would be the suckers), as rule violation reached such a level as to make detection and punishment impossible. In other words, there was a danger that some people's perception of the situation would change to resemble a Prisoners' Dilemma. It was just at that time that the Kottapalle council increased the number of guards and sent repeated warnings to the village via the village crier that no one was to interfere with the work of the common irrigators. Violators were subject to stiff fines, and exposed to loss of social reputation through having to plead their case in public before the council. All this activity by the council can be understood as an attempt to assure irrigators that rule breakers would not get away with it, so there would be no sucker's payoff; the situation would not be allowed to become a Prisoners' Dilemma.

Hardin's tragedy of the common

Although Hardin does not use Prisoners' Dilemma, his argument shares similar assumptions, and indeed can be formally represented as a Prisoners' Dilemma game (Dawes 1975). Just as Prisoners' Dilemma assumes that each prisoner has no information about the other's choice, so Hardin's parable assumes that the individual herder has no information about the aggregate state of the commons and its nearness to the point of collapse. This assumption permits Hardin to have the herder make a decision just prior to collapse that is against his own self-interest – to add another animal thereby precipitating the collapse, with the consequence that he, as well as the others, loses all. At issue is the amount of information people have about the larger situation in which they operate (Kimber 1983). Empirically, there may be situations of extensive common grazing lands used by scattered communities which come close to the information assumption of Hardin's model; and ocean whaling prior to the International Whaling Convention may be another case in point. But the information assumption clearly does not make sense where resource, group, and state characteristics are as described for the villages of this study. Here monitoring the condition of the commons, and of cheating, is relatively easy.

Similarly, just as Prisoners' Dilemma says nothing about how the calculations are affected by different *absolute* values of the payoff, so Hardin's parable does not distinguish between commons where the resource is vital for the individuals' survival, and those where it is not. It is more likely that Hardin's relentless logic will operate where the resource is not vital than where it is (Kimber 1983). Where survival is at stake, the rational individual will exercise restraint at some point. In our villages water and grazing are both vital.

Olson's logic of collective action

Mancur Olson's theory can also be seen as a variant of Prisoners' Dilemma, although Olson himself does not use it in his exposition. The theory says, it will be recalled, that (1) voluntary collective action will not produce public goods, and (2) collective action based on selective (that is, excludable) positive or negative incentives may produce public goods. Existing cases of common interest groups are thus to be explained in terms of selective punishments or inducements. The compelling simplicity of this argument, stated without qualification at the start of Olson's book, has made it one of the touchstones of debate about collective action questions. Later in the book, however, the argument is restricted to 'large' interest groups only, in a three-fold taxonomy.[5] A 'small' group is one in which a single individual has an interest in providing the public good irrespective of the contribution of others. 'Intermediate' and 'large' groups are those where no one individual has this interest and where some cooperation is therefore necessary. Intermediate groups differ from large groups in that the

---

[5] I ignore Olson's distinction between 'privileged' and 'latent' groups, which in his argument has a confused relationship with his distinction between 'small' and 'large' groups.

actions of a single member with regard to whether he contributes or not are noticeable to others in an intermediate group, but not to others in a large group. In Olson's words, an intermediate group is one 'in which no single member gets a share of the benefit sufficient to give him an incentive to provide the good himself, but which does not have so many members that no one member will notice whether any other member is or is not helping to provide the collective good' (1971:50). So intermediate groups can detect free riding more readily than large groups can, because 'noticeability' is higher for intermediate groups than for large groups.

Olson argues that the likelihood of voluntary collective action (without selective punishments or inducements) is high for small interest groups, low for large ones, and *indeterminate* for intermediate ones. However, he gives little guidance as to how to distinguish the three types of groups on the ground. His own examples of large groups are organizations like trade unions or professional associations with a widely scattered membership, and against this standard, interest groups in peasant communities are presumably typically intermediate groups. If so, the implication is that Olson's theorem simply does not apply to the kind of situation with which we have been dealing (Ostrom 1985a).[6]

It is still worth drawing attention to two of our findings which run counter to the spirit of Olson's argument, putting aside the difference in group size. We find, first of all, that the main factor explaining the presence or absence of collective organization in these villages is the net collective benefit of that action. This hardly seems surprising – it would be astonishing if it were not true. Its interest comes from the failure of

[6] Olson's own interest is largely confined to large groups. 'In no major country are large groups without access to selective incentives generally organized – the masses of consumers are not in consumers' organizations, the millions of taxpayers are not in taxpayers' organizations, the vast number of those with relatively low incomes are not in organizations for the poor, and the sometimes substantial numbers of unemployed have no organized voice' (1982:34). Where large common interest groups do exist it is because they provide selective incentives, Olson asserts. 'The common characteristic which distinguishes all of the large economic groups with significant lobbying organizations is that these groups are also organized for some other purpose' (1971:132). This 'other purpose' constitutes the reason for the organization's existence, and the public good of lobbying is a *by-product* of the organization. Olson's only evidence for this thesis is the claim that existing large organized groups tend to have selective incentives; which does not show that the organizations form or are maintained *because* of those selective incentives (Dowding and Kimber 1984:3). Notice too that Olson does not make a clear distinction between group formation and group maintenance or growth. His theory of group 'existence' purports to cover both, but it is unclear how selective incentives could explain the formation of an organization. If an organization is necessary to provide the selective incentive, the latter can hardly explain the former. On the other hand, selective incentives might be used to explain increase in membership, once the organization was formed (Dowding and Kimber 1984:32).

Olson's argument – as well as Prisoners' Dilemma, Hardin's tragedy of the commons, and explanations based on classic sociological variables – to explain the same pattern of inter-village variation. Olson's argument would lead us to account for non-cooperation in terms of free riding, and to account for cooperation in terms of punishments or inducements which overcome free riding. Yet in these villages selective inducements are completely lacking, and selective punishments (as in fines or even social opprobrium) are present but are hardly the central motivating factor. Presence or absence of selective punishments cannot bear much weight in an explanation of variation between villages. They are not the ingredient that ensures the provision of the public good in the Olsonian manner.

In short, these villages exemplify the proposition that it is possible for an interest group organization to emerge voluntarily and be sustained largely voluntarily – that is, without selective benefits or costs – if the net collective benefit is high enough. This runs counter to the spirit of Olson's argument.

A corollary is that the supply of leadership is not a constraint here. Olson himself is not particularly concerned with leadership, but many other writers have emphasized the difficulties of leadership in peasant societies. Popkin sees the temptations to free ride with respect to leadership as typically being so strong that insufficient leadership is normally available within peasant communities; and accordingly emphasizes the need for it to come from outside the local community if peasants are voluntarily to concert their actions (1979). Foster too, from a different perspective, identifies the difficulties of leadership as a major reason why peasant societies tend to be individualistic, unable to support cooperative approaches to village problems. He draws attention to a wide range of observations which suggest 'the peasant's reluctance to accept leadership roles. The peasant feels – for good reason – that his motives will be suspect and that he will be subject to the criticism of neighbours. A "good" man therefore usually shuns community responsibilities (other than of a ritual nature); by so doing he protects his reputation' (1965:303). We have seen that Kottapalle's council members are sensitive to the criticism they attract, and some have resigned from a formal role in the council's activities for this reason. But overall there seems to be no shortage of men who fail to make the calculation that Foster and Popkin take to be typical.

Another corollary is that Olson's own argument places too much weight on the size of the *selective* benefits and costs (those that can discriminate between people according to whether they contribute to the provision of the public good or not) and too little on the size and nature of the *collective* benefits and costs.[7] It simply assumes the net collective benefit to be high, since free riders must by definition be a sub-set of those who value the public good highly. So the argument inclines one to interpret evidence of non-cooperation *faute de mieux* as evidence for the free rider hypothesis, rather than for the hypothesis of low collective benefit.

That interest group organization can emerge and be sustained largely voluntarily is the first major qualification to Olson. The second concerns the source of punishment. Olson's key proposition, it will be recalled, is that existing cases of collective action groups are to be explained in terms of the response to selective punishments or inducements. This differs from the more conventional formulation (as in Prisoners' Dilemma) where joint behaviour is explained by the presence of an external enforcer of agreements. One of the merits of Olson's version is that it leaves open the question of whether the source of selective punishment or induce-ment is inside the group or outside; it thus avoids the *prima facie* silliness of the conventional picture of people facing congestion of the commons and necessarily doing nothing to alleviate it for themselves. However, Olson himself is not clear on whether he thinks his 'selective coercion' must come from outside the group. If one interprets his argument in the friendliest of ways, he is simply saying that negative selective sanctions are an essential part of the organizational design needed to sustain collective action. But he can also be read as suggesting that the sanctions must be organized from outside the group itself, specifically from the state. Whatever Olson's position, this is the position adopted by many writers on the tragedy of the commons, and the Prisoners' Dilemma model appears to provide an analytical justification.

Here my findings and those of many others are contra. We have many examples where villagers have established rules, monitored the con-dition of the commons, monitored cheating, and assigned punishment. We also have, of course, many more examples of where attempts to do this have failed, and where in the absence of state regulation or private property the commons has degenerated. But the cases of success of locally devised rule systems indicate, to repeat, that it is not *necessary* for regulation of the commons to be imposed from the outside (McKean 1984:56, Ostrom 1986). The critical question is what are the conditions

---

[7] It is not that Olson says or implies that the size of the collective net benefit is irrelevant; he simply does not give it much attention. Occasional passages like the following suggest that it is important: 'A group which has members with highly unequal degrees of interest in a collective good, and which wants a collective good that is (at some level of provision) extremely valuable in relation to its cost, will be more apt to provide itself with a collective good than other groups with the same number of members' (1971:45).

in which success is likely. But this is not a question which the more popular collective action theories encourage one to ask.

Where Olson and other collective action pessimists are surely right is in the need for some coercion to back up agreements. Their emphasis on the difficulties of strictly voluntary collective action – that which proceeds from moral commitment, or habit, or a calculation of the benefits to each if each complies – is a useful counter to the simple optimism of those who believe that community development projects, people's participation, water users' associations and the like are mainly a matter of teaching people what their real common interests are, or a matter of changing their values in the direction of less individualism. On the contrary, the ability to make people do what they may not immediately want to do, by means of sanctioned rules, is a necessary ingredient of any arrangement for common-pool resource management. The present study provides much evidence consistent with this argument, as do studies by Ostrom (1986) and many others. But perhaps the most telling evidence comes from Japan. Japanese villagers have had a strong community identity and have been very concerned about social reputation and bonds within the group. They have also, according to McKean, internalized the preservation of the commons as a vital goal. Yet 'even this most cooperative, compliant group of people were vulnerable to temptations to bend, evade, and violate the rules governing the commons. Thus there had to be a scheme of penalties and these had to be enforced' (McKean 1984:54). A great deal of care went into the design and operation of the – village, not state-based – penalty mechanism.

The issue of the voluntariness of collective action therefore has to be considered at two levels. At the constitutional level people can voluntarily negotiate a set of rules of restrained access or financial contributions, their incentive to do so being the prospective net collective benefit. At the action level, most of the compliance with the rules must also be voluntary, not the result of a calculus of evasion and punishment. But the rules must be backed by a system of punishment, the existence of which helps to assure any one person that if he follows the rules he will not be suckered, and which at times of crisis can directly deter. This argument makes the size of the prospective net collective benefit the major factor in explaining the presence or absence of corporate organization in groups like our Indian villages.[8] It suggests that

---

[8] This argument is in line with some of the early writings in public choice theory, notably Buchanan and Tullock 1962 and Ostrom 1968. Later work in the public choice tradition has tended to focus too much on the issue of financial contributions.

Olson's discounting of this factor results from an exaggerated pessimism about the chances that individuals can devise ways to overcome the difficulties of organization which his analysis so well shows. To be fair, however, we must recall that Olson's pessimistic theorem is about large groups, whereas our villages are presumably intermediate groups in his classification, about which his theorem makes no determinate predictions.

Development lessons

Under the impact of fiscal crises, many governments have recently turned to 'beneficiary participation' or 'user groups' as a way of assuring the maintenance and operation of various kinds of rural development projects. What is called 'project sustainability' is argued to be closely dependent upon, in the words of a World Bank report,

fostering the development of grass roots organizations with salient qualities that are embedded in their growth and in their relationship to project activities. Desirable qualities center on increasing assumption by beneficiaries of responsibility for project activities during implementation, and especially following completion. Such responsibility is fostered by an increasing degree of autonomy and self reliance of the grass roots organizations, plus some form of decision-making input into project activities leading to a measure of control over the management of the project (World Bank 1984).

In plainer English, could the Kottapalle type of organization be harnessed for promoting economic development more directly, and could the same kind of organization be induced by the state elsewhere in India? At first sight there seems a ready compatibility between a high level of corporate organization and capacity to take on developmental tasks. After all, an authority structure is well established for raising local funds, for supervising the work of some twenty employees (in Kottapalle), for making decisions about resource use by village households and sanctioning those decisions, and for coping with the demands and opportunities of the state. There is a lot of learning acquired in this type of activity which would be available in other contexts. Could the council not simply add on other functions, such as promoting improved agricultural techniques, health care, nutrition, family planning, and so on?

The short answer is that the type of organization described here could not readily be enlarged to embrace these more developmental functions; and certainly could not be used to channel aid to the poorest, one of the other more recently added objectives of the community development movement. The fact of the matter is that individuals have made a series of specific consignments of power to a village authority *without* building momentum for further grants of power to the authority. What is more, the more corporate or active villages have reached about the same point in terms of the range of goods and services provided through the council; which suggests there are indeed inherent difficulties in going further. The reasons have been discussed at length and need only be summarized. The leaders are anxious above all to avoid conflict, to maintain the status quo. They see government as something to be avoided, tricked or implored. The council confines itself to activities with a high degree of publicness, for the reason that to enter activities where some can be excluded from the benefits would lead to quarrels over the allocation of the benefits, threatening the organization of what the council does already. Many of the community development programmes do involve privatizable benefits, and the council, as a stability-seeking, risk-avoiding organization would find it hard to deal with them. It is also constrained by the organizational difficulties of raising revenue through levies per person or per acre (except for common irrigator services). Its revenue base is therefore dependent on ways of raising money which avoid individual contributions.

Nor is it likely that the Kottapalle organization could be made a model for *widespread* state-promoted adoption elsewhere. The second most striking finding of this study, after the fact that such organization exists at all in village India, is that it is found *only* where the net collective benefit is relatively very high. Which suggests that villagers will deliberately concert their actions only to achieve intensely felt needs which could not be met by individual responses (Johnston and Clark 1982). These are likely to be concerned primarily with the defence of production, secondarily with increasing income, and lastly by a long way, with education, nutrition, health, and civic consciousness. This is not only what is suggested by my data, but is also a more specific statement of what Eckstein identifies as the basic motive force in the early stages of political development. 'Struggles for establishing an "efficient" domain (he argues) are only resolved when an urgent societal need for such resolution arises' (1982:485). In the West that need arose from the differentiation of society into distinct but overlapping 'corporations' in virtually continuous collision. In our case, the need arises from the collision of individuals over grazing and water. The common denominator is that an active public domain concerned with accomplishing substantive tasks emerges only when it is critical to social integration that it occur. Those who suppose that beneficiary groups can be sprung into existence wherever the state wishes them to take over operational and maintenance responsibilities are ignoring this elementary point.

This is to caution against false hopes. But the conclusion is too severe, left at this point. For one thing, the Kottapalle type of organization might plausibly be used to carry out several kinds of collective innovations which have organizational requirements similar to those of the tasks which the councils already perform. Supposing, say, that villages were offered equipment to furnish a health care centre if they provided the building (even one operated on a charge-for-service basis once established). The learning effect from successful financing of water and grazing control would make it easier to organize financing for the cost of the building. The same applies to installation of electricity and telephone link-ups. (It would however be unlikely that the council could get households to contribute labour or materials for such tasks; even such a routine and decentralized activity as field channel maintenance tends to be done not by a cooperative workgroup of affected farmers, but by a contractor using hired labourers, and the same is true for all the labour-requiring tasks which the councils undertake.)

Social forestry is another case in point. Social forestry projects aim to induce small farmers systematically to plant fuelwood trees on their own lands or on 'common' lands, instead of relying on the natural regeneration of trees (Cernea 1985). Where the trees are planted on private lands, some pooling of user rights is typically required, perhaps in the form of leasing to a larger entity for a given period of time. So whether the trees are planted on private lands or on commons, cooperation is needed. Many social forestry projects have failed because the project designers simply assumed that once they had demonstrated the sizable potential additions to farmers' real incomes the farmers would organize themselves appropriately. The key question of what social unit would carry out the collective innovation was then treated too lightly. This is the easy optimism which collective action theories have tried to counter.

In the Kottapalle type of organization we do have a social unit which seems well suited to social forestry tasks. The most important and difficult of those tasks is rule enforcement, so as to prevent premature exploitation of the trees. Kottapalle organizes plenty of rule enforcement already. And if the trees are to be exploited by a franchise holder, the Kottapalle council is used to auctioning franchises and putting the proceeds to public uses. On the other hand, the earlier discussion of types of collective benefits and costs suggests reasons why the social forestry case is, nevertheless, different in important ways from what the

Kottapalle council does already. For one thing, the council is primarily concerned to help households avoid loss on crop investments already made, whereas the social forestry project would concern net increases in non-crop income. For another, the council operates primarily by requiring individuals to change their behaviour from what it might otherwise be (that is, to follow general rules); the social forestry project requires expenditures now in return for income some 8 to 10 years hence. Both characteristics of social forestry benefits tend to make collective action more difficult. The main point, however, is that the Kottapalle type of organization might be suitable for undertaking an expanded set of activities where those activities are organizationally congruent with what it does already.

The second and more important qualification concerns our base of knowledge. It is, as I have said, remarkably thin on the question of how Indian villagers organize the public aspects of resource use. My argument and evidence suggest there may be much more autonomous group action in the Indian countryside than is usually thought. Planners and scholars need to analyze the conditions in which various kinds of organization are and are not found, and the effectiveness of those organizations in implementing rules of restrained access to common-pool resources or raising funds for collective economic purposes. We will then have a basis for judging where government efforts to facilitate 'beneficiary groups' might sensibly be directed.

Where autonomously evolved rule systems are found for common-pool resource management, we need to know about the conditions of emergence and maintenance, and effects on resource use. Successful rule systems can provide the basis for the design of organization prompted from the outside, by the government. They can tell us, in particular, about the relative causal importance of different kinds of viables; about the relative importance for organizational design of ecological and sociological factors, for example. Consider water organization. The only corporate water organization in our villages is based on the village rather than the outlet. Yet the outlet-based unit would mobilize the common interests arising from ecology alone more effectively than the whole village unit. If villages are nevertheless the only units, this argues for the greater importance of existing social ties in relation to strictly ecologically-defined interests; especially the existing authority structure as well as economies of organizational scale achieved by combining water and grazing. It also argues, to complicate matters, for the importance of canal design and land tenure, irrigation outlets being here designed to serve the land of only one village, and land holdings being divided into plots scattered over the whole village area. However, the government of Andhra Pradesh ignored such considerations in its program to form water users' associations under canal systems, simply assuming that the hydrologically-defined outlet unit was appropriate. Some irrigation sociologists have supported the same assumption. Walter Coward, for example, a leading scholar in this field, generalizes Asia-wide that 'for purposes of irrigation organization the critical unit is the 'irrigation community', composed of field neighbours, and not the village community, composed of residential neighbours' (1980:208). The complete failure of the Andhra Pradesh program[9] highlights the need to move beyond generalizations of this kind, to the conditions in which alternative social units are likely to be more or less appropriate. Coward's generalization may work when one or more of the conditions making for village water organization in our cases are different.

My argument, it bears repeating, is not that sociological and collective action variables are unimportant for explaining the form of common interest corporations in the countryside; only that they are unimportant for explaining why some villages have that form of organization while others do not. For the latter, an explanation based on variations in scarcity and risk is sufficient within my sample. For the former it is obviously not. The answer to why institutionalization takes place with respect to village rather than blocks of field neighbours, or why the supply of public goods is arranged through a conciliar rather than a dominant family form of organization, or why the council cannot depend on household levies for financing public goods, relates not to ecology but to features of social organization.

Likewise, if we consider the private enclosure of grazing land – an issue of major importance in other parts of the world though not in our villages – we have to refer to several other variables in addition to the increasing scarcity and value of grazing land. One is the cost of enclosure, and specifically the economies of scale to fencing which lower the wealthy individual's cost-per-animal of appropriating land rights (though by how much depends on the extent of scattering). A second variable is the power relations between those who wish to enclose the commons and those who do not. For the same increase in scarcity and value which encourages some to want to privatize also gives rise to opposing demands from those who benefit from the commons to insist on their retention. A third variable is the credibility of an enforcer of cooperative agreements, whether a council clan leader, a colonial state, or an independent state. In some parts of the world the modern state has undermined locally-based authorities which formerly enforced stinting

---

[9] This is generally agreed by those familiar with Andhra Pradesh irrigation.

or cattle taxation, but lacks the command over punishments or popular confidence to be able to replace them. Each individual is therefore likely to feel more dubious about trusting his neighbours not to over-graze, and other things being equal, to favour privatization (Lipton 1985).

On what, then, does successful collective action depend? My argument suggests that, as an extreme case, we would *not* expect to find effective rules of restrained access organized by the users themselves when there are many users, when the boundaries of the common-pool resources are unclear, when the users live in groups scattered over a large area, when undiscovered rule-breaking is easy, and so on. In these circumstances a degradation of the commons can confidently be expected, and privatization or state regulation may be the only options. The further an actual case deviates from this extreme the more likely will the people who face the problem be able to organize a solution. To spell it out in more detail, the likelihood of successful organization depends on:[10]

1 *The resources*
>the smaller and more clearly defined the boundaries of the common-pool resources the greater the chances of success.

2 *The technology*
>the higher the costs of exclusion technology (such as fencing) the better the chances of success.

3 *Relationship between resources and user group*
>(i) Location: the greater the overlap between the location of the common-pool resources and the residence of the users the greater the chances of success.
>
>(ii) Users' demands: the greater the demands (up to a limit) and the more vital the resource for survival the greater the chances of success.
>
>(iii) Users' knowledge: the better their knowledge of sustainable yields the greater the chances of success.

4 *User group*
>(i) Size: the smaller the number of users the better the chances of success, down to a minimum below which the tasks able to be performed by such a small group cease to be meaningful (perhaps because, for reasons to do with the nature of the resource, action to mitigate common property problems must be done, if at all, by a larger group).
>
>(ii) Boundaries: the more clearly defined are the boundaries of the group, the better the chances of success.

[10] See also Ostrom's list of variables (1985b), the starting point for my own.

(iii) Relative power of sub-groups: the more powerful are those who benefit from retaining the commons, and the weaker are those who favour sub-group enclosure or private property, the better the chances of success.

(iv) Existing arrangements for discussion of common problems: the better developed are such arrangements among the users the greater the chances of success.

 (v) Extent to which users are bound by mutual obligations: the more concerned people are about their social reputation the better the chances of success.

(vi) Punishments against rule-breaking: the more the users already have joint rules for purposes other than common-pool resource use, and the more bite behind those rules, the better the chances of success.

5 *Noticeability*

Ease of detection of rule-breaking free riders: the more notice-able is cheating on agreements the better the chances of success. Noticeability is a function partly of 1, 3(i), and 4(i).

6 *Relationship between users and the state*

 (i) Ability of state to penetrate to rural localities, and state tolerance of locally based authorities: the less the state can, or wishes to, undermine locally based authorities, and the less the state can enforce private property rights effectively, the better the chances of success.

Many of these facilitating conditions are found in the situations in which Asian peasant villagers typically use common-pool resources. The more they are present, the more promising is the collective action route. But as the list itself implies, there can be no presumption that the collective action route will generally work, any more than there can be a presumption that private property or state regulation will generally work. Indeed, some of the large-scale and long-term changes occurring in the rural areas of developing countries may be lowering the average probability of cooperative solutions. Rapidly rising person/land pressures may increase the dangers of trusting people and increase the number of people to be trusted; migration may reduce 'recurrence and noticeability'; state penetration of rural areas may only undermine old systems of authority without permitting or establishing new ones, resulting in a hiatus of confidence (Lipton 1985). My argument is only that (a) the propensity to descend into anarchy or destruction is neither as strong nor as general as the Prisoners' Dilemma model and its variants imply, and (b) that where a situation looks promising for collective action according to the above criteria, government officials should treat this option as seriously as the other two.

One good reason for taking it seriously is that collective action is likely to be much cheaper in terms of state resources than the other two (Runge 1986). Both private property regimes and state control regimes are expensive to make effective. Already over-stretched states in developing countries may not be able to provide the necessary resources to make them work across myriad micro locations. A malfunctioning approximation to a formalized system of state control or private property rights, based on a distant authority only dimly aware of local conditions, may be worse in terms of resource management than a strategy which aims to improve, or at least not impair, local systems of rules.

The government can help these local systems by providing a legal framework, and perhaps technical assistance. The legal framework should make it possible for local collective action organizations to obtain legally enforceable recognition of their identity and rights within the society, and to call upon the state as an enforcer of last resort (Korten, forthcoming). Obvious as it may sound, few countries in Asia have given much attention to this task, with respect to rural as distinct from modern urban organizations. If governments move in this direction, their efforts should widen the range of situations in which locally based common property regimes can be expected to work.

APPENDIX

Water supply and the irrigation network

The layout of the main distributary system as it comes through Kottapalle's land is shown in map A.1. The map shows the location of sluice outlets from the main channel, plus the unofficial and ungated 'cuts' made by farmers, together with the boundaries of the zoned blocks or irrigable land. Two blocks each have a zoned area of about 900 acres (not all of which is irrigated); the remaining five blocks average about 270 zoned acres (table A.1). Neither in Kottapalle nor in other canal irrigated villages is there any significant use of ground water for irrigation. Neither the distributary nor the field channels are lined.

The whole of the zoned area of about 3,100 gross acres (and actual gross irrigated area of a little over 2,000 acres) is served by 12 sluices or other water outlets. Of these 12, 7 are official (gated) sluices and appear on the Irrigation Department's detailed maps of the area. Of the remaining 5 'unofficial' outlets (which do not appear on the maps), one is a proper sluice (an imposing concrete structure with an adjustable steel shutter), and the others are simple lined or unlined cuts through the channel bank. These latter (numbers 3, 6, 7 and 9 in map A.1) are on the side opposite the inspection road, this being the narrower; here as elsewhere in the system, if the farmers want to get water through an unofficial opening on the road side of the channel they have to make a proper concrete sluice (as is no. 4) and pay to obtain the connivance of the Irrigation Department. Simple cuts, on the other hand, are concealed, if possible, from the Irrigation Department. The purpose of the unofficial outlets is to allow the farmers under them to take water to their fields by a more direct route than would be possible from the official sluice; or to take water to unzoned land which could not be reached from an official sluice; or to reach land which though zoned is too high in elevation for water from the official sluice to reach. The outlets are all named, and the names are used by villagers as terms of reference. The name is in most cases derived from the name of the nearest field road, which is derived from the name of the location to which the road leads. Officials use numbers as terms of reference, but have no numbers for the unofficial outlets.

It is interesting to note that in this one village there are 70 per cent more water outlets on the ground than the official records show; and that the locations of the official sluices as shown on the maps are 0.5 to 1 inch inaccurate on a scale of 4 inches to the mile. As instruments for water control purposes, the Irrigation Department's site maps leave much to be desired.

Water supply where the channel enters Kottapalle's land fluctuates considerably. At this point the design discharge – the normal 'Full Supply' flow according to the design – is 28 cusecs, and the design dimensions of the channel

Table A.1 Zoned and actual irrigated area (acres), by blocks. (Actual irrigated area given as average of 1978/9 – 1980/1.)

Outlet no.	Block	Zoned land		Actual area					
		Paddy (First season)	Upland (Second season)	First season			Second season		
				Paddy	Upland	Total	Paddy	Upland	Total
1	4		365	29	37	66	2	106	108
2	3	882		637	1	638	84	317	401
5	8		409	149		149	11	78	89
9	9		904	81	8	89	42	164	206
8	11	253	209	199	1	200	4	57	61
11	10		129	42	7	49		106	106
12	12			16	13	29		33	33
		1,135	2,016	1,153	67	1,220	143	861	1,004

Notes: Outlet and block numbers refer to the map. Whereas the map shows all the outlets, official and unofficial, the table gives data arranged in terms of the seven official outlets and blocks (which include the unofficial blocks within the area of the official ones). The data on actual (as well as zoned) irrigated area by crop type comes from the Irrigation Department. Revenue Department figures for irrigated area over the same period as covered in the table come to 47 per cent of the Irrigation Department's figures, which may reflect some overstatement by the Irrigation Department but mostly reflects concealment by the Revenue Department officials (who are able to receive part of what the farmers would otherwise have had to pay in water rate). See further, Wade 1981; 1985a.

Appendix map A.1 Irrigation channel layout. Kottapalle village are: 18 feet from bank top to bank top, 5 feet wide at bed level, and 5 feet deep from bed level to bank top. Most of the time the actual flow is 20 cusecs or less. At times of heavy rainfall the flow at this point might be as much as 37 cusecs. In the second season the flow may dwindle to less than 10 cusecs. (No records are made of flows this far down the distribution network; these figures are based on a few spot calculations and casual observation.)

Most of what enters Kottapalle's land is used within it. Except during or soon after periods of heavy rain, little water in either season goes below the boundary of Kottapalle's land to the next and final village (MNC – 1). Kottapalle farmers and common irrigators cross-bund the channel near the boundary (outlet 12 in map A.1) and divert water through their own field channel network, even if they don't need the water. MNC – 1 is entitled to a sizeable share of the channel water, having a zoned area of 400 acres and 950 acres in the first and second seasons. If this entitlement were to be met, Kottapalle would find itself even more squeezed for water than at present. So Kottapalle people take care to ensure that only when supply in the channel is too great to be put through Kottapalle's field channel system is water let down to MNC – 1 in any quantity. The result is that it has only about 145 and 65 acres in the first and second seasons under irrigation; and at times of heavy rainfall, its lands are inundated with channel water let down from Kottapalle, sometimes with consequent crop damage. If MNC – 1 were able to plant larger areas with irrigated crops in line with its entitlement under the crop zoning, it would be able to exert much stronger pressure on the Irrigation Department to supply enough water to bring the crop to harvest than it is able to exert merely because of its 'rights', 'save the standing crop' is a more powerful lever than 'give to those with water rights'. Hence Kottapalle people take steps to ensure this does not happen. They are prepared to put up with some inconvenience to themselves, as when the road beside the village is used as a drainage route and becomes a veritable torrent; better this than allow enough water down to MNC – 1 for them to plant irrigated crops.

The field channels below the outlets are unlined earthen ditches (like the main channel itself). Within each block water is controlled by means of stone slabs and/or mud barriers, placed against the direction of flow and removed when not needed. In a few places are solid stone drop structures built by the adjacent farmers themselves.

Rice irrigation in India is normally characterized as 'from-field-to-field,' rather than 'from-field-channel-to-field'; water is let in at the head of a service area, fills up the adjacent paddies, then is allowed to fill up the paddies next lower down, and so on, in a slow cascade (Ishikawa 1978:70–1; Wade 1976). Kottapalle, however, has a fairly dense network of field channels: roughly 80 metres per cropped hectare, which compares favourably with the conventional figure for 'adequate' density in Asian paddy irrigation of 'more than 50 metres' (Colombo *et al.* 1977; Svendsen 1981). Most paddy fields are connected directly to or are one or two removed from a field channel, as are most fields for lightly irrigated crops. While the Irrigation Department constructed the 'parent' field channel running some way from the outlet into the block, the farmers constructed the maze of smaller field channels themselves (almost certainly using gangs of contract labourers).

The field channel network also serves for drainage, especially to get rid of torrential storm water which would otherwise quickly break down the paddy bunds. Drainage problems persist, however, especially in some areas close to the channel which are affected by seepage from the channel, and where, in consequence, yields are *less* than further away. A bigger, more purpose-built drainage network and/or lining, would be needed to eliminate this problem. Drainage problems can also occur in places on rainfed land because of the heavy, concentrated nature of the rainfall. On the other hand, most of the village area, and most of the canal command generally, has good natural drainage. So we are not dealing with a case familiar in northern India, where land has actually gone out of production after the arrival of irrigation because insufficient attention was given to ways to offset poor natural drainage (Wade 1980a; Whitcombe 1972; Vohra 1971; Center for Science and Environment 1981).

BIBLIOGRAPHY

Agarwal, S., 1971, *Economics of Land Consolidation in India*. New Delhi: S. Chand.

Akerlof, G., 1980, 'A theory of social custom, of which unemployment may be one consequence', *Quarterly Journal of Economics* 44(4) June: 749–75.

Alexander, K., G. Verma, E. Jayakumar, 1981, 'Social development of weaker sections in Krishna District, Andhra Pradesh', *Behavioral Sciences and Rural Development* (Hyderabad), 4(2) pp. 246–79.

Althusser, L., 1971, *Lenin and Philosophy and Other Essays*, London: New Left Books.

Attwood, D., 1979, 'Conflict cycles: the interaction of local and regional politics in India', *Man* (N.S.), 14: 145–60.

Ault, W., 1972, *Open-Field Farming in Medieval England: A Study of Village By-Laws*. London: George Allen and Unwin.

Axelrod, R., 1981, 'The evolution of cooperation among egoists', *American Political Science Review*, 75 (June): 306–18.

Bailey, F., 1957, *Caste and the Economic Frontier*. Manchester: Manchester University Press.

1963, *Politics and Social Change: Orissa in 1959*. London: University of California Press.

1969, *Stratagems and Spoils*. Oxford: Blackwell.

Bailey, F.G., 1971, 'The peasant view of the bad life', in Shanin, T. (ed.), *Peasants and Peasant Societies*. Penguin Modern Sociology Readings, Penguin: Harmondsworth.

Baker, A., 1969, 'Some terminological problems in studies of British field systems', *Agricultural History Review*, 17.

Baker, A., and R. Butlin (eds.), 1973, *Studies of Field Systems in the British Isles*. Cambridge: Cambridge University Press.

Baker, C., 1976, *The politics of South India 1920–1937*. New Delhi: Vikas.

1979, 'Madras headmen', in Chaudhuri, K. and C. Dewey (eds.), *Economy and Society: Essays in Indian Economic and Social History*. Delhi: Oxford University Press.

1981, 'Economic reorganization and the slump in South and Southeast Asia', *Comparative Studies in Society and History*. 23(3): 325–49.

Baker, G., 1974, 'A theory of social interactions', *Journal of Political Economy*, 83: 1063–93.

Banaji, J., 1978, 'Capitalist domination and the small peasantry. Deccan districts in the late nineteenth century', in *Studies in the Development of*

Capitalism in India, U. Patnaik *et al.*, Lahore: Vanguard Books Ltd.

Banfield, E., 1968, *The Moral Basis of a Backward Society*. New York: The Free Press.

Barkley, P. and D. Seckler, 1972, *Economic Growth and Environmental Decay: The Solution Becomes the Problem*. New York: Harcourt Brace Jovanovich.

Barnett, S., 1973, 'The process of withdrawal in a South Indian caste', in Singer, M. (ed.), *Entrepreneurship and the Modernisation of Occupations*. Duke University Press.

Barry, B., 1973, *The Liberal Theory of Justice*. Oxford: Clarendon Press.

Barth, F., 1965, *Models of Social Organization*. Occasional Paper 23, Royal Anthropological Institute of Great Britain and Ireland. London.

Beals, A., 1963, *Gopalpur: A South Indian Village*. New York: Holt, Rinehart and Winston.

1969, 'Social structure and the prediction of conflict: a test of two hypotheses', *Contributions to Indian Sociology* (New Series), No. 3, December.

1974, *Village Life in South India: Cultural Design and Environmental Variation*. Chicago: Aldine.

Beals, A. and B. Siegel, 1967, *Divisiveness and Social Conflict: An Anthropological Approach*. Bombay: Oxford University Press.

Beardsley, R., 1964, 'Ecological and social parallels between rice-growing communities of Japan and Spain', in *Symposium on Community Studies in Anthropology* (eds.) V. Garfield and E. Friedl. Seattle: University of Washington Press.

Bennett, J., 1974, 'Anthropological contributions to the cultural ecology and management of water resources', in *Men and Water: The Social Sciences and Water Management* (ed.) L. James. Lexington, University of Kentucky Press.

Benson, C., 1889, *An Account of the Kurnool District based on an Analysis of Statistical Information Relating Thereto and on Personal Observation*. Madras: Government Press.

Berreman, G., 1963, *Hindus of the Himalayas*. Bombay: Oxford University Press.

Beteille, A., 1977, *Inequality Among Men*. Oxford: Blackwells.

Bhaduri, A., 1973, 'A study in agricultural backwardness under semi-feudalism', *The Economic Journal*, March, 120–37.

Bhalla, S., 1980, *Measurement of poverty: issues and methods*, mimeo, The World Bank.

Binswanger, H., V. Doherty, T. Balaramaiah, M. Shehde, K. Kshirsagar, V. Rao, and P. Raju, 1980, *Common features and contrasts in labor relations in the semi-arid tropics of India*, March. ICRISAT Research Paper Series.

Bloch, M., 1966 (1931), *French Rural History*. Berkeley and Los Angeles.

Blomquist, W. and E. Ostrom, 1985, 'Institutional capacity and the resolution of a commons dilemma', *Policy Studies Review*, 5(2):383–93.

Blum, J., 1978, *The End of the Old Order in Rural Europe*. Princeton: Princeton University Press.

Borude, S. and N. Joglekar, 1971, 'Crop insurance to protect farmers under dry farming conditions in Maharashtra', *Indian Journal of Agricultural Economics*, 26(4).

Boserup, E., 1965, *The Conditions of Agricultural Growth: The Economics of Agrarian Change Under Population Pressure*. New York: Aldine.

1981, *Population and Technology*. Oxford: Blackwell.

Brackenbury, C., 1915, *Cuddappah*, Madras District Gazatteers, Madras, Government Press.

Braudel, F., 1981, *The Structures of Everyday Life: the Limits of the Possible*. Vol. 1 of *Civilization and Capitalism, 15th–18th century*. London: Collins.

Buchanan, J. and G. Tullock, 1962, *The Calculus of Consent*. Ann Arbor: University of Michigan Press.

Campbell, Bruce, 1981, 'Common-field agriculture – the regional dimension', in T.R. Rowley (ed.) *The Origins of Open-field Agriculture*. London: Croom Helm.

Campbell, Bruce and R. Godoy, 1985, 'Common-field agriculture: the Andes and medieval England compared'. Geography Dept., Queens University of Belfast, mimeo.

Carruthers, I., and R. Stoner, 1981, 'Economic aspects and policy issues in groundwater development.' World Bank Staff Working Paper No. 496 Washington, DC, The World Bank.

Carstairs, G.M., 1958, *The Twice-Born: a Study of a Community of High-Caste Hindus*. Bloomington: Indiana University Press.

Center for Science and Environment, 1981, '*An irrigation project that has reduced farm production*', New Delhi: A. Mishra.

Cernea, M., 1985, 'Alternative units of social organization sustaining afforestation strategies', in M. Cernea (ed.) *Putting People First: Sociological Variables in Rural Development*. Oxford: Oxford University Press.

Chambers, J. and G. Mingay, 1966, *The Agricultural Revolution 1750–1880*. London: Batsford.

Clark, C. and M. Haswell, 1970, *The Economics of Subsistence Agriculture*. London: Macmillan.

Coase, R., 1960, 'The problem of social cost', *Journal of Law and Economics* 3 (Oct.).

Cohen, B., 1965, 'Anthropological notes on disputes and law in India', *American Anthropologist* 67(6):82–122.

Colombo, U., D. Johnson, T. Shishido, 1977, 'Reducing malnutrition in developing countries: increasing rice production in South and Southeast Asia', report of Trilateral North–South Food Task Force to the Trilateral Commission. Trilateral Commission, New York.

Coward, E.W., 1977, 'Irrigation management alternatives: themes from indigenous irrigation systems', *Agricultural Administration* 4:223–37.

1980, 'Management themes in community irrigation systems', in E.W. Coward (ed.).

1980 (ed.), *Irrigation and Agricultural Development in Asia: Perspectives from the Social Sciences*. Ithaca: Cornell University Press.

Cowgill, G., 1975, 'On causes and consequences of ancient and modern population changes', *American Anthropologist*, 73(3):505–25.

Dawes, R., 1975, 'Formal models of dilemmas in social decision-making', in *Human Judgement and Decision Processes* (eds.) M. Kaplan and S. Swartz. New York: Academic Press.

Demsetz, H., 1967, 'Toward a theory of property rights', *American Economic Review* 57:347–59.

Dore, R., 1971, 'Modern cooperatives in traditional communities', in P. Worsley (ed.), *Two Blades of Grass*, Manchester: Manchester University Press.

1978, *Shinohata: A Portrait of a Japanese Village*. London: Allen Lane.

Dowding, K. and R. Kimber, 1984, 'The by-product theory of groups', Keele Research Papers No. 18, Dept. of Politics, University of Keele.

Dube, G., 1968, *Rural Economy and Country Life in the Medieval West*. Transl. C. Postan. Columbia, University of South Carolina Press.

Dube, S., 1955, *Indian Village*. London: Routledge and Kegan Paul.

Dumont, L., 1972 (1966), *Homo Hierarchicus: The Caste System and its Implications*. London: Paladin.

Durkheim, E., 1964, *The Elementary Forms of the Religious Life*. London: Allen and Unwin.

Durnin, J., O. Edholm, D. Miller, J. Waterlow, 1973, 'How much food does man require?', *Nature*, 242(Apr. 6) 418.

Dutt, R.C., 1963 (1901), *The Economic History of India*. Vol. 1. New Delhi: Government of India, Ministry of Information and Broadcasting.

Eckstein, H., 1982, 'The idea of political development: from dignity to efficiency', *World Politics*, 34(4):451–86.

Ehrenfeld, D., 1972, *Conserving Life on Earth*. New York: Oxford University Press.

Elliott, C., 1970, 'Caste and faction among the dominant caste: the Reddis and Kammas of Andhra', in R. Kothari (ed.), *Caste in Indian Politics*. New Delhi: Orient Longmans.

Epstein, T.S., 1962, *Economic Development and Social Change in South India*. Manchester: Manchester University Press.

Eyre, J., 1955, 'Water controls in a Japanese irrigation system', *Geographic Review*, 45(2): 197–216.

Farmer, B., 1960, 'On not controlling sub-division of paddy land', *Transactions and Papers*, Institute of British Geographers, No. 28.

(ed.), 1977, *Green Revolution? Technology and Change in Rice Growing Areas of Tamil Nadu and Sri Lanka*. London: Macmillan.

Foster, G., 1948, *Empire's Children: The People of Tzintzuntzan*. Smithsonian Institution, Institute of Social Anthropology, Publication No. 6.

1965, 'Peasant society and the Image of Limited Good', *American Anthropologist*, 67.

Frankel, F., 1971, *India's Green Revolution: Economic Gains and Political Costs*. Princeton: Princeton University Press.

Frohlich, N., J. Oppenheimer, O. Young, 1971, *Political Leadership and Collective Goods*. Princeton: Princeton University Press.

Gaikwad, V.R., 1981, 'Community development in India', in *Community Development: Comparative Case Studies in India, the Republic of Korea, Mexico and Tanzania*, (eds.) R. Dore and Z. Mars. London: Croom Helm.

Gopalakrishnamah Chetty, N., 1886, *A Manual of the Kurnool District*. Madras: Government Press.

Gopalan, C., B. Rama Sastri, S. Balasubramanian, 1978, *Nutritive Value of Indian Foods*, National Institute of Nutrition, Indian Council of Medical Research, Hyderabad.

Gough, K., 1961 (1955). 'The social structure of a Tanjore village', in M. Marriott (ed.), *Village India: Studies in the Little Community*. Delhi: Asia Publishing House.

Government of Andhra Pradesh, 1973, *Census 1971*, Series 2, *District Census Handbook, Kurnool District*, Hyderabad.

Government of Andhra Pradesh, Andhra Pradesh Irrigation Committee, 1974, *Report*, Hyderabad.

Government of Andhra Pradesh, Bureau of Economics and Statistics, 1979, *Handbook of Statistics, Andhra Pradesh, 1978-79*, Hyderabad.

Government of Andhra Pradesh, Bureau of Economics and Statistics, *Season and Crop Reports*, various issues, Hyderabad.

Government of Andhra Pradesh, Finance and Planning Dept., 1973, *Perspective Plan for Rayalseema*, Vol. 1. Hyderabad.

Government of Andhra Pradesh, 1975, *Kurnool District Handbook of Statistics 1974/75*. Hyderabad.

Government of India, Directorate of Economics and Statistics, 1980. *Agricultural Situation in India*, Sept. New Delhi.

Government of India, Ministry of Irrigation and Power, Irrigation Commission, 1972, *Report*. New Delhi.

Government of India, Registrar General and Census Commissioner, 1978, *Census of India, 1971*, Series I, India, Part II-B (ii). New Delhi.

Grist, D., 1975, *Rice*. Fifth Edition, London: Longman.

Habib, Irfan, 1963, *The Agrarian System of Mughal India (1556-1707)*. New York: Asia Publishing House.

Hardin, G., 1968, 'The tragedy of the commons', *Science* 162 (Dec.): 1343-8.

Hardin, R., 1982, *Collective Action*. Baltimore: The Johns Hopkins Press.

Harriss, J., 1982, *Capitalism and Peasant Farming: Agrarian Structure and Ideology in Northern Tamil Nadu*. New Delhi: Oxford University Press.

Hart, H., 1967, 'The village and development administration', mimeo, Comparative Administration Group, American Society for Public Administration.

Hayami, Y., 1980, 'Economic approach to village community and institution', *Journal of Rural Development*. 3 (April): 27-49.

Hiebert, P., 1971, *Konduru: Structure and Integration in a South Indian Village*. Minneapolis: University of Minnesota Press.

Hoffman, R., 1975, 'Medieval origins of the common fields', in Parker and Jones (eds.), pp. 23-71.

Hofstede, G., 1980, *Culture's Consequences: International Differences in Work-Related Values*. Beverley Hills: Sage.

Honigmann, J., 1968, 'Interpersonal relations in atomistic communities', *Human Organization*, 27:224–5.

Hume, David, 1965 (1888), *A Treatise of Human Nature*, Book 3, *Of Morals* (ed.) L. Selby-Bigge. Oxford: Clarendon Press.

Hunt, R., 1985, 'Appropriate social organization? Water users associations in bureaucratic canal irrigation systems', mimeo, Dept. of Anthropology, Brandeis University.

Hunt, R., and E. Hunt, 1976, 'Canal irrigation and local social organization', *Current Anthropology*, 17(3):389–411.

International Crop Research Institute for the Semi-Arid Tropics, National Institute of Nutrition, and Home Science College of Andhra Pradesh Agricultural University, 1982, untitled report on diets, health, nutrition, household time allocation in six villages of upland peninsula India in 1976–8. Mimeo, ICRISAT.

Ishikawa, S., 1975, 'Peasant families and the agrarian community in the process of economic development', in L. Reynolds (ed.), *Agriculture in Development Theory*. Economic Growth Center, New Haven: Yale University.

1978, *Labour Absorption in Asian Agriculture*. Asian Regional Program for Employment Promotion, International Labour Office, Bangkok.

Ishwaran, K., 1966, *Tradition and Economy in Village India*. Bombay: Allied Publishers.

1968, *Shivapur, A South Indian Village*. London: Routledge and Kegan Paul.

ISVIP (International Studies of Values in Politics), 1971, *Values and the Active Community: A Cross-National Study of the Influence of Local Leadership*. New York: The Free Press.

Jodha, N., 1985, 'Population growth and the decline of common property resources in India', *Population and Development Review*, 11(2):247–64.

Johnson, O., 1972, 'Economic analysis, the legal framework and land tenure systems', *Journal of Law and Economics* 15:259–76.

Johnston, B. and W. Clark, 1982, *Redesigning Rural Development: A Strategic Perspective*. Baltimore: The John Hopkins University Press.

Kahlon, A., S. Miglani and H. Singh, 1971, 'A comparative analysis of dry and irrigated farming in Ferozepur district, Punjab', *Indian Journal of Agricultural Economics*, 26(4).

Kakar, S., 1981, *The Inner World: A Psycho-analytic Study of Childhood and Society in India*, 2nd edn. Delhi, Oxford University Press.

Kelly, W., 1982, *Water Control in Tokugawa Japan: Irrigation Organization in a Japanese River Basin, 1600–1870*. East Asia Paper Series. Ithaca: Cornell University China–Japan Program.

Kerridge, E., 1953–4, 'The sheepfold in Wiltshire and the floating of the watermeadows', *Economic History Review* (2nd ser.), 6:282–9.

Kimber, R., 1981, 'Collective actions and the fallacy of the liberal fallacy', *World Politics*, 33(2): 178–96.

1983, 'The tragedy of the commons reappraised', Department of Politics, University of Keele, mimeo.

Kimber, R., and J. Richardson, 1974, *Compaigning for the Environment*. London: Routledge and Kegan Paul.

Korten, D. and F. Alfonso (eds.), 1981, *Bureaucracy and the Poor: Closing the Gap*. Singapore: McGraw-Hill.

Korten, F., forthcoming, 'The policy framework for community management', in *Community Management: Asian Experiences and Perspectives* (ed.) D. Korten, New Hartford: Kumarian Press.

Laver, M. 1981, *The Politics of Private Desires*. Harmondsworth: Penguin.

Leach, E., 1961, *Pul Eliya*. Cambridge: Cambridge University Press.

Levine, G., 1977, 'Management components in irrigation system design and operation', *Agricultural Administration*, 4(1).

Levine, G., P. Oram and J. Zapata, 1979, 'Water', paper prepared for conference, 'Agricultural Production: Research and Development Strategies for the 1980s'. Bonn, October 8–12.

Lewis, O., 1951, *Life in a Mexican Village: Tepoztlan Restudied*. University of Illinois Press.

Lipton, M., 1968, 'The theory of the optimizing peasant', *Journal of Development Studies*, 4:327–51.

1983, 'Poverty, undernutrition and hunger', World Bank Staff Working Paper No. 597, Washington, DC: The World Bank.

1985, 'Prisoners' Dilemma and Coase's theorem: a case for democracy in less developed countries?', in R. Matthews (ed.), *Economics and Democracy*, published for British Association for the Advancement of Science. London: Macmillan.

Maass, A., and R. Anderson, 1978, *. . . and the Desert Shall Rejoice: Conflict, Growth, and Justice in Arid Environment*. Cambridge, MA.: The MIT Press.

McCloskey, D., 1975, 'The persistence of English common fields', in Parker and Jones (eds.), 73–119.

1976, 'English open fields as behavior towards risk', in P. Uselding (ed.), Research in Economic History. Greenwich, Conn., JAI Press.

Macfarlane, A., 1978, *The Origins of English Individualism: The Family, Property and Social Transition*. Oxford: Blackwell.

McKean, M., 1984, 'Management of traditional common lands in Japan', Dept. of Political Science, Duke University, mimeo.

Maine, Sir Henry, 1905, *Ancient Law: Its Connection with the Early History of Society and its Relation to Modern Ideas*. London: Routledge.

Mair, L., 1964, *Primitive Government*. Harmondsworth: Penguin.

Mann, H., 1968, *The Social Framework of Agriculture: India, Middle East, England*. London: Frank Cass.

Marx, K., 1853, Dispatch to *New York Daily Tribune*, 10 June.

1973, 'The future results of British rule in India', in *Surveys from Exile*, London.

Marwell, G. and R. Ames, 1981, 'Economists free-ride, does anyone else?

Experiments in the provision of public goods IV', *Journal of Public Economics*, 15:295–310.

Masefield, G., 1977, 'Food resources and production', in J. Garlick and R. Keay (eds.), *Human Ecology in the Tropics*. London: Taylor and Francis.

Mayhew, A., 1973, *Rural Settlement and Farming in Germany*. London.

Mencher, J., 1975, 'Land ceilings in Tamil Nadu: facts and fictions', *Economic and Political Weekly*, Annual Number, Feb., 241–54.

Mohr, E., F. van Baren, J. van Schuylenborgh, 1972, *Tropical Soils: A Comprehensive Study of Their Genesis*. The Hague: Mouton.

Moore, B.. 1967, *Social Origins of Dictatorship and Democracy*. Harmondsworth: Penguin.

Moore, M., 1972, 'On not defining peasants', *Peasant Studies Newsletter*, 1(4): 156–7.

Moore, M., J. Connel, C. Lambert, 1976, *Village Studies: Data Analysis and Bibliography, Vol. I: India 1950–1975*. Institute of Development Studies. Epping: Bowker.

Naik, B., 1981, 'Evolution of an approach for off and on farm development', *Wamana* 1(3):3–5, Indian Institute of Management, Bangalore.

Netting, R., 1972, 'Of men and meadows: strategies of Alpine land use', *Anthropological Quarterly* 45(3):132–44.

North, D., and R. Thomas, 1977, 'The first economic revolution', *Economic History Review*, 30:229–41.

Nozick, R., 1974, *Anarchy, State and Utopia*. Oxford: Blackwell.

Oakerson, R., 1985, 'A model for the analysis of common property problems', paper for Common Property Steering Committee, National Research Council (USA).

Olson, M., 1971, *The Logic of Collective Action*, Cambridge, Mass.: Harvard University Press.

1982, *The Rise and Decline of Nations: Economic Growth, Stagflation, and Social Rigidities*. New Haven: Yale University Press.

Ophuls, W., 1973, 'Leviathan or oblivion', in Herman Daley (ed.), *Toward a Steady State Economy*. San Francisco: W.H. Freeman.

Oppenheimer, J., 1981, 'Does the route to development pass through public choice?', in Russell and Nicholson (eds.).

Orans, M., 1968, 'Maximizing in jajmaniland: a model of caste relations', *American Anthropologist*, 70:875–97.

Orenstein, H., 1965, *Gaon: Conflict and Cohesion in an Indian Village*. Princeton: Princeton University Press.

Ostrom, E., 1968, 'Some postulated effects of learning on constitutional behavior', *Public Choice* 5(Fall):87–104.

1985a, 'Are successful efforts to manage common-pool resources a challenge to the theories of Garrett Hardin and Mancur Olson?', Working paper W85–31, Workshop in Political Theory and Policy Analysis, Indiana University.

1985b, 'The rudiments of a revised theory of the origins, survival, and performance of institutions for collective action', Working paper W85–32,

Workshop in Political Theory and Policy Analysis, Indiana University.

1986, 'Institutional arrangements for resolving the commons dilemma: some contending approaches', in *Capturing the Commons*, B. McKay and J. Acheson (eds.). Tucson: University of Arizona Press.

Parker, W., and E. Jones (eds.), 1975, *European Peasants and Their Markets: Essays in Agrarian Economic History*. Princeton: Princeton University Press.

Picardi, A., and W. Siefert, 1976, 'A tragedy of the commons in the Sahel', *Technology Review*, 78:42–51.

Poggi, G., 1978, *The Development of the Modern State: A Sociological Introduction*. London: Hutchinson.

Popkin, S., 1979, *The Rational Peasant: The Political Economy of Rural Society in Vietnam*. Berkeley: University of California Press.

Pye, L., 1985, *Asian Power and Politics: The Cultural Dimensions of Authority*, Cambridge: Belknap Press.

Rajagopal, M., 1974, *Andhra Pradesh District Gazetteers, Kurnool* (Revised Edition), Government of Andhra Pradesh, Hyderabad.

Randall, A., 1983, 'The problem of market failure', *Natural Resources Journal* 23(1):131–48.

Rao, G., 1977, 'Agrarian relations in coastal Andhra under early British rule', *Social Scientist* 6(1), August:29.

Rapoport, A. and A. Chammah, 1965, *Prisoner's Dilemma*. Ann Arbor: University of Michigan Press.

Rawls, J., 1971, *A Theory of Justice*. Cambridge, MA: Harvard University Press.

Redfield, R., 1956, *Peasant Society and Culture*. Chicago: University of Chicago Press.

Runge, C. Ford, 1984, 'Institutions and the free rider: the assurance problem in collective action', *The Journal of Politics*, 46:154–81.

1986, 'Common property and collective action in economic development', *World Development*, forthcoming.

Russell, C., 1981, 'Introduction', in Russell and Nicholson (eds.).

Russell, C. and N. Nicholson (eds.) 1981, *Public Choice and Rural Development*. Washington, DC: Resources for the Future.

Ruthenberg, H., 1980, *Farming Systems in the Tropics*, (3rd edn). Oxford: Clarendon Press.

Ryan, J., R. Ghodake, R. Sarin, 1980, 'Labor use and labor markets in semi-arid tropical rural villages of peninsular India', Proceedings, International Workshop on Socio-economic Constraints to Development of Semi-Arid Tropical Agriculture, ICRISAT, 19–23 Feb., 1979, Hyderabad, India.

Sungeetha Rao, R., 1980, 'Trends in the behaviour of costs of cultivation/production of paddy in Andhra Pradesh during 1971–72 to 1975–76', in *Agricultural Situation in India*, May, Government of India, Ministry of Agriculture, Directorate of Economics and Statistics, New Delhi.

Scott, J., 1972, *Comparative Political Corruption*. Englewood Cliffs: Prentice-Hall.

1976, *The Moral Economy of the Peasant*. New Haven: Yale University Press.

Seckler, D., 1980, '"Small but healthy": a crucial hypothesis in the theory, measurement and policy of malnutrition', mimeo. Ford Foundation, New Delhi.

Sen, A., 1983, 'How is India doing?', *Mainstream*, Republic Day.

Shanin, T. (ed.), 1971, Peasants and Peasant Societies. Harmondswarth: Penguin.

Sharma, B. and K. Madhusudhan Reddy, 1979, 'Electoral politics and voting behaviour', in G. Ram Reddy and B. Sharma (eds.) 1979, *State Government and Politics: Andhra Pradesh*. New Delhi: Sterling Publishers Pvt. Ltd.

Sharma, M., 1978, *The Politics of Inequality: Competition and Control in an Indian Village*. Honolulu: University of Hawaii Press.

Silverman, S., 1968, 'Agricultural organization, social structure and values in Italy: Amoral familism reconsidered', *American Anthropologist* 70:1–20.

Slicher van Bath, B., 1963, *The Agrarian History of Western Europe*. New York: St Martin Press.

Smith, R., 1981, 'Resolving the tragedy of the commons by creating private property rights in wildlife, *CATO Journal*, 1(2):439–68.

Snidal, D., 1985, 'Coordination versus Prisoners' Dilemma: implications for international cooperation and regimes', *American Political Science Review* 79:923–47.

Sproule-Jones, M., 1982, 'Public choice theory and natural resources: methodological explication and critique', *American Political Science Review* 76(4):790–804.

Srinivas, S., 1976, *The Remembered Village*. Delhi: Oxford University Press.

Stein, B., 1980, *Peasant State and Society in South India*. Delhi: Oxford University Press.

Sugden, R., 1984, 'Reciprocity: the supply of public goods through voluntary contributions', *Economic Journal* 94:772–87.

Svendsen, M., 1981, 'Irrigator behavior in three Phillippine irrigation systems', memeo. paper to seminar on 'Investment decisions to further develop and make use of Southest Asia's irrigation resources', sponsored by Agricultural Development Council and Royal Irrigation Department of Thailand, Kasetsart University, Bangkok, 17–21 August.

Thirsk, J., 1973, 'Field systems of the east Midlands', in Baker, A. and R. Butlin (eds.), *Studies of Field Systems in the British Isles*. Cambridge: Cambridge University Press.

1967, 'Preface', in C. and C. Orwin, *The Open Fields*, Oxford: Clarendon Press.

Tinker, H., 1954, *The Foundations of Local Self-Government in India, Pakistan and Burma*. London: Athlone Press.

Tocqueville, A., 1969, *Democracy in America*. Trans. G. Lawrence. New York: Doubleday Anchor.

Triandis, H., *et al.*, 1972, *The Analysis of Subjective Culture*. New York: Wiley-Interscience.

Truman, D., 1951, *The Governmental Process: Political Interests and Public Opinion*. New York: Knopf.

Bibliography

Vohra, B.B., 1971, *A Charter for the Land*. New Delhi: Ministry of Agriculture.

Wade, R., 1975a, 'The base of a "centrifugal democracy": party allegiance in rural Central Italy', in J. Boissevain and J. Friedl (eds.), *Beyond the Community: Social Process in Europe*. The Hague: Ministrie van Onderwijs en Wetenschappen.

1975b, 'Administration and the distribution of irrigation benefits', *Economic and Political Weekly*, 10(29), 19 July.

1976, 'How not to redistribute with growth: the case of India's command area development programme', *Pacific Viewpoint*, 17(2):95–104.

1979, 'The social response to irrigation: an Indian case study', *Journal of Development Studies* 16(1):3–26.

1980a, 'On substituting management for water in canal irrigation: a South Indian case', *Economic and Political Weekly*, 15(52), Review of Agriculture, Dec. 27.

1980b, (1975), 'India's changing strategy of irrigation development', in E.W. Coward (ed.).

1981, 'The information problem of South Indian canals', *Water Supply and Management*, 5:31–51.

1982a, 'The system of administrative and political corruption: canal irrigation in South India', *Journal of Development Studies*, 18(3), May: 287–328.

1982b, 'The World Bank and India's irrigation reform', *Journal of Development Studies*, 18(2), Jan: 171–84.

1982c, *Irrigation and Politics in South Korea*. Boulder: Westview Press.

1982d, 'Employment, water control and irrigation institutions: South India and South Korea', Asian Regional Employment Program Working Paper, ILO, Bangkok; IDS Discussion Paper No. 182.

1982e, 'Group action for irrigation', *Economic and Political Weekly*, 17(39), Review of Agriculture, Sept. 25.

1984a, Review of J. Toye, *Public Expenditure and India's Development Policy 1969–1970. Economic Development and Cultural Change*, 32(2), Jan:437–44.

1984b, 'Irrigation reform in conditions of populist anarchy: a South Indian case', *Journal of Development Economics*, 14(3), April:285–303.

1984c, 'Managing a drought with canal irrigation: a South Indian case', *Agricultural Administration.* 17(4):177–201.

1985a, 'On the sociology of irrigation statistics: how do we know the truth about canal performance?', *Agricultural Administration.* 19(2):63–79.

1985b, 'The market for public office: why the Indian state is not better at development', *World Development* 13(4):467–97.

Wagner, R., 1983, 'The theory of games and the problem of international cooperation', *American Political Science Review* 77:330–46.

Washbrook, D., 1975, 'Introduction', in Baker, C. and D. Washbrook (eds.), *South India: Political Institutions and Political Change 1880–1940*. Delhi: Macmillan.

1977 (1976), *The Emergence of Provincial Politics: The Madras Presidency, 1870–1920*. New Delhi: Vikas Publishing House.

Bibliography

Weiner, M., 1967, *Party Building in a New Nation: The Indian National Congress*. Chicago: University of Chicago Press.

Whitcombe, E., 1972, *Agrarian Condition in Northern India*, Vol. 1: *The United Provinces Under British Rule, 1860–1900*. Berkeley: University of California Press.

Wiser, W. and C. Wiser, 1971, *Behind Mud Walls, 1930–1960, with a sequel: The Village in 1970*. Berkeley: University of California Press.

Wittfogel, K., 1963 (1957), *Oriental Despotism, A Comparative Study of Total Power*. New Haven: Yale University Press.

Wolf, E., 1957, 'Closed corporate communities in Meso-America and Java', *Southwestern Journal of Anthropology* 13:1–18.

1966, *Peasants*. Englewood Cliffs: Prentice-Hall.

1971 (1956), 'Aspects of group relations in a complex society: Mexico', in Shanin (ed.).

World Bank, 1984, *Tenth Annual Review of Project Performance Audit Results*, Vol. 1, Chapter 3, Washington, DC: The World Bank.

Wurfel, D., 1963, 'The Philippines', in R. Rose and A. Heidenheimer (eds.), 'Comparative Studies in Political Finance: A Symposium', *Journal of Politics*, 25(4).

INDEX

All page references in italics are to maps, figures or tables.

CAMBRIDGE SOUTH ASIAN STUDIES

These monographs are published by the Syndics of Cambridge University Press in association with the Cambridge University Centre for South Asian Studies. The following books have been published in this series:

Cambridge South Asian Studies

Printed in the United States
By Bookmasters